First Arabic Reader for Beginners

Saher Ahmed Salama

First Arabic Reader for Beginners
Bilingual for Speakers of English
Beginner and Elementary (A1 A2)

LANGUAGE
PRACTICE
PUBLISHING

First Arabic Reader for Beginners
by Saher Ahmed Salama

Audio tracks www.lppbooks.com/Book/Arabic-1/

Homepage www.audiolego.com

Graphics: Audiolego Design

Copyright © 2010 2018 2023 Language Practice Publishing

Copyright © 2018 2023 Audiolego

This book is in copyright. Subject to statutory exception and to the provisions of relevant collective licensing agreements, no reproduction of any part may take place without the written permission of Language Practice Publishing.

Table of contents

Arabic alphabet	7
The playback speed	12
Beginner Course	13
Chapter 1	14
Bruce has a dog	16
Chapter 2	19
They live in Alexandria	20
Chapter 3	23
Are they Egyptians?	24
Chapter 4	28
Can you help, please?	29
Chapter 5	34
Bruce lives in Egypt now	35
Chapter 6	40
Bruce has many friends	41
Chapter 7	46
Omar buys a bike	47
Chapter 8	51
Hanan wants to buy a new DVD	52
Chapter 9	55
Hiroshi listens to American songs	56
Chapter 10	61
Hiroshi buys textbooks on design	62
Chapter 11	67
Bruce wants to earn some money (part 1)	68
Chapter 12	73
Bruce wants to earn some money (part 2)	74
It is time to go to college	77
Elementary Course	79
Chapter 13	80
The name of the hotel	81
Chapter 14	84
Aspirin	85

- Chapter 15 89
  - Mariam and kangaroo 90
- Chapter 16 95
  - Parachutists 97
- Chapter 17 104
  - Turn the gas off! 106
- Chapter 18 110
  - A job agency 112
- Chapter 19 117
  - Omar and Bruce wash the truck 119
- Chapter 20 123
  - Omar and Bruce wash the truck (part 2) 125
- Chapter 21 130
  - A lesson 131
- Chapter 22 135
  - Hiroshi works at a publishing house 137
- Chapter 23 142
  - Cat rules 143
- Chapter 24 148
  - Team work 150
- Chapter 25 154
  - Bruce and Omar are looking for a new job 155
- Chapter 26 164
  - Applying to "Alexandria today" 165
- Chapter 27 172
  - The police patrol (part 1) 173
- Chapter 28 181
  - The police patrol (part 2) 182
- Chapter 29 190
  - FLEX and Au pair 192
- Arabic-English vocabulary 197
- English-Arabic vocabulary 223

Arabic alphabet

The Arabic alphabet contains 28 letters. Arabic is written from right to left. In Arabic short vowels are generally not written. Arabic letters change their shape according to their position in a word. Arabic is a *cursive-only* script, which is to say that Arabic cannot be written with unconnected, separated letters. All letters must be connected together in general.

Many letters look similar but are distinguished from one another by dots above or below their central part, called *i'jam*. These dots are an integral part of a letter, since they distinguish between letters that represent different sounds. For example, the Arabic letters transliterated as *b* and *t* have the same basic shape, but *b* has one dot below, ب, and *t* has two dots above, ت.

Both printed and written Arabic are cursive, with most of the letters within a word directly connected to the adjacent letters. Unlike cursive writing based on the Latin alphabet, the standard Arabic style is to have a substantially different shape depending on whether it will be connecting with a preceding and/or a succeeding letter, thus all primary letters have conditional forms for their *glyphs*, depending on whether they are at the beginning, middle or end of a word, so they may exhibit four distinct forms (initial, medial, final or isolated). However, six letters have only isolated or final form, and so force the following letter (if any) to take an initial or isolated form, as if there were a word break. These six letters (أ,د,ذ,ر,ز,و) are not connected to the letter following them, therefore their initial form matches the isolated and their medial form matches the final.

Some letters look almost the same in all four forms, while others show considerable variation. Generally, the initial and middle forms look similar except that in some letters the middle form starts with a short horizontal line on the right to ensure that it will connect with its preceding letter. The final and isolated forms, are also similar in appearance but the final form will also have a horizontal stroke on the right and, for some letters, a loop or longer line on the left with which to finish the word with a subtle ornamental flourish. In addition, some letter combinations are written as ligatures (special shapes), including *lām-'alif*.

The phonetic values given are those of the pronunciation of literary Arabic, the standard which is taught in universities.

The names of the Arabic letters can be thought of as abstractions of an older version where they were meaningful words in the Proto-Semitic language.

Arabic uses a diacritic sign, ء, called *hamza*, to denote the glottal stop, written alone or with a carrier:

- alone: ء ;
- with a carrier: أ ,إ (above and under a *'alif*), ؤ (above a *wāw*), ئ (above a dotless *yā'* or *yā' hamza*).

Letters lacking an initial or medial version are never connected to the following letter, even within a word. As to the *hamza*, it has only a single form, since it is never connected to a preceding or following letter. However, it is sometimes combined with a *wāw*, *yā'*, or *'alif*, and in that case the carrier behaves like an ordinary *wāw*, *yā'*, or *'alif*.

Contextual forms				Name	Translit.	Phonemic Value (IPA)
Isolated	End	Middle	Beginning			
ا	ـا	ـا	ا	'alif	' / ā	various, including /a:/
ب	ـب	ـبـ	بـ	bā'	b	/b/, also /p/ in some loanwords
ت	ـت	ـتـ	تـ	tā'	t	/t/
ث	ـث	ـثـ	ثـ	ṯā'	ṯ	/θ/
ج	ـج	ـجـ	جـ	ǧīm	ǧ (also j, g)	[g~dʒ~ʒ]
ح	ـح	ـحـ	حـ	ḥā'	ḥ	/ħ/
خ	ـخ	ـخـ	خـ	ḫā'	ḫ (also kh, x)	/x/
د	ـد	ـد	د	dāl	d	/d/
ذ	ـذ	ـذ	ذ	ḏāl	ḏ (also dh, ð)	/ð/
ر	ـر	ـر	ر	rā'	r	/r/
ز	ـز	ـز	ز	zāy	z	/z/
س	ـس	ـسـ	سـ	sīn	s	/s/
ش	ـش	ـشـ	شـ	šīn	š (also sh)	/ʃ/
ص	ـص	ـصـ	صـ	ṣād	ṣ	/sˤ/
ض	ـض	ـضـ	ضـ	ḍād	ḍ	/dˤ/
ط	ـط	ـطـ	طـ	ṭā'	ṭ	/tˤ/

ظ	ظ	ظ	ظ	ẓāʾ	ẓ	[ðˤ~zˤ]
ع	ع	ـعـ	عـ	ʿayn	ʿ	/ʕ/
غ	غ	ـغـ	غـ	ġayn	ġ (also gh)	/ɣ/ (/g/ in many loanwords)
ف	ف	ـفـ	فـ	fāʾ	f	/f/, also /v/ in some loanwords
ق	ق	ـقـ	قـ	qāf	q	/q/
ك	ك	ـكـ	كـ	kāf	k	/k/
ل	ل	ـلـ	لـ	lām	l	/l/, (/lˤ/ in *Allah* only)
م	م	ـمـ	مـ	mīm	m	/m/
ن	ن	ـنـ	نـ	nūn	n	/n/
ه	ه	ـهـ	هـ	hāʾ	h	/h/
و	و	و	و	wāw	w / ū / aw	/w/ / /uː/ / /au/, sometimes /u/, /o/ and /oː/ in loanwords
ي	ي	ـيـ	يـ	yāʾ	y / ī / ay	/j/ / /iː/ / /ai/, sometimes /i/, /eː/ and /e/ in loanwords

Arabic word	Pronunciation	Translation
إنترنت	i n t r n t	internet
كتشب	k t sh b	ketchup
تلفون	t l f w n	telephone
أمريكا	a m r y k aa	America
بريطانيا	b r y T aa n y aa	Britain
نيويورك	n y w y w r k	New York
ليمونادة	l y m w n aa d ah	lemonade
كيلومتر	k y l w m t r	kilometer
تلفزيون	t l f z y w n	television
استراليا	u s t r aa l y aa	Australia
وشنطن	w sh n T n	Washington
لوس انجلس	l w s a n j l s	Los Angeles

The playback speed

The book is equipped with audio tracks. With the help of QR codes, call up an audio track in no time, without typing a web address manually. VLC media player is an app to control the playback speed.

Beginner Course

الفَصْلُ الأَوَّل
Chapter 1

Audio track

بروس يَمْتَلِك كَلْباً

Bruce has a dog

A

الكَلِمَاتُ

Words

1. أَخْضَرٌ - green
2. أَرْبَعَةٌ - four
3. أَزْرَقٌ - blue
4. أَسْرَةٌ - beds
5. أَسْوَدٌ - black
6. أَقْلامُ حِبْرٍ - pens
7. الإِسْكَنْدَرِيَّةُ - Alexandria
8. أَنَا - I
9. أَنْفٌ - nose
10. أُولئِكَ - those

11.	بْروس - Bruce		31.	قَليلٌ - little
12.	جِدّاً، أيْضاً - too		32.	كَبيرٌ - big
13.	جَديدٌ - new		33.	كِتابٌ – book
14.	حُلْمٌ - dream		34.	كَثيرٌ - many, much
15.	دَرّاجَةٌ - bike		35.	كَلْبٌ – dog
16.	ذلِكَ - that		36.	كَلِماتٌ - words
17.	سَريرٌ - bed		37.	كَلِمَةٌ - word
18.	شارِعٌ - street		38.	لَطيفٌ - nice
19.	شَوارِعُ - streets		39.	لَهُ، مُلِكُهُ - his
20.	طالِبٌ - student		40.	سَريرُهُ - his bed
21.	طَلَبَةٌ - students		41.	مَلِكي لي - my
22.	عُمَر - Omar		42.	لَيْسَ - not
23.	عَيْنٌ - eye		43.	مَتاجِرٌ - shops
24.	عُيُونٌ - eyes		44.	مَتْجَرٌ - shop
25.	غُرَفٌ، حُجُراتٌ - rooms		45.	مُتَنَزَّهٌ، حَديقَةٌ - park
26.	غُرْفَةٌ، حُجَرَةٌ - room		46.	مُتَنَزَّهاتٌ، حَدائِقُ - parks
27.	فَنادِقُ - hotels		47.	مُفَكِّراتٌ - notebooks
28.	فُنْدُقٌ - hotel		48.	مُفَكِّرَةٌ - notebook
29.	قِطَّةٌ - cat		49.	مَناضِدُ - tables
30.	قَلَمُ حِبْرٍ - pen		50.	مِنْضَدَةٌ - table

15

51. نافِذَةٌ - window	56. هٰذا - this
52. نَجْمٌ - star	57. هٰذا الكِتابٌ - this book
53. نَصٌّ - text	58. هُمْ - they
54. نَوافِذٌ - windows	59. هُوَ - he
55. هٰؤُلاءِ - these	60. هِيروشِي - Hiroshi

B

Bruce has a dog	berwes yemtelk kelbaan	بروس يَمْتَلِكُ كَلْباً
1. This student has a book.	1. heda aletaleb yemlek ketabaan.	1. هٰذا الطالِبُ يَمْلِكُ كِتاباً.
2. He has a pen too.	2. yemlek qelm hebr ayedaan.	2. يَمْلِكُ قَلَمَ حِبْرٍ أَيْضاً.
3. Alexandria has many streets and parks.	3. yewjed baleseknedreyh alektheyr men aleshewar' walheda'eq.	3. يُوجَدُ بِالإِسْكَنْدَرِيَّةِ الكَثِيرُ مِنَ الشَوارِعِ وَالحَدائِقِ.
4. This street has new hotels and shops.	4. yewjed bheda aleshar' fenadeq wemtajer jedyedh.	4. يُوجَدُ بِهٰذا الشارِعِ فَنادِقُ وَمَتاجِرُ جَدِيدَةٌ.
5. This hotel has four stars.	5. heda alefnedq men areb' nejwem.	5. هٰذا الفُنْدُقُ مِنْ أَرْبَعِ نُجُومٍ.
6. This hotel has many nice big rooms.	6. leda heda alefnedq alektheyr men alegherf alekbeyrh alelteyfh.	6. لَدَى هٰذا الفُنْدُقِ الكَثِيرُ مِنَ الغُرَفِ الكَبِيرَةِ اللَطِيفَةِ.

7. That room has many windows.	7. yewjed betlek alegherfh alektheyr men alenwafed.	٧. يُوجَدُ بِتِلكَ الغُرْفَةِ الكَثِيرُ مِنْ النَوافِذِ.
8. And these rooms do not have many windows.	8. whedh alegherf la yewjed bha newafed ketheyrh.	٨. وَهٰذِهِ الغُرَفُ لا يُوجَدُ بِها نَوافِذٌ كَثِيرَةٌ.
9. These rooms have four beds.	9. yewjed bhedh alegherf areb'eh aserh.	٩. يُوجَدُ بِهٰذِهِ الغُرَفِ أَرْبَعَةُ أَسِرَةٍ.
10. And those rooms have one bed.	10. weywejd betlek alegherf seryer wahed.	١٠. وَيُوجَدُ بِتِلكَ الغُرَفِ سَرِيرٌ واحِدٌ.
11. That room does not have many tables.	11. telk alegherfh la yewjed bha al'edeyd men alemnaded.	١١. تِلكَ الغُرْفَةُ لا يُوجَدُ بِها العَدِيدُ مِنْ المَناضِدِ.
12. And those rooms have many big tables.	12. weywejd betlek alegherf ketheyraan men alemnaded alekbeyrh.	١٢. وَيُوجَدُ بِتِلكَ الغُرَفِ كَثِيراً مِنْ المَناضِدِ الكَبِيرَةِ.
13. This street does not have hotels.	13. heda aleshar' la yewjed bh fenadeq.	١٣. هٰذا الشارِعُ لا يُوجَدُ بِهِ فَنادِقُ.
14. That big shop has many windows.	14. yewjed bheda alemtejr alekbeyr ketheyraan men alenwafed.	١٤. يُوجَدُ بِهٰذا المَتْجَرِ الكَبِيرِ كَثِيرٌ مِنْ النَوافِذِ.
15. These students have notebooks.	15. h'ela' aletlebh ledyhem mefkerat.	١٥. هٰؤُلاءِ الطَلَبَةُ لَدَيْهِم مُفَكِّراتٌ.
16. They have pens too.	16. ledyhem aqelam hebr ayedaan.	١٦. لَدَيْهِمْ أَقْلامُ حِبرٍ أَيْضاً.
17. Bruce has one little black notebook.	17. leda berwes mefkerh wahedh segheyrh sewda'.	١٧. لَدَى بروس مُفَكِّرَةٌ واحِدَةٌ صَغِيرَةٌ سَوْداءُ.

18. Hiroshi has four new green notebooks.	18. leda heyrewshey areb' mefkerat khedra' jedyedh.	18. لَدَى هِيرُوشِي أَرْبَعُ مُفَكِّراتٍ خَضْراءَ جَدِيدَةٍ.
19. This student has a bike.	19. heda aletaleb ledyh derajh.	19. هٰذا الطالِبُ لَدَيْهِ دَرّاجَةٌ.
20. He has a new blue bike.	20. ledyh derajh zerqa' jedyedh.	20. لَدَيْهِ دَرّاجَةٌ زَرْقاءُ جَدِيدَةٌ.
21. Omar has a bike too.	21. leda 'emer derajh ayedaan.	21. لَدَى عُمَرَ دَرّاجَةٌ أَيضاً.
22. He has a nice black bike.	22. ledyh derajh sewda' letyefh.	22. لَدَيْهِ دَرّاجَةٌ سَوْداءُ لَطيفَةٌ.
23. Hiroshi has a dream.	23. leda heyrewshey helmaan.	23. لَدَى هِيرُوشِي حُلْمٌ.
24. I have a dream too.	24. ledy helm ayedaan.	24. لَدَيَّ حُلْمٌ أَيضاً.
25. I do not have a dog.	25. la amelk kelbaan.	25. لا أَمْلِكُ كَلْباً.
26. I have a cat.	26. amelk qeth.	26. أَمْلِكُ قِطَّةً.
27. My cat has nice green eyes.	27. 'eyewn qettey khedra' letyefh.	27. عُيُونُ قِطَّتِي خَضْراءُ لَطيفَةٌ.
28. Bruce does not have a cat.	28. berwes la yemlek qeth.	28. برُوس لا يَمْلِكُ قِطَّةً.
29. He has a dog.	29. ledyh kelbaan.	29. لَدَيْهِ كَلْبٌ.
30. His dog has a little black nose.	30. kelbh ledyh anef asewd segheyr.	30. كَلْبُهُ لَدَيْهِ أَنْفٌ أَسْوَدُ صَغِيرٌ.

الفَصْلُ الثَّانِي
Chapter 2

يَعِيشُونَ فِي الإِسْكَنْدِرِيَّةِ

They live in Alexandria

A

الكَلِمَاتُ

Words

1. اِثْنَانِ - two
2. أَخٌ ، شَقِيقٌ - brother
3. أُخْتٌ ، شَقِيقَةٌ - sister
4. أَسْبانِي - Spanish
5. أَسْبانِيا - Spain
6. الآنَ - now
7. الوِلاياتُ المُتَّحِدَةُ الأَمْرِيكِيَّةُ - the USA
8. أُمٌّ - mother
9. أَمْرِيكِيٌّ - American
10. أَنْتَ، أَنْتُما ، أَنْتُمْ - you
11. جائِعٌ - hungry
12. حَنان - Hanan (name)
13. سُوبَر مارْكت - supermarket
14. شَطِيرَةٌ ، شندويتش - sandwich
15. فِي - in

19

16. كَبِيرٌ- big	21. نَحْنُ - we	
17. مَدِينَةٌ- city	22. هِيَ - she	
18. مِصْرُ - Egypt	23. يَشْتَرِي - to buy	
19. مِصْرِيٌّ - Egyptian	24. يَعِيش ، يُقِيمُ - to live	
20. مِنْ - from		

B

They live in Alexandria	y'eyeshewn fey aleseknedreyh	يَعِيشُونَ فِي الإِسْكَنْدَرِيَّةِ
1. Alexandria is a big city.	1. aleseknedreyh medyenh kebyerh.	1. الإِسْكَنْدَرِيَّةُ مَدِينَةٌ كَبِيرَةٌ.
2. Alexandria is in Egypt.	2. enha fey mesr.	2. إِنَّها فِي مِصْرَ.
3. This is Bruce.	3. enh berwes.	3. إِنَّهُ بْرُوس.
4. Bruce is a student.	4. enh taleb.	4. إِنَّهُ طالِبٌ.
5. He is in Alexandria now.	5. enh fey aleseknedreyh alan.	5. إِنَّهُ فِي الإِسْكَنْدَرِيَّةِ الآنَ.
6. Bruce is from the USA.	6. enh men alewlayat alemthedh alameryekyh.	6. إِنَّهُ مِنَ الوِلاياتِ المُتَّحِدَةِ الأَمْرِيكِيَّةِ.
7. He is American.	7. enh ameryeky.	7. إِنَّهُ أَمْرِيكِيٌّ.
8. Bruce has a mother, a father, a brother and a sister.	8. ledyh am wab wakh wakhet.	8. لَدَيهِ أُمٌّ وَأَبٌ وَأَخٌ وَأُخْتٌ.
9. They live in the USA.	9. y'eyeshewn fey alewlayat alemthedh alameryekyh.	9. يَعِيشُونَ فِي الوِلاياتِ المُتَّحِدَةِ الأَمْرِيكِيَّةِ.
10. This is Hiroshi.	10. enh heyrewshey.	10. إِنَّهُ هِيرُوشِي.
11. Hiroshi is a student	11. enh taleb ayedaan.	11. إِنَّهُ طالِبٌ أَيضاً.

too.	12. enh men aleyaban.	12. إِنَّهُ مِنْ اليابانِ.
12. He is from Japan.	13. enh yabaney.	13. إِنَّهُ يابانِيٌّ.
13. He is Japanese.	14. ledyh am wab wakhetyen.	14. لَدَيْهِ أُمٌّ وَأَبٌ وَأُخْتَيْنِ.
14. Hiroshi has a mother, a father and two sisters.	15. enhem y'eyeshewn fey aleyaban.	15. إِنَّهُمْ يَعِيشُونَ فِي اليابانِ.
15. They live in Japan.	16. berwes wheyrewshey fey aleswebr marekt alan.	16. بْرُوس وَهِيرُوشِي فِي السُوبَر مارِكِت الآنَ.
16. Bruce and Hiroshi are in a supermarket now.	17. enhem ja'e'ewen.	17. إِنَّهُمْ جائِعُونَ.
17. They are hungry.	18. yeshetrewn sheta'er.	18. يَشْتَرُونَ شَطائِرَ.
18. They buy sandwiches.	19. enha henan.	19. إِنَّها حَنانٌ.
19. This is Hanan.	20. enha mesreyh.	20. إِنَّها مِصرِيَّةٌ.
20. Hanan is Egyptian.	21. enha t'eyesh fey aleseknedreyh ayedaan.	21. إِنَّها تَعِيشُ فِي الإِسْكَنْدَرِيَّةِ أَيْضاً.
21. Hanan lives in Alexandria too.	22. enha leyset talebh.	22. إِنَّها لَيْسَتْ طالِبَةً.
22. She is not a student.	23. ana taleb.	23. أَنا طالِبٌ.
23. I am a student.	24. ana men alewlayat alemthedh alameryekyh.	24. أَنا مِنْ الوِلاياتِ المُتَّحِدَةِ الأَمْرِيكِيَّةِ.
24. I am from the USA.	25. ana fey aleseknedreyh alan.	25. أَنا فِي الإِسْكَنْدَرِيَّةِ الآنَ.
25. I am in Alexandria now.	26. ana lest ja'e'eaan.	26. أَنا لَسْتُ جائِعاً.
26. I am not hungry.	27. anet taleb.	27. أَنْتَ طالِبٌ.
27. You are a student.	28. anet ameryeky.	28. أَنْتَ أَمْرِيكِيٌّ.
28. You are American.		

29. You are not in the USA now.	29. enek lest fey alewlayat alemthedh alameryekyh alan.	29. إِنَّكَ لَسْتَ فِي الوِلاياتِ المُتَّحِدَةِ الأَمْريكِيَّةِ الآنَ.
30. You are in Egypt.	30. enek fey mesr.	30. إِنَّكَ فِي مِصْرَ.
31. We are students.	31. nhen telab.	31. نَحْنُ طُلّابٌ.
32. We are in Egypt now.	32. enena fey mesr alan.	32. إِنَّنا فِي مِصْرَ الآنَ.
33. This is a bike.	33. hedh derajh.	33. هٰذِهِ دَرّاجَةٌ.
34. The bike is blue.	34. enha zerqa'.	34. إِنَّها زَرْقاءُ.
35. The bike is not new.	35. enha leyset jedyedh.	35. إِنَّها لَيْسَتْ جَديدَةً.
36. This is a dog.	36. heda kelb.	36. هٰذا كَلْبٌ.
37. The dog is black.	37. enh asewd.	37. إِنَّهُ أَسْوَدُ.
38. The dog is not big.	38. enh leys kebyeraan.	38. إِنَّهُ لَيْسَ كَبيراً.
39. These are shops.	39. hedh metajer.	39. هٰذِهِ مَتاجِرُ.
40. The shops are not big.	40. enha leyset kebyerh.	40. إِنَّها لَيْسَتْ كَبيرَةً.
41. They are little.	41. enha qelyelh.	41. إِنَّها قَليلَةٌ.
42. That shop has many windows.	42. yewjed betlek alemtejr newafed ketheyrh.	42. يُوجَدُ بِتِلْكَ المَتْجَرِ نَوافِذُ كَثيرَةٌ.
43. Those shops do not have many windows.	43. la yewjed bha newafed ketheyrh.	43. لا يُوجَدُ بِها نَوافِذُ كَثيرَةٌ.
44. That cat is in the room.	44. telk aleqth fey alegherfh.	44. تِلْكَ القِطَّةُ فِي الغُرْفَةِ.
45. Those cats are not in the room.	45. telk aleqtet leyset fey alegherfh.	45. تِلْكَ القِطَطُ لَيْسَتْ فِي الغُرْفَةِ.

الفَصْلُ الثَالِثُ
Chapter 3

هَلْ هُمْ مَصرِيُّونَ؟

Are they Egyptians?

A

الكَلِمَاتُ

Words

1. إمْرَأَةٌ - woman
2. أَنْتَ ، أَنْتُما ، أَنْتُمْ - you
3. انجليزِي - English
4. أَيْنَ - where
5. حَيَوانٌ - animal
6. خَرِيطَةٌ - map
7. هو - it
8. عَلَى - on
9. فِي ، عِنْدَ - at
10. قَدِيمٌ - old
11. رَجُلٌ - man
12. كِتابُها - her book

23

13. كُلُّ ، جَمِيعُ - all
14. كَيْفَ - how
15. لا - no
16. مَشْغَلُ أسْطُواناتٍ - CD player
17. مَقْهَى - café
18. مَلِكُنا - our
19. مَنْزِلُ - house
20. نَعَمْ - yes
21. وُلَدَ ، غُلام - boy

B

Are they Egyptians?	hel hem mesreywen?	هَل هُمْ مِصْرِيُّونَ؟
–I am a boy. I am in the room.	- ana weld. eneny fey alegherfh.	- أَنا وَلَدٌ. إِنَّنِي فِي الغُرْفَةِ.
–Are you Egyptian?	- hel anet mesrey?	- هَل أَنْتَ مِصْرِيٌّ؟
–No, I am not. I am American.	- la. ana ameryeky.	- لا. أَنا أَمرِيكِيٌّ.
–Are you a student?	- hel anet taleb?	- هَل أَنْتَ طالِبٌ؟
–Yes, I am. I am a student.	- n'em. ana taleb.	- نَعَمْ. أَنا طالِبٌ.
–This is a woman. The woman is in the room too.	- hedh emerah. enha fey alegherfh kedlek.	- هٰذِهِ إِمرَأَةٌ. إِنَّها فِي الغُرْفَةِ كَذٰلِكَ.
–Is she American?	- hel hey ameryekyh?	- هَل هِيَ أَمرِيكِيَّةٌ؟
–No, she is not. She is Egyptian.	- la. enha mesreyh.	- لا. إِنَّها مِصْرِيَّةٌ.
–Is she a student?	- hel hey talebh?	- هَل هِيَ طالِبَةٌ؟
–No, she is not. She is not a student.	- la. enha leyset talebh.	- لا. إِنَّها لَيْسَتْ طالِبَةً.

–This is a man. He is at the table. –Is he Egyptian? –Yes, he is. He is Egyptian.	- heda rejl. enh yejles ela alemneddh. - hel hew mesrey? - n'em. enh mesrey.	- هٰذا رَجُلٌ. إنَّهُ يَجلِسُ إلَى المِنضَدَةِ. - هَل هُوَ مِصرِيٌّ؟ - نَعَم. إنَّهُ مِصرِيٌّ.
–These are students. They are in the park. –Are they all Egyptians? –No, they are not. They are Egyptians, Americans and Japanese.	- h'ela' telab. enhem fey alhedyeqh. - hel jemy'ehem mesreyyen? - la. enhem mesreywen wameryekyewn weyabaneywen.	- هٰؤُلاءِ طُلّابٌ. إنَّهُم فِي الحَدِيقَةِ. - هَل جَمِيعُهُم مِصرِيِّينَ؟ - لا. إنَّهُم مِصرِيُّونَ وَأَمرِيكِيُّونَ وَيابانِيُّونَ.
–This is a table. It is big. –Is it new? –Yes, it is. It is new.	- hedh mendedh. enha kebyerh. - hel hey jedyedh? - n'em. enha jedyedh.	- هٰذِهِ مِنضَدَةٌ. إنَّها كَبِيرَةٌ. - هَل هِيَ جَدِيدَةٌ؟ - نَعَم. إنَّها جَدِيدَةٌ.
–This is a cat. It is in the room. –Is it black? –Yes, it is. It is black and nice.	- hedh qeth. enha fey alegherfh. - hel hey sewda'? - n'em. enha sewda' welteyfh.	- هٰذِهِ قِطَّةٌ. إنَّها فِي الغُرفَةِ. - هَل هِيَ سَوداءُ؟ - نَعَم. إنَّها سَوداءُ وَلَطِيفَةٌ.
–These are bikes. They are at the house. –Are they black? –Yes, they are. They are black.	- hedh derajat. enha fey alemnezl. - hel hey sewda'? - n'em. enha sewda'.	- هٰذِهِ دَرّاجاتٌ. إنَّها فِي المَنزِلِ. - هَل هِيَ سَوداءُ؟ - نَعَم. إنَّها سَوداءُ.

–Do you have a notebook? –Yes, I do. –How many notebooks do you have? –I have two notebooks.	- hel 'enedk mefkerh? - n'em. - kem mefkerh? - mefkertan.	- هَلْ عِنْدَكَ مُفَكِّرَةٌ؟ - نَعَمْ. - كَمْ مُفَكِّرَةً؟ - مُفَكِّرَتانِ.
–Does he have a pen? –Yes, he does. –How many pens does he have? –He has one pen.	- hel 'enedh qelm hebr? - n'em. - kem qelm hebr? - qelm hebr wahed.	- هَلْ عِنْدَهُ قَلَمُ حِبْرٍ؟ - نَعَمْ. - كَمْ قَلَمَ حِبْرٍ؟ - قَلَمُ حِبْرٍ واحِدٍ.
–Does she have a bike? –Yes, she does. –Is her bike blue? –No, it is not. Her bike is not blue. It is green.	- hel 'enedha derajh? - n'em. - hel hey zerqa'? - la. leyset zerqa'. enha khedra'.	- هَلْ عِنْدَها دَرّاجَةٌ؟ - نَعَمْ. - هَلْ هِيَ زَرْقاءُ؟ - لا. لَيْسَتْ زَرْقاءَ. إنَّها خَضْراءُ.
–Do you have an English book? –No, I do not. I do not have an English book. I have no book.	- hel 'enedk ketab leghh enejleyzeyh? - la. leys 'enedy ketab leghh enejleyzeyh. leys 'enedy ay ketab.	- هَلْ عِنْدَكِ كِتابُ لُغَةٍ إنجليزِيَّةٍ؟ - لا. لَيْسَ عِنْدِي كِتابُ لُغَةٍ إنجليزِيَّةٍ. لَيْسَ عِنْدِي أيُّ كِتابٍ.
–Does she have a cat? –No, she does not. She does not have a cat. She has no animal.	- hel 'enedha qeth? - la. leys 'enedha qeth. leys 'enedha ay heywan.	- هَلْ عِنْدَها قِطَّةٌ؟ - لا. لَيْسَ عِنْدَها قِطَّةٌ. لَيْسَ عِنْدَها أيُّ حَيَوانٍ.

–Do you have a CD player?
–No, we do not. We do not have a CD player. We have no player.

–Where is our map?
–Our map is in the room.
–Is it on the table?
–Yes, it is.

–Where are the boys?
–They are in the café.
–Where are the bikes?
–They are at the café.
–Where is Hiroshi?
–He is in the café too.

- hel 'enedkem mesheghel asetwanat?
- la. leys 'enedna. leys 'enedna ay mesheghel asetwanat.

- ayen kheryettena?
- enha fey alegherfh.
- hel hey 'ela alemneddh?
- n'em, hey kedlek.

- ayen alawelad?
- enhem fey alemqha.
- ayen aledrajat?
- enha 'ened alemqha.
- ayen heyrewshey?
- enh fey alemqha kedlek.

- هَلْ عِنْدَكُمْ مَشْغَلُ أُسْطُواناتٍ؟
- لا. لَيْسَ عِنْدَنا. لَيْسَ عِنْدَنا أَيُّ مَشْغَلِ أُسْطُواناتٍ.

- أَيْنَ خَرِيطَتُنا؟
- إِنَّها فِي الغُرْفَةِ.
- هَلْ هِيَ عَلَى المِنْضَدَةِ؟
- نَعَمْ، هِيَ كَذٰلِكَ.

- أَيْنَ الأَوْلادُ؟
- إِنَّهُمْ فِي المَقْهَى.
- أَيْنَ الدَرّاجاتُ؟
- إِنَّها عِنْدَ المَقْهَى.
- أَيْنَ هِيرُوشِي؟
- إِنَّهُ فِي المَقْهَى كَذٰلِكَ.

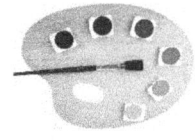

الفَصْلُ الرَّابِعُ
Chapter 4

أَيُمْكِنُكَ أَنْ تُساعِدَ مِنْ فَضْلِكَ؟
Can you help, please?

A

الكَلِمَاتُ
Words

1. أَذْهَبُ إِلَى البَنْكِ. - I go to the bank.
2. أَوْ - or
3. رُبَّما أَذْهَبُ إِلَى البَنْكِ. - I may go to the bank. أَيُمْكِنِي مُساعَدَتُكَ؟ - May I help you?
4. رُوسي (m), رُوسِيَّة (f), رُوسي (adj.) - Russian
5. رُوسيا - Russia
6. عَمَلُ - work; يَعْمَلُ - to work
7. عُنْوانُ - address
8. لِأَجْلِ - for

9. لٰكِنْ - but
10. لِي - to me
11. مُساعِدُ - to help; مُساعَدَةُ - help
12. مَصْرِفُ - بَنْكٌ - bank
13. مَكانٌ - place; يَضَعُ - to place
14. مِن فضلك - please
15. يَأْخُذُ - to take
16. يَتَعَلَّمُ - learn
17. يَتَكَلَّمُ - يَتَحَدَّثُ - to speak
18. يَجِبُ - must
   يَجِبُ أَنْ أَذْهَبَ. - I must go.
19. يَجْلِسُ - to sit
20. يَذْهَبُ (عَلَى الأَقْدامِ) - to go (on foot); يَذْهَبُ (بِوَسيلَةِ إنتِقال) - to go (by a transport)
21. يَسْتَطِيعُ - can
   أَسْتَطِيعُ القِراءَةَ - I can read.
22. يَشْكُرُ - to thank; شُكْراً لَكَ - Thank you. شُكْراً - thanks
23. يُعْطِي - to give
24. يَقْرَأُ - to read
25. يَكْتُبُ - to write
26. يَلْعَبُ - to play

B

Can you help, please?	aymknk an tsa'ed mn fdlk?	أَيُمْكِنُكَ أَنْ تُساعِدَ مِنْ فَضْلِكَ؟
- Can you help me, please?	- aymknk msa'edty mn fdlk?	- أَيُمْكِنُكِ مُساعَدَتِي مِنْ فَضْلِكِ؟
- Yes, I can.	- n'em, astty'e.	- نَعَم، أَسْتَطِيعُ.
- I cannot write the address in Arabic. Can you write it for me?	- laastty'e ktabh al'enwan bal'erbyyh. aymknk ktabth ly?	- لاِأَسْتَطِيعُ كِتابَةَ العُنْوانِ بِالعَرَبِيَّةِ. أَيُمْكِنُكَ كِتابَتَهُ لِي؟
- Yes, I can.	- n'em, astty'e.	- نَعَم، أَسْتَطِيعُ.
- Thank you.	- shkraan lk.	- شُكْراً لَكَ.

- Can you play tennis?
- No, I cannot. But I can learn. Can you help me to learn?
- Yes, I can. I can help you to learn to play tennis.
- Thank you.

- aymknk l'eb altns?
- la, wlkn mmn almmkn an at'elm. aymknk msa'edty lat'elm?
- n'em. ymknny msa'edtk fy t'elm l'eb altns.
- shkraan lk.

- أَيُمْكِنُكَ لَعِبُ التِنِسِ؟
- لَا، وَلَكِنْ مِمَّنْ المُمْكِنِ أَنْ أَتَعَلَّمَ. أَيُمْكِنُكَ مُسَاعَدَتِي لِأَتَعَلَّمَ؟
- نَعَمْ. يُمْكِنُنِي مُسَاعَدَتُكَ فِي تَعَلُّمِ لَعِبِ التِنِسِ.
- شُكْراً لَكَ.

- Can you speak Arabic?
- I can speak and read Arabic but I cannot write.
- Can you speak English or Russian?
- I can speak, read and write English and Russian.

- aymknk althdth bal'erbyh?
- astty'e althdth walqra'h bal'erbyh wlkn la astty'e an aktb.
- aymknk althdth balenjlyzyh aw alrwsyh?
- astty'e an athdth waqra waktb balenjlyzyh aw alrwsyh.

- أَيُمْكِنُكَ التَحَدُّثَ بِالعَرَبِيَّةِ؟
- أَسْتَطِيعُ التَحَدُّثَ وَالقِرَاءَةَ بِالعَرَبِيَّةِ وَلَكِنْ لَا أَسْتَطِيعُ أَنْ أَكْتُبَ.
- أَيُمْكِنُكَ التَحَدُّثَ بِالإنجليزِيَّةِ أَوْ الرُوسِيَّةِ؟
- أَسْتَطِيعُ أَنْ أَتَحَدَّثَ وَأَقْرَأَ وَأَكْتُبَ بِالإنجليزِيَّةِ أَوْ الرُوسِيَّةِ.

- Can Hanan speak Russian too?
- No, she cannot. She is Egyptian.
- Can they speak Arabic?
- Yes, they can a little.

- hl tthdth hnan alrwsyh aydaan?
- la, enha msryh.
- hl ythdthwn al'erbyh?
- n'em, qlylaan. enhm tlab, whm yt'elmwn

- هَلْ تَتَحَدَّثُ حَنان الرُوسِيَّةُ أَيْضاً؟
- لَا، إِنَّها مِصْرِيَّةٌ.
- هَلْ يَتَحَدَّثُونَ العَرَبِيَّةَ؟
- نَعَمْ، قَلِيلاً. إِنَّهُمْ طُلَّابٌ، وَهُمْ

They are students and they learn Arabic. - This boy cannot speak Arabic.	al'erbyh. - hda alghlam la ythdth al'erbyh.	يَتَعَلَّمُونَ العَرَبِيَّةَ. - هٰذا الغُلامُ لا يَتَحَدَّثُ العَرَبِيَّةَ.
- Where are they? - They play tennis now. - May we play too? - Yes, we may.	- ayn hm? - enhm yl'ebwn altns alan. - hl ymknna all'eb aydaan? - n'em ymknna.	- أَيْنَ هُمْ؟ - إِنَّهُمْ يَلْعَبُونَ التِنِسَ الآنَ. - هَلْ يُمكِنُنا اللَعِبُ أَيْضاً؟ - نَعَمْ يُمْكِنُنا.
- Where is Bruce? - He may be at the café.	- ayn brws? - rbma ykwn fy almqha.	- أَيْنَ بْرُوس؟ - رُبَّما يَكُونُ فِي المَقْهَى.
- Sit at this table, please. - Thank you. May I place my books on that table? - Yes, you may.	- ajls ela hdh almnddh mn fdlk. - shkraan lk. aymknny an ad'e ktby 'elyha? - n'em, ymknk.	- اِجْلِسْ إِلَى هٰذِهِ المِنْضَدَةِ مِنْ فَضْلِكِ. - شُكْراً لَكَ. أَيُمْكِنُنِي أَنْ أَضَعَ كُتُبِي عَلَيْها؟ - نَعَمْ، يُمْكِنُكَ.
- May Hiroshi sit at her table? - Yes, he may. - May I sit on her bed? - No, you must not. - May Hanan take his	- hl ymkn lhyrwshy an yjls ela mnddtha? - n'em, ymknh. - aymknny an ajls 'ela sryrha? - la, 'elyk ala tf'el. - hl ymkn lhnan an	- هَلْ يُمْكِنُ لِهيروشِي أَنْ يَجْلِسَ إِلَى مِنْضَدَتِها؟ - نَعَمْ، يُمْكِنُهُ. - أَيُمْكِنُنِي أَنْ أَجْلِسَ عَلَى سَرِيرِها؟ - لا، عَلَيْكَ أَلّا تَفْعَلَ.

CD player? - No. She must not take his CD player. - May they take her map? - No, they may not.	takhd mshghl astwanath? - la, 'elyha ala tf'el. - hl ymknhm akhd khryttha? - la, la ymknhm.	- هَلْ يُمْكِنُ لِحنانٍ أَنْ تَأْخُذَ مَشْغَلَ أَسْطُواناتِهِ؟ - لا، عَلَيْها أَلّا تَفْعَلَ. - هَلْ يُمْكِنُهُمْ أَخْذُ خَريطَتِها؟ - لا، لا يُمَكِّنُهُمْ.
- You must not sit on her bed. - She must not take his CD player. - They must not take these notebooks.	- yjb ala tjls 'ela sryrha. - yjb ala takhd mshghl astwanath. - yjb ala yakhdwa hdh almfkrat.	- يَجِبُ أَلّا تَجْلِسَ عَلَى سَريرِها. - يَجِبُ أَلّا تَأْخُذَ مَشْغَلَ أَسْطُواناتِهِ. - يَجِبُ أَلّا يَأْخُذوا هٰذِهِ المُفَكِّراتِ.
- I must go to the bank. - Must you go now? - Yes, I must.	- yjb an adhb ela albnk. - hl yjb an tdhb alan? - n'em, yjb.	- يَجِبُ أَنْ أَذْهَبَ إِلَى البَنْكِ. - هَلْ يَجِبُ أَنْ تَذْهَبَ الآنَ؟ - نَعَمْ، يَجِبُ.
- Must you learn English? - I need not learn English. I must learn Arabic.	- hl yjb an tt'elm alenjlyzyh? - la ahtaj lt'elm lenjlyzyh. yjb an at'elm al'erbyh.	- هَلْ يَجِبُ أَنْ تَتَعَلَّمَ الإِنْجليزِيَّةَ؟ - لا أَحْتاجُ لِتَعَلُّمِ الإِنْجليزِيَّةِ. يَجِبُ أَنْ أَتَعَلَّمَ العَرَبِيَّةَ.
- Must she go to the bank? - No. She need not go to the bank.	- hl yjb 'elyha aldhab ela albnk? - la, la thtaj an tdhb elyh.	- هَلْ يَجِبُ عَلَيْها الذَهابُ إِلَى البَنْكِ؟ - لا، لا تَحْتاجُ أَنْ تَذْهَبَ إِلَيْهِ.

- May I take this bike?
- No, you must not take this bike.

- aymknny an aakhd hdh aldrajh?
- la, la yjb an takhdha.

- أَيُمْكِنُنِي أَنْ أَأْخُذَ هٰذِهِ الدَّرَاجَةَ؟
- لَا، لَا يَجِبُ أَنْ تَأْخُذَها.

- May we place these notebooks on her bed?
- No. You must not place the notebooks on her bed

- hl ymknna an nd'e hdh almfkrat 'ela sryrha?
- la, la yjb wd'e almfkrat 'ela sryrha.

- هَلْ يُمْكِئُنَا أَنْ نَضَعَ هٰذِهِ المُفَكِّرَاتِ عَلَى سَرِيرِها؟
- لَا، لَا يَجِبُ وَضْعُ المُفَكِّرَاتِ عَلَى سَرِيرِها.

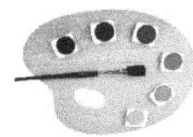

الفَصْلُ الخَامِسُ
Chapter 5

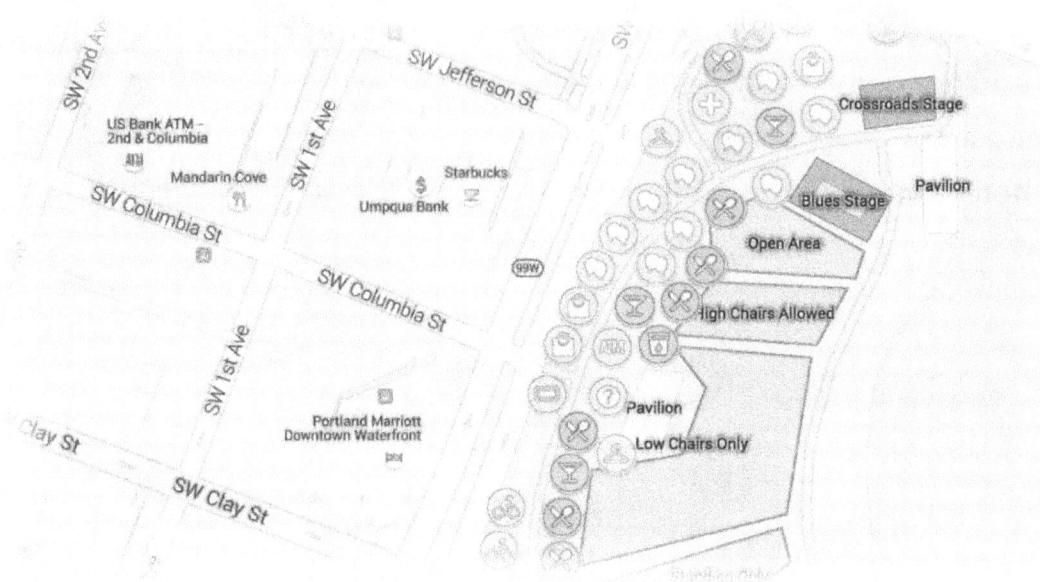

بروس يَعِيشُ فِي مِصْرَ الآنَ
Bruce lives in Egypt now

A

الكَلِمَاتُ
Words

1. أَثاثُ - furniture
2. أَيْ - any
3. بَعْضٌ - some
4. ثَلاثَةُ - three
5. ثَمانِيَةُ - eight
6. جَيِّدٌ - good
7. حاجَةُ - need
8. حَسَناً - جَيِّداً - well
9. خَمْسَةُ - five
10. سَبْعَةُ - seven
11. سِتَّةُ - six
12. شايُ - tea

13. صَحِيفَة - جَرِيدَة - newspaper
14. فَتاةٌ - بِنْت - girl
15. فَطُورٌ - breakfast; يَتَناوَلُ الفَطُورَ - have breakfast
16. كُرْسِيٌّ - chair
17. مَزْرَعَةٌ - farm
18. مُوسِيقَى - music
19. مَيْدانٌ - مُرَبَّعٌ - square
20. ناس - شَعْبٌ - people
21. هُناكَ (لِلمَكانِ) - there (place)
22. هُناكَ (لِلإتْجاهِ) - there (direction)
23. يَأْكُلُ - to eat
24. يُحِبُّ - to like, to love
25. يَسْتَمِعُ - يُصْغِي - to listen; يَسْتَمِعُ إلَى المُوسِيقَى - I listen to music.
26. يَشْرَبُ - to drink

B

Bruce lives in Egypt now	berwes y'eyesh fey mesr alan	بروس يَعِيشُ فِي مِصْرَ الآنَ
Hanan reads English well. I read English too. The students go to the park. She goes to the park too.	henan teqra alenejleyzeyh jeydaan. wana aqera alenejleyzeyh ayedaan. yedheb aletlab ela alhedyeqh. whey tedheb eleyha ayedaan.	حَنان تَقْرَأُ الإنجليزيَّةَ جَيِّداً. وَأَنا أَقْرَأُ الإنجليزيَّةَ أَيْضاً. يَذْهَبُ الطُّلَّابُ إلَى الحَدِيقَةِ. وَهِيَ تَذْهَبُ إلَيْها أَيْضاً.
We live in Alexandia. Hiroshi lives in Alexandria now too. His father and mother live in Japan. Brucec lives in Egypt now. His	enena n'eyesh fey aleseknedreyh. ayedaan y'eyesh heyrewshey bha haleyaan. y'ebesh abewh wamh baleyaban. y'eyesh berwes fey mesr haleyaan. y'eyesh abewh wamh fey	إنَّنا نَعِيشُ فِي الإسْكَنْدَرِيَّةِ. أَيْضاً يَعِيشُ هِيروشِي بِها حالِيّاً. يَعِيشُ أَبُوهُ وَأُمُّهُ بِاليابانِ. يَعِيشُ بروس فِي مِصْرَ حالِيّاً. يَعِيشُ أَبُوهُ وَأُمُّهُ فِي الوِلاياتِ

father and mother live in the USA.	alewlayat alemthedh alameryekyh.	المُتَّحِدَةِ الأَمْريكِيَّةِ.
The students play tennis. Hiroshi plays well. Bruce does not play well.	yel'eb aletlab aletnes. heyrewshey yel'eb jeydaan. berwes la yel'eb jeydaan.	يَلْعَبُ الطُّلّابُ التِنِس. هِيروشِي يَلْعَبُ جَيِّداً. بْروس لا يَلْعَبُ جَيِّداً.
We drink tea. Hanan drinks green tea. Omar drinks black tea. I drink black tea too.	enena nesherb aleshay. henan tesherb aleshay alakhedr. 'emer yesherb aleshay alasewd. wana asherb aleshay alasewd ayedaan.	إِنَّنا نَشْرَبُ الشايَ. حَنان تَشْرَبُ الشايَ الأَخْضَرَ. عُمْرْ يَشْرَبُ الشايَ الأَسْوَدَ. وَأَنا أَشْرَبُ الشايَ الأَسْوَدَ أَيْضاً.
I listen to music. Sarah listens to music too. She likes to listen to good music.	asetm' ela alemwesyeqa. sarh testem' eleyha ayedaan. enha theb an testem' ela alemwesyeqa alejyedh.	أَسْتَمِعُ إِلَى المُوسِيقَى. سارَّة تَسْتَمِعُ إِلَيْها أَيْضاً. إِنَّها تُحِبُّ أَنْ تَسْتَمِعَ إِلَى المُوسِيقَى الجَيِّدَةِ.
I need six notebooks. Omar needs seven notebooks. Hanan needs eight notebooks.	ahetaj seth mefkerat. 'emer yhetaj seb'eh mefkerat. henan thetaj themaneyh mefkerat.	أَحْتاجُ سِتَّةَ مُفَكِّراتٍ. عُمْرْ يَحْتاجُ سَبْعَةَ مُفَكِّراتٍ. حَنانْ تَحْتاجُ ثَمانِيَةَ مُفَكِّراتٍ.
Sarah wants to drink. I want to drink too. Hiroshi wants to eat.	sarh teryed an tesherb. areyd an asherb ayedaan. heyrewshey yeryed an yakel.	سارَّة تُرِيدُ أَنْ تَشْرَبَ. أُرِيدُ أَنْ أَشْرَبَ أَيْضاً. هِيروشِي يُرِيدُ أَنْ يَأْكُلَ.

There is a newspaper on the table. Hiroshi takes it and reads. He likes to read newspapers.

henak sheyfh 'ela alemneddh. heyrewshey yakhedha weyqera. enh yheb an yeqra aleshef.

هُناكَ صَحِيفَةٌ عَلَى المِنْضَدَةِ. هِيروشي يَأْخُذُها وَيَقْرَأُ. إِنَّهُ يُحِبُّ أَنْ يَقْرَأَ الصُّحَفَ.

There is some furniture in the room. There are six tables and six chairs there.

yewjed b'ed alathath fey alegherfh. henak seth menaded westh kerasey.

يُوجَدُ بَعْضُ الأَثاثِ فِي الغُرْفَةِ. هُناكَ سِتَّةُ مَناضِدَ وَسِتَّةُ كَراسِي.

There are three girls in the room. They eat breakfast.
Sarah eats bread and drinks tea. She likes green tea.

henak thelathh fetyat fey alegherfh. enhem yetnawelwen aleftewr. sarh takel khebzaan wetsherb aleshay. enha theb aleshay alakhedr.

هُناكَ ثَلاثَةُ فَتَياتٍ فِي الغُرْفَةِ. إِنَّهُمْ يَتَناوَلُونَ الفُطُورَ. سارَة تَأْكُلُ خُبْزاً وَتَشْرَبُ الشايَ. إِنَّها تُحِبُّ الشايَ الأَخْضَرَ.

There are some books on the table. They are not new. They are old.

henak b'ed alekteb 'ela alemneddh. enha leyset jedyedh. enha qedyemh.

هُناكَ بَعْضُ الكُتُبِ عَلَى المِنْضَدَةِ. إِنَّها لَيْسَتْ جَدِيدَةً. إِنَّها قَدِيمَةٌ.

- Is there a bank in this street?
- Yes, there is. There are five banks in this street. The banks are not big.

- hel henak benkaan fey heda aleshar'e?
- n'em, yewjed. henak khemsh benwek fey heda aleshar'e. whedh alebnewk gheyr kebyerh.

-هَلْ هُناكَ بَنْكاً فِي هٰذا الشارِعِ؟
-نَعَمْ، يُوجَدُ. هُناكَ خَمْسَةُ بُنُوكِ فِي هٰذا الشارِعِ. وَهٰذِهِ البُنُوكُ غَيْرُ كَبِيرَةٍ.

- Are there people in

- hel henak anas fey alemyedan?

-هَلْ هُناكَ أَناسٌ فِي المَيْدانِ؟

the square? - Yes, there are. There are some people in the square.	- n'em, yewjed. henak b'ed alenas fey alemyedan.	-نَعَم، يُوجَدُ. هُناكَ بَعْضُ الناسِ فِي المَيدانِ.
- Are there bikes at the café? - Yes, there are. There are four bikes at the café. They are not new.	- hel henak derajat 'ened alemqha? - n'em, yewjed. henak areb'eh derajat 'ened alemqha. enha leyset jedyedh.	-هَل هُناكَ دَرّاجاتٌ عِنْدَ المَقْهَى؟ -نَعَم، يُوجَدُ. هُناكَ أَرْبَعَةُ دَرّاجاتٍ عِنْدَ المَقْهَى. إنَّها لَيْسَت جَديدَةً.
- Is there a hotel in this street? - No, there is not. There are no hotels in this street.	- hel henak fendeqaan fey heda aleshar'e? - la, la yewjed. la tewjed fenadeq fey heda aleshar'e.	-هَل هُناكَ فُنْدُقاً فِي هٰذا الشارِعِ؟ -لا، لا يُوجَدُ. لا تُوجَدُ فَنادِقُ فِي هٰذا الشارِعِ.
- Are there any big shops in that street? - No, there are not. There are no big shops in that street.	- hel henak metajer kebyerh fey telk aleshar'e? - la, la tewjed. la tewjed metajer kebyerh fey telk aleshar'e.	-هَل هُناكَ مَتاجِرُ كَبيرَةٌ فِي تِلْكَ الشارِعِ؟ -لا، لا تُوجَدُ. لا تُوجَدُ مَتاجِرُ كَبيرَةٌ فِي تِلْكَ الشارِعِ.
- Are there any farms in Egypt? - Yes, there are. There are many farms in Egypt.	- hel henak ay mezar' fey mesr? - n'em, tewjed. henak mezar' ketheyrh fey mesr.	-هَل هُناكَ أَيُّ مُزارِعَ فِي مِصْرَ؟ -نَعَم، تُوجَدُ. هُناكَ مَزارِعُ كَثيرَةٌ فِي مِصْرَ.

- Is there any furniture in that room?
- Yes, there is. There are four tables and some chairs there.

- hel henak aa athath fey telk alegherfh?
- n'em, yewjed. henak areb'eh menaded web'ed alekrasey.

-هَلْ هُناكَ أَى أَثاثٍ فِي تِلْكَ الغُرْفَةِ؟
-نَعَمْ، يُوجَدُ. هُناكَ أَرْبَعَةُ مَناضِدَ وَبَعْضُ الكَراسِي.

الفَصْلُ السَادِسُ
Chapter 6

بُروس لَدَيْهِ الكَثِيرُ مِنَ الأَصْدِقَاء

Bruce has many friends

A

الكَلِمَاتُ
Words

1. أبٌ - dad
2. أُسْطُوانَةٌ مُدْمَجَةٌ - CD
3. إلَى - نَحْوَ - into
4. إناءٌ لِلطَهْيِ - cooker
5. أَيْضاً - as well
6. بابٌ - door
7. تَحْتَ - under

8. عادِل - Adel
9. حُرٌّ - مَجّاناً - free
10. خاصٌّ بالأُمّ - mother's
11. خاصٌّ بالمَرْأةِ - woman's
12. خاصٌّ ببُروس - Bruce's
13. خاصٌّ بِعُمَرٍ - Omar's;
    كِتابُ عُمَر - Omar's book

14. خاصٌّ بِهِيرُوشِي - Hiroshi's	21. مَارِي - Mariam	
15. خَرِيطَةُ الرَجُلِ - man's map	22. نَظِيفٌ - clean; يُنَظِّفُ - to clean	
16. سَيَّارَةٌ - car	23. وَظِيفَةٌ - job; وَكَالَةُ تَوْظِيفٍ - job agency	
17. صَدِيقٌ - friend	24. وَكَالَةٌ - مَكْتَبٌ - agency	
18. قَهْوَةٌ - coffee	25. يَذْهَبُ - go; يَأْتِي - come	
19. كَثِيرٌ - much, many	26. يَعرِفُ - to know	
20. كُمْبْيُوتَر - حَاسُوبٌ - computer		

B

Bruce has many friends	berwes ledyh alektheyr men alasedqa'	بْرُوس لَدَيْهِ الكَثِيرُ مِنَ الأَصْدِقَاء
Bruce has many friends. Bruce's friends come to the café. They like to drink coffee. Bruce's friends drink a lot of coffee.	berwes ledyh alektheyr men alasedqa'. asedqa' berwes yatewn ela alemqha. enhem yhebwen tenawel aleqhewh. asedqa' berwes yetnawelwen alektheyr men aleqhewh.	بْرُوس لَدَيْهِ الكَثِيرُ مِنَ الأَصْدِقَاءِ. أَصْدِقَاءُ بْرُوس يَأْتُونَ إِلَى المَقْهَى. إِنَّهُمْ يُحِبُّونَ تَنَاوُلَ القَهْوَةِ. أَصْدِقَاءُ بْرُوس يَتَنَاوَلُونَ الكَثِيرَ مِنْ القَهْوَةِ.
Hiroshi's dad has a car. The dad's car is clean but old. Hiroshi's dad drives a lot. He has a good job	waled heyrewshey ledyh seyarh. alesyarh nezyefh welkenha qedyemh. waled heyrewshey yeqwed alesyarh ketheyraan. whew y'emel fey wezyefh jeydh weldeyh alektheyr	وَالِدُ هِيرُوشِي لَدَيْهِ سَيَّارَةٌ. السَيَّارَةُ نَظِيفَةٌ وَلَكِنَّها قَدِيمَةٌ. وَالِدُ هِيرُوشِيٌّ يَقُودُ السَيَّارَةَ كَثِيراً. وَهُوَ يَعْمَلُ فِي وَظِيفَةٍ جَيِّدَةٍ وَلَدَيْهِ الكَثِيرُ مِنْ العَمَلِ

and he has a lot of work now.	men al'emel alan.	الأَنَّ.
Omar has a lot of CDs. Omar's CDs are on his bed. Omar's CD player is on his bed as well.	'emer ledyh ketheyraan men alasetwanat. whey 'ela seryerh. wemsheghel alasetwanat 'ela seryerh ayedaan.	عُمَرُ لَدَيْهِ كَثِيراً مِن الأسْطُواناتِ. وَهِيَ عَلَى سَرِيرِهِ. وَمُشْغِلُ الأسْطُواناتِ عَلَى سَرِيرِهِ أَيْضاً.
Bruce reads Egyptian newspapers. There are many newspapers on the table in Bruce's room.	berwes yeqra shefaan mesreyh. henak alektheyr men aleshef 'ela alemneddh fey gherfeth.	برُوس يَقْرَأُ صُحُفاً مِصْرِيَّةً. هُناكَ الكَثِيرُ مِنَ الصُحُفِ عَلَى المِنْضَدَةِ فِي غُرْفَتِهِ.
Mariam has a cat and a dog. Mariam's cat is in the room under the bed. Mariam's dog is in the room as well.	marey ledyha qethan weklebaan. qettha fey alegherfh thet alesreyr. weklebha fey alegherfh kedlek.	مارِي لَدَيْها قِطَّةٌ وَكَلْباً. قِطَّتُها فِي الغُرْفَةِ تَحْتَ السَرِيرِ. وَكَلْبُها فِي الغُرْفَةِ كَذَلِكَ.
There is a man in this car. This man has a map. The man's map is big. This man drives a lot.	henak rejl bhedh alesyarh. heda alerjel m'eh kheryeth. wekheryetth kebyerh. hew yeqwed ketheyraan.	هُناكَ رَجُلٌ بِهَذِهِ السَيّارَةِ. هَذا الرَجُلُ مَعَهُ خَرِيطَةٌ. وَخَرِيطَتُهُ كَبِيرَةٌ. وَهُوَ يَقُودُ كَثِيراً.

I am a student. I have a lot of free time. I go to a job agency. I need a good job.

eneny taleb. w'enedy alektheyr men weqt alefragh. adheb ela wekalh tewzeyf. eneny bhajh ela wezyefh jeydh.

إِنَّنِي طالِبٌ. وَعِنْدِي الكَثِيرُ مِنْ وَقْتِ الفَراغِ. أَذْهَبُ إِلَى وَكالَةِ تَوْظِيفٍ. إِنَّنِي بِحاجَةٍ إِلَى وَظِيفَةٍ جَيِّدَةٍ.

Hiroshi and Bruce have a little free time. They go to the job agency as well. Hiroshi has a computer. The agency may give Hiroshi a good job.

heyrewshey webrews ledyhema aleqleyl men weqt alefragh. whema yedheban ela wekalh aletwezyef kedlek. heyrewshey ledyh kembeywetr. rebma t'eteyh alewkalh wezyefh jeydh.

هِيرُوشِي وَبرُوس لَدَيْهِما القَلِيلُ مِنْ وَقْتِ الفَراغِ. وَهُما يَذْهَبانِ إِلَى وِكالَةِ التَوْظِيفِ كَذَلِكَ. هِيروشي لَدَيْهِ كَمْبِيُوتَرٌ. رُبَّما تُعْطِيهِ الوَكالَةُ وَظِيفَةً جَيِّدَةً.

Hanan has a new cooker. Hanan's cooker is good and clean. She cooks breakfast for her children. Mariam and Omar are Hanan's children. Hanan's children drink a lot of tea. The mother drinks a little coffee. Mariam's mother can speak very few English words. She

henan ledyha ena' jedyed. ena'eha jeyd wenzeyf. enha tethew t'eam aleftewr latefalha. meryem w'emer hem awelad henan. whem yesherbewn aleshay bektherh. alam tesherb aleqleyl men aleqhewh. am meryem testety' an tethedth beklemat enejleyzeyh qelyelh jedaan. hey tethedth aleqleyl jedaan

حَنانٌ لَدَيْها إِناءٌ جَدِيدٌ. إِناؤُها جَيِّدٌ وَنَظِيفٌ. إِنَّها تَطْهُو طَعامَ الفُطُورِ لِأَطْفالِها. مَرْيَمُ وَعُمَرُ هُمْ أَوْلادُ حَنانٍ. وَهُمْ يَشْرَبُونَ الشايَ بِكَثْرَةٍ. الأُمُّ تَشْرَبُ القَلِيلَ مِنْ القَهْوَةِ. أُمُّ مَرْيَمَ تَسْتَطِيعُ أَنْ تَتَحَدَّثَ بِكَلِماتٍ إِنجِلِيزِيَّةٍ قَلِيلَةٍ جِدّاً. هِيَ تَتَحَدَّثُ القَلِيلَ جِدّاً مِنَ الإِنجِلِيزِيَّةِ. حَنانٌ لَدَيْها

speaks English very little. Hanan has a job. She has little free time.

men alenejleyzeyh. henan ledyha wezyefh. weldeyha aleqleyl men weqt alefragh.

وَظِيفَةٌ. وَلَدَيْها القَلِيلُ مِن وَقْتِ الفَراغِ.

Bruce can speak Arabic little. Bruce knows very few Arabic words. I know a lot of English words. I can speak English a little. This woman knows many English words. She can speak English well.

berwes yestety' alethedth bal'erebyh qelyelaan. fhew y'eref kelmat 'erebyh qelyelh jedaan. a'eref aletheyr men aleklemat alenejleyzeyh. asettey' alethedth balenejleyzeyh qelyelaan. hedh alesyedh t'eref kelmat enejleyzeyh ketheyrh. testety' alethedth balenejleyzeyh jeydaan.

بْرُوس يَسْتَطِيعُ التَحَدُّثَ بِالعَرَبِيَّةِ قَلِيلاً. فَهُوَ يَعرِفُ كَلِماتٍ عَرَبِيَّةً قَلِيلَةً جِدّاً. أَعرِفُ الكَثِيرَ مِن الكَلِماتِ الإنجليزِيَّةِ. أَسْتَطِيعُ التَحَدُّثَ بِالإنجليزِيَّةِ قَلِيلاً. هٰذِهِ السَّيِّدَةُ تَعرِفُ كَلِماتٍ إنجليزِيَّةً كَثِيرَةً. تَسْتَطِيعُ التَحَدُّثَ بِالإنجليزِيَّةِ جَيِّداً.

Adel works at a job agency. This job agency is in Alexandria. Adel has a car. Adel's car is in the street. Adel has a lot of work. He must go to the agency. He drives there. Adel comes into the agency. There are a lot of students there. They need jobs. Adel's

y'emel 'eadel fey wekalh tewzeyf. whedh alewkalh tewjed baleseknedreyh. 'eadel ledyh seyarh. wesyareth fey aleshar'e. 'eadel ledyh aletheyr men al'emel. yejb an yedheb ela alewkalh. yeqwed seyareth ela henak. yatey 'eadel ela alewkalh. henak aletheyr men aletlebh. enhem yetlebwen weza'ef.

يَعمَلُ عادِلٌ فِي وَكالَةِ تَوظِيفٍ. وَهٰذِهِ الوَكالَةُ تُوجَدُ بِالإِسْكَنْدَرِيَّةِ. عادِلٌ لَدَيهِ سَيّارَةٌ. وَسَيّارَتُهُ فِي الشارِعِ. عادِلٌ لَدَيهِ الكَثِيرُ مِنَ العَمَلِ. يَجِبُ أَنْ يَذهَبَ إِلَى الوَكالَةِ. يَقُودُ سَيّارَتَهُ إِلَى هُناكَ. يَأتِي عادِلٌ إِلَى الوَكالَةِ. هُناكَ الكَثِيرُ مِنَ الطَلَبَةِ. إِنَّهُم يَطلُبُونَ وَظائِفَ. وَظِيفَةُ

job is to help the students.	wezyefh 'eadel hey mesa'edh aletlebh.	عادِلٌ هِيَ مُساعَدَةُ الطَّلَبَةِ.
There is a car at the hotel. The doors of this car are not clean.	henak seyarh 'ened alefnedq. abewab hedh alesyarh gheyr nezyefh.	هُناكَ سَيّارَةٌ عِنْدَ الفُنْدُقِ. أَبوابُ هٰذِهِ السَّيّارَةِ غَيْرُ نَظِيفَةٍ.
Many students live in this hotel. The rooms of the hotel are little but clean. This is Bruce's room. The window of the room is big and clean.	y'eyesh alektheyr men aletlebh fey heda alefnedq. gherf alefnedq qelyelh welkenha nezyefh. hedh gherfh berwes. nafedh alegherfh kebyerh wenzeyfh.	يَعِيشُ الكَثِيرُ مِنْ الطَّلَبَةِ فِي هٰذا الفُنْدُقِ. غُرَفُ الفُنْدُقِ قَلِيلَةٌ وَلٰكِنَّها نَظِيفَةٌ. هٰذِهِ غُرْفَةُ بْروس. نافِذَةُ الغُرْفَةِ كَبِيرَةٌ وَنَظِيفَةٌ.

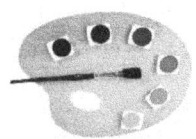

الفَصْلُ السَّابِعُ
Chapter 7

عُمَرُ يَشْتَرِي دَرَّاجَة
Omar buys a bike

A

الكَلِمَاتُ
Words

1. اليَوْمَ - today
2. بِواسِطَةٍ - مَعَ - with
3. بَعْدَ ذَلِكَ - ثُمَّ - إِذَنْ - after, then, that
4. جِدّاً - لِذَلِكَ - so
5. حافِلَةٌ - bus
6. مَتْجَرُ أَدَواتٍ رِياضَة - sport; رِياضِيَّةٍ - sport shop, دَرَّاجَةٌ رِياضِيَّةٌ - sport bike
7. شَرِكَةٌ - firm
8. صَباحُ - morning
9. طابُورُ - صَفٌّ - queue
10. عامِلٌ - worker

11. غُرْفَةُ الحَمّامِ - bathroom;
12. حَمّامٌ يَسْتَحِمُّ - bath
13. غَسّالَةُ - washer
14. مَطْبَخٌ - kitchen
15. مَكْتَبٌ - office
16. مَنْزِلٌ - بَيْتٌ - home, house
17. مِنْضَدَةُ الحَمّامِ - bathroom table
18. وَجْبَةٌ خَفِيفَةٌ - snack
19. وَجْهُ - face
20. وَسَطَ - مَرْكَزٌ - centre
    وَسَطَ المَدِينَةِ - city centre

21. وَقْتٌ - مَرَّةً - time;
    الوَقْتُ يَمْضِي - time goes
    مَرَّتانِ - two times
22. يَرْكَبُ - to go by, to ride
23. يركب الحافلة - to go by bus
24. يُعَدُّ - يُصْنَعُ - يَعْمَلُ - to make
    ماكِينَةُ الشاي - tea-maker
25. يَغْسَلُ - to wash
26. فَطُورُ الأَحَدِ; يَوْمَ الأَحَدِ - Sunday; Sunday breakfast

B

Omar buys a bike

'emer yeshetrey derajh

عُمَرْ يَشْتَرِي دَرَاجَةً

It is Sunday morning. Omar goes to the bathroom. The bathroom is not big. There is a bath, a washer and a bathroom table there. Omar washes his face. Then he goes to the kitchen. There is a tea-maker on the kitchen

enh sebah yewm alahed. yedheb 'emer ela alhemam. enh leys kebyeraan. henak hemam weghesalh wemneddh hemam. yeghesl 'emer wejhh. them yedheb ela alemtebkh. henak makeynh shay 'ela mendedh alemtebkh. yetnawel 'emer fetwerh.

إِنَّهُ صَبَاحُ يَوْمِ الأَحَدِ. يَذْهَبُ عُمَرُ إِلَى الحَمّامِ. إِنَّهُ لَيْسَ كَبِيراً. هُنَاكَ حَمّامٌ وَغَسّالَةٌ وَمِنْضَدَةُ حَمّامٍ. يَغْسِلُ عُمَرُ وَجْهِهِ. ثُمَّ يَذْهَبُ إِلَى المَطْبَخِ. هُنَاكَ ماكِينَةُ شاي عَلَى مِنْضَدَةِ المَطْبَخِ. يَتَنَاوَلُ عُمَرْ

table. Omar eats his breakfast. Omar's Sunday breakfast is not big. Then he makes some tea with the tea-maker and drinks it. He wants to go to a sport shop today. Omar goes into the street. He takes bus seven. It takes Omar a little time to go to the shop by bus.

Omar goes into the sport shop. He wants to buy a new sport bike. There are a lot of sport bikes there. They are black, blue and green. Omar likes blue bikes. He wants to buy a blue one. There is a queue in the shop. It takes Omar a lot of time to buy the bike. Then he goes to the street and rides the

fetwer yewm alahed leys kebyeraan. them y'ed b'ed aleshay bewaseth makeynh aleshay weysherbh. enh yeryed an yedheb ela metjer leladewat aleryadeyh aleywem. yentelq 'emer ela aleshar'e. yakhed alhafelh reqm (7). yhetaj 'emer lewqet qelyel leydheb ela alemtejr balhafelh.

yedkhel 'emer ela metjer aladewat aleryadeyh. yeryed an yeshetrey derajh reyadeyh jedyedh. henak alektheyr men aledrajat aleryadeyh. enha sewda', wezreqa', wekhedra'. yheb 'emer aledrajat alezreqa'. enh yeryed an yeshetrey derajh zerqa'. henak tabewr fey alemtejr. yhetaj 'emer lelketheyr men alewqet leyshetrey aledrajh. b'ed delk yentelq ela aleshar' weyrekb aledrajh. yentelq

فُطُورِهِ. فُطُورُ يَوْمِ الأَحَدِ لَيْسَ كَبِيراً. ثُمَّ يُعِدُّ بَعْضَ الشَايِ بِوَاسِطَةِ مَاكِينَةِ الشَايِ وَيَشْرَبُهُ. إِنَّهُ يُرِيدُ أَنْ يَذْهَبَ إِلَى مَتْجَرٍ لِلْأَدَوَاتِ الرِيَاضِيَّةِ الْيَوْمَ. يَنْطَلِقُ عُمَرُ إِلَى الشَارِعِ. يَأْخُذُ الحَافِلَةَ رَقْمَ (7). يَحْتَاجُ عُمَرُ لِوَقْتٍ قَلِيلٍ لِيَذْهَبَ إِلَى المَتْجَرِ بِالحَافِلَةِ.

يَدْخُلُ عُمَرُ إِلَى مَتْجَرِ الأَدَوَاتِ الرِيَاضِيَّةِ. يُرِيدُ أَنْ يَشْتَرِيَ دَرَّاجَةً رِيَاضِيَّةً جَدِيدَةً. هُنَاكَ الكَثِيرُ مِنَ الدَرَّاجَاتِ الرِيَاضِيَّةِ. إِنَّها سَوْدَاءُ، وَزَرْقَاءُ، وَخَضْرَاءُ. يُحِبُّ عُمَرُ الدَرَّاجَاتِ الزَرْقَاءِ. إِنَّهُ يُرِيدُ أَنْ يَشْتَرِيَ دَرَّاجَةً زَرْقَاءَ. هُنَاكَ طَابُورٌ فِي المَتْجَرِ. يَحْتَاجُ عُمَرُ لِلْكَثِيرِ مِنَ الوَقْتِ لِيَشْتَرِيَ الدَرَّاجَةَ. بَعْدَ ذَلِكَ يَنْطَلِقُ إِلَى الشَارِعِ وَيَرْكَبُ الدَرَّاجَةَ.

bike. He rides to the city centre. Then he rides from the city centre to the city park. It is so nice to ride a new sport bike!

It is Sunday morning but Adel is in his office. He has a lot of work today. There is a queue to Adel's office. There are many students and workers in the queue. They need a job. They go one by one into Adel's room. They speak with Adel. Then he gives addresses of firms.

It is snack time now. Adel makes some coffee with the coffee maker. He eats his snack and drinks some coffee. There is no queue to his office now. Adel can go home. He goes into the

ela west alemdeynh. b'ed delk yentelq men west alemdeynh ela mentezh alemdeynh. enh letyef jedaan an terkeb derajh reyadeyh jedyedh!

enh sebah yewm alahed lekn 'eadel henak bemketbh. ledyh alektheyr men al'emel aleywem. henak tabewr amam mekteb 'eadel. yewjed alektheyr men aletlebh wal'emal fey aletabewr. enhem yhetajewn wezyefh. yedkhelwen wahedaan b'ed alakher ela hejrh 'eadel. yethedthewn eleyh. them y'eteyhem 'enaweyn lesherkat.

enh weqt alewjebh alekhefyefh alan. y'ed 'eadel b'ed aleqhewh bewaseth makeynh aleqhewh. yakel wejbeth alekhefyefh weysherb b'ed aleqhewh. la yewjed tabewr amam mektebh alan. yestety' 'eadel al'ewedh lelmenzel.

يَنْطَلِقُ إِلَى وَسَطِ المَدِينَةِ. بَعْدَ ذَلِكَ يَنْطَلِقُ مِنْ وَسَطِ المَدِينَةِ إِلَى مُنْتَزَهِ المَدِينَةِ. إِنَّهُ لَطِيفٌ جِدّاً أَنْ تَرْكَبَ دَرَّاجَةً رِيَاضِيَّةً جَدِيدَةً!

إِنَّهُ صَبَاحُ يَوْمِ الأَحَدِ لَكِنْ عَادِلٌ هُنَاكَ بِمَكْتَبِهِ. لَدَيْهِ الكَثِيرُ مِنَ العَمَلِ اليَوْمَ. هُنَاكَ طَابُورٌ أَمَامَ مَكْتَبِ عَادِلٍ. يُوجَدُ الكَثِيرُ مِنَ الطَّلَبَةِ وَالعُمَّالِ فِي الطَّابُورِ. إِنَّهُمْ يَحْتَاجُونَ وَظِيفَةً. يَدْخُلُونَ وَاحِداً بَعْدَ الآخَرِ إِلَى حُجْرَةِ عَادِلٍ. يَتَحَدَّثُونَ إِلَيْهِ. ثُمَّ يُعْطِيهِمْ عَنَاوِينَ لِشَرِكَاتٍ.

إِنَّهُ وَقْتُ الوَجْبَةِ الخَفِيفَةِ الآنَ. يُعَدُّ عَادِلٌ بَعْضَ القَهْوَةِ بِوَاسِطَةِ مَاكِينَةِ القَهْوَةِ. يَأْكُلُ وَجْبَتَهُ الخَفِيفَةَ وَيَشْرَبُ بَعْضَ القَهْوَةِ. لَا يُوجَدُ طَابُورٌ أَمَامَ مَكْتَبِهِ الآنَ. يَسْتَطِيعُ عَادِلٌ العَوْدَةِ لِلْمَنْزِلِ. يَنْطَلِقُ إِلَى

49

street. It is so nice today! Adel goes home. He takes his children and goes to the city park. They have a nice time there.

yentelq ela aleshar'e. en aletqes letyef jedaan aleywem! y'ewed 'eadel lelmenzel. yakhed atefalh weydheb ela mentezh alemdeynh. yetmet'ewen bewqet letyef henak.

الشارِعِ. إِنَّ الطَقْسَ لَطيفٌ جِدّاً اليَوْمَ! يَعُودُ عادِلٌ لِلمَنْزِلِ. يَأْخُذُ أَطْفالَهُ وَيَذْهَبُ إِلَى مُنْتَزَهِ المَدينَةِ. يَتَمَتَّعُونَ بِوَقْتٍ لَطيفٍ هُناكَ.

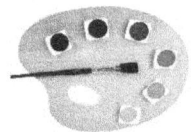

الفَصْلُ الثَامِنُ
Chapter 8

تُرِيدُ حَنَانُ أَنْ تَشْتَرِي فِيلماً جَدِيداً
Hanan wants to buy a newer film

A

الكَلِمَاتُ
Words

1. أَكْثَرُ - more
2. أَنْ - that
3. خَمْسَةَ عَشَرَ - fifteen
4. دِي فِي دِي - DVD
5. سَاعَةُ - hour
6. شَرِيطُ فِيدِيو - videocassette
7. شَيِّقٌ ، مُمْتِعٌ - interesting
8. صَغِيرٌ - young
9. صُنْدُوقٌ ، عُلْبَةٌ - box
10. طَوِيلٌ - long
11. عِشْرُونَ - twenty
12. حَوالَيْ ; عَنْ ، بِشَأْنِ - about

13. فِيلْمُ - film
14. كُوبٌ ، كَأْسُ - cup
15. مَتْجَرُ أَفْلامِ فِيدِيو - video-shop
16. مُساعِدٌ فِي مَتْجَرٍ - shop assistant
17. مُعْظَمُ - most
18. مُغامَرَةٌ - adventure
19. مُفَضَّلٌ - favorite

20. عادِلُ أَكْبَرُ مِنْ حَنانٍ، مِنْ - than,
Adel is older than Hanan.
21. وَدُودٌ ، بودٌ - friendly
22. يَبْتَعِدُ - to go away
23. يُبَيِّنُ ، يَظْهَرُ - to show
24. يَدٌ - يُناوِلُ - hand
25. يَسْأَلُ ، يَطْلُبُ - to ask
26. يَقُولُ - to say

B

Hanan wants to buy a new DVD

teryed henan an teshetrey dey fey dey jedyed

تُرِيدُ حَنان أَنْ تَشْتَرِيَ دِي فِي دِيٍّ جَدِيدا

Omar and Mariam are Hanan's children. Mariam is the youngest child. She is five years old. Omar is fifteen years older than Mariam. He is twenty. Mariam is much younger than Omar.

'emer wemreym hem awelad henan. meryem hey aletfelh alasegher. 'emerha khems senwat. 'emer akebr men meryem bekhemsh 'esher senh. 'emerh 'esheryen senh. meryem asegher ketheyraan men 'emer.

عُمَرُ وَمَرْيَمُ هُمْ أَوْلادُ حَنانٍ. مَرْيَمُ هِيَ الطِّفْلَةُ الأَصْغَرُ. عُمْرُها خَمْسُ سَنَواتٍ. عُمَرُ أَكْبَرُ مِنْ مَرْيَمَ بِخَمْسَةَ عَشَرَ سَنَةً. عُمْرُهُ عِشْرِينَ سَنَةً. مَرْيَمُ أَصْغَرُ كَثِيراً مِنْ عُمَرٍ.

Mariam, Hanan and Omar are in the kitchen. They drink tea. Mariam's cup is big. Hanan's cup is

meryem whenan w'emer fey alemtebkh. yesherbewn aleshay.

مَرْيَمُ وَحَنانٌ وَعُمَرُ فِي المَطْبَخِ. يَشْرَبُونَ الشَّايَ. كُوبُ مَرْيَمَ كَبِيرٌ. كُوبُ حَنانٍ

bigger. Omar's cup is the biggest.

Hanan has a lot of videocassettes and DVDs with interesting films. She wants to buy a newer film. She goes to a video-shop. There are many boxes with videocassettes and DVDs there. She asks a shop assistant to help her. The shop assistant hands Hanan some cassettes. Hanan wants to know more about these films but the shop assistant goes away.

There is one more shop assistant in the shop and she is friendlier. She asks Hanan about her favorite films. Hanan likes romantic films and adventure films. The film "Titanic" is her most favorite film. The shop assistant shows Hanan a

kewb meryem kebyer. kewb henan akebr. kewb 'emer hew alakebr. henan ledyha alektheyr men shera'et alefyedyew waledy fey dey lafelam sheyqh. teryed an teshetrey feylemaan jedyedaan. tedheb ela metjer afelam alefyedyew. henak alektheyr men 'eleb shera'et alefyedyew waledy fey dey. tetleb men mesa'ed alemtejr alemsa'edh. yenawelha alemsa'ed b'ed aleshera'et. teryed henan m'erefh alemzeyd 'en hedh alafelam welken alemsa'ed yebt'ed.

henak mesa'edh akhera fey alemtejr whey akether wedaan. tesal henan 'en afelamha alemfedlh. henan theb alafelam alerwemanesyh wafelam alemghamerat. feylem "teytaneyk" hew akether feylem tefdelh. tezher lha

أَكْبَرُ. كُوبُ عُمَرٍ هُوَ الأَكْبَرُ.

حَنانٌ لَدَيْهَا الكَثِيرُ مِنْ شَرائِطِ الفِيدِيو والِدِي في دِي لِأَفْلامٍ شَيِّقَةٍ. تُرِيدُ أَنْ تَشْتَرِيَ فِيلْماً جَدِيداً. تَذْهَبُ إِلَى مَتْجَرِ أَفْلامِ الفِيدِيو. هُناكَ الكَثِيرُ مِنْ عُلَبِ شَرائِطِ الفِيدِيو والِدِي في دِي. تَطْلُبُ مِنْ مُساعِدِ المَتْجَرِ المُساعِدَةِ. يُناوِلُها المُساعِدُ بَعْضَ الشَرائِطِ. تُرِيدُ حَنانَ مَعْرِفَةِ المَزِيدِ عَنْ هَذِهِ الأَفْلامِ وَلَكِنَّ المُساعِدَ يَبْتَعِدُ.

هُناكَ مُساعَدَةٌ أُخْرَى في المَتْجَرِ وَهِيَ أَكْثَرُ وُدّاً. تَسْأَلُ حَنان عَنْ أَفْلامِها المُفَضَّلَةِ. حَنانٌ تُحِبُّ الأَفْلامَ الرومانِسِيَّةَ وَأَفْلامَ المُغامَراتِ. فِيلَمُ "تِيتانِيك" هُوَ أَكْثَرُ فِيلَمٍ تُفَضِّلُهُ. تَظْهَرُ

cassette with the newest Hollywood film "The Mexican Friend". It is about romantic adventures of a man and a young woman in Mexico.

She shows Hanan a DVD with the film "The Firm" as well. The shop assistant says that the film "The Firm" is one of the most interesting films. And it is one of the longest films as well. It is more than three hours long. Hanan likes longer films. She says that "Titanic" is the most interesting and the longest film that she has. Hanan buys a DVD with the film "The Firm". She thanks the shop assistant and goes.

mesa'edh alemtejr ahedth feylem lhewleywewd "alesdeyq alemkesyeky". enh 'en meghamerat rewmanesyh rejl wamerah shabh fey alemkesyek. ayedaan tezher lhenan dey fey dey lefyelm "alem'esesh". teqwel alemsa'edh an feylem "alem'esesh" men akether alafelam teshewyeqaan. whew men atewl alafelam kedlek. enh akether men thelath sa'eat. henan theb alafelam aletweylh. teqwel an "teytaneyk" hew alefyelm alakether teshewyeqaan walatewl ledyha. teshetrey henan dey fey dey lefyelm "alem'esesh". teshekr mesa'edh alemtejr wetdheb.

لَها مُساعَدَةُ المَتجَرِ أَحْدَثَ فيلِم لِهوليوود "الصَّديقُ المَكسيكِيُّ". إِنَّهُ عَنْ مُغامَراتٍ رومانسِيَّةِ رَجُلٍ وَاِمْرَأَةٍ شابَّةٍ فِي المَكسيكِ.

أَيْضاً تَظْهَرُ لِحَنان دي فِي دي لِفيلم "المُؤَسَّسَةِ". تَقُولُ المُساعَدَةُ أَنَّ فيلمَ "المُؤَسَّسَةِ" مِنْ أَكْثَرِ الأَفْلامِ تَشْويقاً. وَهُوَ مِنْ أَطْوَلِ الأَفْلامِ كَذَلِكَ. إِنَّهُ أَكْثَرُ مِنْ ثَلاثِ ساعاتٍ. حَنانٌ تُحِبُّ الأَفْلامَ الطَويلَةَ. تَقُولُ أَنَّ "تيتانيك" هُوَ الفيلمُ الأَكْثَرُ تَشْويقاً وَالأَطْوَلُ لَدَيها. تَشْتَري حَنانُ دي فِي دي لِفيلِم "المُؤَسَّسَةِ". تَشْكُرُ مُساعَدَةَ المَتجَرِ وَتَذْهَبُ.

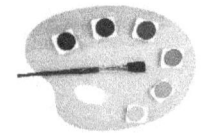

الفَصْلُ التاسِعُ
Chapter 9

هِيرُوشِي يَسْتَمِعُ إِلَى أَغَاني أَمْرِيكِيّةٍ
Hiroshi listens to American songs

A

الكَلِمَاتُ
Words

1. أَسْبانْيا - Spain
2. أُسْرَةٌ ، عائِلَةٌ - family
3. يُسَمِّي ، يُحَدِّدُ ؛ اِسْمُ - to name; name
4. أنجيلا - Angela
5. بَسِيطٌ - simple
6. جِدّاً - very
7. حَقِيبَةٌ - bag
8. خُبْزٌ - bread
9. دَقِيقَةٌ - minute
10. رَأْسٌ - head
11. زَبَدٌ - butter
    يَدْهَنُ بِالزَبَدِ - to butter
12. عِبارَةٌ - phrase
13. قُبَّعَةٌ - hat
14. قَبْلَ - before

55

15. قُرْبٌ - near
16. كارول - Carol
17. كُلُّ - every
18. لِأَنَ ، بِسَبَبِ - because
19. مَساكِنُ - dorms
20. مُعَطَّلٌ - out of order
21. مُغَنِّي ، مُطْرِبٌ - singer
22. هاتِفٌ - telephone; يَتَّصِلُ هاتِفِيّاً - to telephone
23. يَبْدَأُ - to begin
24. يَجْرِي - to run
25. يَخْجَلُ - to be ashamed; إِنَّهُ خَجْلانِ - he is ashamed
26. يَطْلُبُ عَلَى الهاتِفِ - to call on the phone; مُكالَمَةً هاتِفِيَّةً - call
27. يُغَنِّي - sing
28. يَقْفِزُ - to jump; قَفْزَةٌ - jump
29. يَوْمَ - day

B

Hiroshi listens to American songs

heyrewshey yestem' ela aghaney ameryekyh

هِيروشِي يَسْتَمِعُ إِلَى أَغاني أَمْرِيكِيَّةٍ

Carol is a student. She is twenty years old. Carol is from Spain. She lives in the student dorms. She is a very nice girl. Carol has a blue dress on. There is a hat on her head.

Carol wants to telephone her family today. She heads to the call centre because her

karewl talebh. 'emerha 'esheryen senh. hey men asebaneya. t'eyesh bemsaken aletlab. enha fetah jemyelh jedaan. tertedy festan azerq. tewjed qeb'eh 'ela rasha.

teryed karewl an tetsel hatefyaan basertha aleywem. tentelq ela merkez alatesalat lan

كارول طالِبَةٌ. عُمْرُها عِشْرِينَ سَنَةً. هِيَ مِنْ أَسْبانيا. تَعِيشُ بِمَساكِنِ الطُّلّابِ. إِنَّها فَتاةٌ جَمِيلَةٌ جِدّاً. تَرْتَدِي فُسْتانٌ أَزْرَقَ. تُوجَدُ قُبَّعَةٌ عَلَى رَأْسِها.

تُرِيدُ كارولُ أَنْ تَتَّصِلَ هاتِفِيّاً بِأُسْرَتِها اليَوْمَ. تَنْطَلِقُ إِلَى مَرْكَزِ الاِتِّصالاتِ لِأَنَّ هاتِفَها

telephone is out of order. The call centre is in front of the café. Carol calls her family. She speaks with her mother and father. The call takes her about five minutes. Then she calls her friend Angela. This call takes her about three minutes.

Bruce likes sport. He runs every morning in the park near the dorms. He runs today too. He jumps as well. His jumps are very long. Hiroshi and Omar run and jump with Bruce. Omar's jumps are longer. Hiroshi's jumps are the longest. He jumps best of all. Then Bruce and Hiroshi run to the dorms and Omar runs home.

Bruce has his breakfast in his room.

hatefha m'etel. merkez alatesalat amam alemqha. tetsel karewl basertha. tethedth m' amha wabeyha. takhed alemkalemh menha hewaley khems deqa'eq. them tetsel besdeyqetha anejyela. takhed hedh alemkalemh menha hewaley thelath deqa'eq.

berwes yheb aleryadh. yejrey kel sebah fey alemnetzh qerb mesaken aletlebh. enh yejrey aleywem ayedaan. enh yeqfez kedlek. qefzath tewyelh jedaan. heyrewshey w'emer yejreyan weyqefzan m' berwes. qefzat 'emer atewl. qefzat heyrewshey hey alatewl. enh yeqfez afedl men alejmey'e. b'ed delk berwes wheyrewshey yejreyan ela alemsekn weyjery 'emer ela alebyet. yetnawel berwes fetwerh begherfeth. yakhed

مُعَطَّل. مَرْكَزُ الاِتِّصالاتِ أَمامَ المَقْهى. تَتَّصِلُ كارول بِأُسْرَتِها. تَتَحَدَّث مَعَ أُمِّها وَأَبِيها. تَأْخُذُ المُكالَمَةَ مِنْها حَوالَيْ خَمْسِ دَقائِقَ. ثُمَّ تَتَّصِلُ بِصَدِيقَتِها أنجيلا. تَأْخُذُ هٰذِهِ المُكالَمَةُ مِنْها حَوالَيْ ثَلاثِ دَقائِقَ.

بْرُوس يُحِبُّ الرِياضَةَ. يَجْرِي كُلَّ صَباحٍ فِي المُنْتَزَهِ قُرْبَ مَساكِنِ الطَلَبَةِ. إِنَّهُ يَجْرِي اليَوْمَ أَيْضاً. إِنَّهُ يَقْفِزُ كَذَلِكَ. قَفَزاتُهُ طَوِيلَةٌ جِدّاً. هِيروشِي وَعُمَرُ يَجْرِيانِ وَيَقْفِزانِ مَعَ بْروس. قَفَزاتُ عُمَرَ أَطْوَلُ. قَفَزاتُ هِيروشِيّ هِيَ الأَطْوَلُ. إِنَّهُ يَقْفِزُ أَفْضَلَ مِنَ الجَمِيعِ. بَعْدَ ذَلِكَ بْروس وَهِيروشِيّ يَجْرِيانِ إِلَى المَسْكَنِ وَيَجْرِي عُمَرُ إِلَى البَيْتِ.

يَتَناوَلُ بْروس فُطُورَهُ

He takes bread and butter. He makes some coffee with the coffee-maker. Then he butters the bread and eats.

Bruce lives in the dorms in Alexandria. His room is near Hiroshi's room. Bruce's room is not big. It is clean because Bruce cleans it every day. There is a table, a bed, some chairs and some more furniture in his room. Bruce's books and notebooks are on the table. His bag is under the table. The chairs are at the table. Bruce takes some CDs in his hand and heads to Hiroshi's because Hiroshi wants to listen to American music. Hiroshi is in his room at the table. His cat is under the table. There is some bread before the cat. The cat eats the khebzaan wezbedaan. y'ed b'ed aleqhewh bewaseth makeynh aleqhewh. them yedhen alekhebz balezbed weyakel.

y'eyesh berwes fey mesaken aletlebh baleseknedreyh. gherfeth qerb gherfh heyrewshey. whey leyset kebyerh. whey nezyefh lanh yenzefha kel yewm. yewjed bha mendedh, wesreyr, web'ed alekrasey web'ed alathath alakher. ketbh wemfekrath tewjed 'ela alemneddh. wheqyebth asefl alemneddh. walekrasey bejwar alemneddh. yakhed berwes b'ed alasetwanat fey yedh weytejh ela gherfh heyrewshey lan heyrewshey yeryed alasetma' ela mewseyqa ameryekyh. heyrewshey begherfeth yejles ela alemneddh. weqteth thet alemneddh. henak b'ed alekhebz amamha. aleqth takel

بِغُرْفَتِهِ. يَأْخُذُ خُبْزاً وَزَبَداً. يُعَدُّ بَعْضَ القَهْوَةِ بِوَاسِطَةِ مَاكِينَةِ القَهْوَةِ. ثُمَّ يَدْهَنُ الخُبْزُ بِالزَبَدِ وَيَأْكُلُ.
يَعِيشُ بْرُوس فِي مَسَاكِنِ الطَلَبَةِ بِالإسْكَنْدَرِيَّةِ. غُرْفَتُهُ قُرْبَ غُرْفَةِ هِيرُوشِي. وَهِيَ لَيْسَتْ كَبِيرَةً. وَهِيَ نَظِيفَةٌ لِأَنَّهُ يُنَظِّفُها كُلَّ يَوْمٍ. يُوجَدُ بِها مِنْضَدَةٌ، وَسَرِيرٌ، وَبَعْضُ الكَرَاسِي وَبَعْضُ الأَثَاثِ الآخَرِ. كُتُبُهُ وَمُفَكِّرَاتُهُ تُوجَدُ عَلَى المِنْضَدَةِ. وَحَقِيبَتُهُ أَسْفَلَ المِنْضَدَةِ. وَالكَرَاسِي بِجِوَارِ المِنْضَدَةِ. يَأْخُذُ بْرُوس بَعْضَ الأُسْطُوانَاتِ فِي يَدِهِ وَيَتَّجِهُ إِلَى غُرْفَةِ هِيرُوشِي لِأَنَّ هِيرُوشِي يُرِيدُ الاسْتِمَاعَ إِلَى مُوسِيقَى أَمْرِيكِيَّةٍ. هِيرُوشِي بِغُرْفَتِهِ يَجْلِسُ إِلَى المِنْضَدَةِ. وَقِطَّتُهُ تَحْتَ المِنْضَدَةِ. هُنَاكَ بَعْضُ الخُبْزِ أَمَامَها. القِطَّةُ تَأْكُلُ الخُبْزَ.

bread. Bruce hands the CDs to Hiroshi. There is the best American music on the CDs. Hiroshi wants to know the names of the American singers as well. Bruce names his favorite singers. He names Michael Jackson, Mariah Carey, Britney Spears and Madonna. These names are new to Hiroshi.

He listens to the CDs and then begins to sing the American songs! He likes these songs very much. Hiroshi asks Bruce to write the words of the songs. Bruce writes the words of the best American songs for Hiroshi. Hiroshi says that he wants to learn the words of some songs

alekhebz. berwes yenawel alasetwanat lheyrewshey. 'eleyha afedl alemwesyeqa alameryekyh. yeryed heyrewshey m'erefh asema' alemghenyeyn alameryekyeyn kedlek. yesmey berwes alemghenyeyn alemfedleyn ledyh. yedker mayekl jakeswen, mareya karey, beryetney sebyerz wemadewna. hedh alasema' jedyedh 'ela heyrewshey. enh yestem' lelasetwanat them yebda fey ghena' alaghaney alameryekyh! fhew yheb hedh alaghaney ketheyraan jedaan. yetleb heyrewshey men berwes an yekteb lh kelmat alaghaney. yekteb berwes kelmat afedl alaghaney alameryekyh lheyrewshey. heyrewshey yeqwel anh yeryed an yet'elem kelmat b'ed alaghaney weytelb men berwes an yesa'edh. berwes yesa'ed heyrewshey

بْرُوس يُناوِلُ الأَسْطُواناتِ لِهِيرُوشِي. عَلَيْها أَفْضَلُ المُوسِيقَى الأَمْرِيكِيَّةِ. يُرِيدُ هِيرُوشِي مَعْرِفَةَ أَسْماءِ المُغَنِّيَيْنِ الأَمْرِيكِيِّيْنَ كَذٰلِكَ. يُسَمِّي بْرُوس المُغَنِّيَيْنِ المُفَضَّلَيْنِ لَدَيْهِ. يَذْكُرُ مايكل جاكسون، مارْيا كارِي، بريتْنِي سبيرز ومادُونا. هٰذِهِ الأَسْماءُ جَدِيدَةٌ عَلَى هِيرُوشِي.

إِنَّهُ يَسْتَمِعُ لِلأَسْطُواناتِ ثُمَّ يَبْدَأُ فِي غِناءِ الأَغانِي الأَمْرِيكِيَّةِ! فَهُوَ يُحِبُّ هٰذِهِ الأَغانِي كَثِيراً جِدّاً. يَطْلُبُ هِيرُوشِي مِنْ بْرُوس أَنْ يَكْتُبَ لَهُ كَلِماتِ الأَغانِي. يَكْتُبُ بْرُوس كَلِماتِ أَفْضَلِ الأَغانِي الأَمْرِيكِيَّةِ لِهِيرُوشِي. هِيرُوشِي يَقُولُ أَنَّهُ يُرِيدُ أَنْ يَتَعَلَّمَ كَلِماتِ بَعْضِ الأَغانِي وَيَطْلُبَ مِنْ بْرُوس أَنْ يُساعِدَهُ. بْرُوس يُساعِدُ

and asks Bruce to help. Bruce helps Hiroshi to learn the English words. It takes a lot of time because Bruce cannot speak Japanese well. Bruce is ashamed. He cannot say some simple phrases! Then Bruce goes to his room and learns Japanese.

leyt'elem aleklemat alenejleyzeyh. wheda yakhed alektheyr men alewqet lan berwes la yestety' alethedth baleyabaneyh jeydaan. berwes yesh'er balekhejl. ha hew la yestety' an yenteq b'ed al'ebarat alebseyth! them yedheb ela gherfeth weyt'elem aleyabaneyh.

هِيروشِي لِيَتَعَلَّمَ الكَلِمَاتِ الإنجليزيَّةَ. وَهٰذا يَأْخُذُ الكَثيرَ مِنْ الوَقْتِ لِأَنَّ بروس لا يَسْتَطِيعُ التَحَدُّثَ بِاليابانِيَّةِ جَيِّداً. بروس يَشْعُرُ بِالخَجَلِ. ها هُوَ لا يَسْتَطِيعُ أَنْ يَنْطِقَ بَعْضَ العِباراتِ البَسيطَةِ! ثُمَّ يَذْهَبُ إلى غُرْفَتِهِ وَيَتَعَلَّمُ اليابانِيَّةَ.

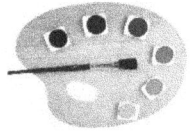

الفَصْلُ العَاشِرُ
Chapter 10

بروس يَشْتَرِي كُتُباً عَنْ التَصْمِيمِ الفَنِّيِّ

Hiroshi buys textbooks on design

A

الكَلِمَاتُ
Words

1. أَصَلِّي - native
2. إلَى اللِقاءِ - bye
3. أَهْلاً ، هُتافُ تَرْحِيبٍ - hello
4. أَيْ - أَيّاً مِنْ - any of
5. بَرْنامَجٌ - program
6. تَصْمِيمٌ فَنِّيٌّ - design
7. دَرْسٌ - lesson
8. دُولار - dollar
9. رائِعٌ - fine
10. صُورَةٌ - picture
11. ضَمِيرٌ غائِبٌ لِلجَمْعِ، هُمْ - them
12. فَقَطْ - only
13. فِي الواقِعِ ، حَقّاً - really
14. كِتابٌ تَعْلِيمِيٌّ - textbook

15. كُلِّيَّةٌ - college
16. لُغَةٌ - language
17. لَهُ ، ضَمِيرٌ لِلْمُفْرَدِ الغائِبِ - him
18. مُجاوِرٌ ، تالٍ - nearby, next
19. نَوْعٌ - kind, type
20. يَخْتارُ - to choose
21. يَدْرُسُ - to study
22. يَدْفَعُ - to pay
23. يَرَى - to see
24. يَشْرَحُ - to explain
25. يُكَلِّفُ - to cost
26. يَنْظُرُ - to look
27. يَوْمَ السَبْتِ - Saturday

B

Hiroshi buys textbooks on design

Hiroshi is Japanese and Japanese is his native language. He studies design at college in Alexandria.

It is Saturday today and Hiroshi has a lot of free time. He wants to buy some books on design. He goes to the nearby book shop. They may have some textbooks on design. He comes into the shop and looks at the

heyrewshey yeshetrey ketbaan 'en aletsemyem

heyrewshey yabaney walelghh aleyabaneyh hey legheth alaselyh. yedres aletsemyem alefney balekleyh fey aleseknedreyh.

enh yewm alesbet welda heyrewshey alektheyr men weqt alefragh. yeryed shera' b'ed alekteb 'en aletsemyem alefney. yedheb ela alemketbh alemjawerh. rebma ledyhem b'ed alekteb alet'eleymeyh 'en aletsemyem alefney.

هِيرُوشِي يَشْتَرِي كُتُباً عَنْ التَصْمِيمِ

هِيرُوشِي يابانِيٌّ وَاللُغَةُ اليابانِيَّةُ هِيَ لُغَتُهُ الأَصْلِيَّةُ. يَدْرُسُ التَصْمِيمَ الفَنِّيَّ بِالكُلِّيَّةِ فِي الإِسْكَنْدَرِيَّةِ.

إِنَّهُ يَوْمُ السَبْتِ وَلَدَى هيروشي الكَثِيرُ مِنْ وَقْتِ الفَراغِ. يُرِيدُ شِراءَ بَعْضِ الكُتُبِ عَنْ التَصْمِيمِ الفَنِّيِّ. يَذْهَبُ إِلَى المَكْتَبَةِ المُجاوِرَةِ. رُبَّما لَدَيْهِمْ بَعْضُ الكُتُبِ التَعْلِيمِيَّةِ عَنْ

tables with books. A woman comes to Hiroshi. She is a shop assistant.

"Hello. Can I help you?" the shop assistant asks him.

"Hello," Hiroshi says, "I study design at college. I need some textbooks. Do you have any textbooks on design?" Hiroshi asks her.

"What kind of design? We have some textbooks on furniture design, car design, sport design, internet design," she explains to him.

"Can you show me some textbooks on furniture design and internet

yedkhel ela alemketbh weynezr ela menaded alekteb. tatey amerah nhewh. enha mesa'edh alemtejr.
"ahelaan. hel asettey' mesa'edetk?" tesalh mesa'edh alemtejr.
"ahelaan," yeqwel heyrewshey. "ana aders aletsemyem alefney fey alekleyh. ahetaj leb'ed alekteb alet'eleymeyh. hel ledyekm ay ketb t'eleymeyh 'en aletsemyem alefney?" yesalha heyrewshey.
"ay new' men aletsemyem?" ledyena b'ed alekteb alet'eleymeyh 'en tesmeym alathath, wetsemyem alesyarat, waletsemyem aleryadey wetsemyem alenetrent" tesherh lh.
"ayemkenk an teryeny b'ed alekteb alet'eleymeyh

التَّصْمِيمِ الفَنِّيِّ. يَدْخُلُ إِلَى المَكْتَبَةِ وَيَنْظُرُ إِلَى مَناضِدِ الكُتُبِ. تَأْتِي اِمْرَأَةٌ نَحْوَهُ. إِنَّها مُساعَدَةُ المَتْجَرِ.
"أَهْلاً. هَلْ أَسْتَطِيعُ مُساعَدَتَكَ؟" تَسْأَلُهُ مُساعَدَةُ المَتْجَرِ.
"أَهْلاً،" يَقُولُ هِيرُوشِي. "أَنا أَدْرُسُ التَّصْمِيمَ الفَنِّيَ فِي الكُلِّيَةِ. أَحْتاجُ لِبَعْضِ الكُتُبِ التَّعْلِيمِيَّةِ. هَلْ لَدَيْكُمْ أَيُّ كُتُبٍ تَعْلِيمِيَّةٍ عَنْ التَّصْمِيمِ الفَنِّيِّ؟" يَسْأَلُها هِيرُوشِي.
"أَيُّ نَوْعٍ مِنَ التَّصْمِيمِ؟" لَدَيْنا بَعْضُ الكُتُبِ التَّعْلِيمِيَّةِ عَنْ تَصْمِيمِ الأَثاثِ، وَتَصْمِيمِ السَّيَّاراتِ، وَالتَّصْمِيمِ الرِّياضِيِّ وَتَصْمِيمِ الإِنْتَرْنِتْ" تَشْرَحُ لَهُ.
"أَيُمْكِنُكِ أَنْ تُرِيِني بَعْضَ الكُتُبِ التَّعْلِيمِيَّةِ عَنْ تَصْمِيمِ الأَثاثِ وَتَصْمِيمِ الإِنْتَرْنِتْ؟"

design?" Hiroshi says to her.

"You can choose the books from the next tables. Look at them. This is a book by Italian furniture designer Palatino. This designer explains the design of Italian furniture. He explains the furniture design of Europe and the USA as well. There are some fine pictures there," the shop assistant explains.

"I see there are some lessons in the book too. This book is really fine. How much is it?" Hiroshi asks her.

"It costs 52 dollars. And with the book you have a CD. There is a computer program for furniture design on the CD," the

'en tesmeym alathath wetsemyem alenetrent?" yeqwel heyrewshey. "yemkenk an tekhetarha men alemnaded alemjawerh. anezr eleyhem. heda ketab lemsemm alathath aleyetaley balateynew. heda alemsemm yesherh tesmeym alathath aleyetaley. weysherh kedlek tesmeym alathath fey awerweba walewlayat alemthedh alameryekyh. wefyh b'ed aleswer alejmeylh," tesherh mesa'edh alemtejr.
" ara feyh b'ed aledrews ayedaan. heda alektab ra'e' heqaan. ma themnh?" yesalha heyrewshey.
" enh yeklef 52 dewlaraan. wem' alektab tewjed asetwanh. henak bernamej letsemyem

يَقُولُ هِيرُوشِي.

"يُمْكِنُكَ أَنْ تَخْتارَها مِنَ المَناضِدِ المُجاوِرَةِ. أَنْظُرْ إِلَيْهِمْ. هٰذا كِتابٌ لِمُصَمِّمِ الأَثاثِ الإِيطالِيِّ بالاتينو. هٰذا المُصَمِّمَ يَشرَحُ تَصْميمَ الأَثاثِ الإِيطالِيِّ. وَيَشرَحُ كَذٰلِكَ تَصْميمَ الأَثاثِ فِي أوروبا وَالوِلاياتِ المُتَّحِدَةِ الأَمْريكِيَّةِ. وَفيهِ بَعْضُ الصُوَرِ الجَميلَةِ," تَشرَحُ مُساعَدَةُ المَتْجَرِ.

" أَرى فيهِ بَعْضَ الدُروسِ أَيْضاً. هٰذا الكِتابُ رائِعٌ حَقّاً. ما ثَمَنُهُ؟" يَسْأَلُها هِيرُوشِي.

" إِنَّهُ يُكَلِّفُ 52 دُولاراً. وَمَعَ الكِتابِ تُوجَدُ أَسْطُوانَةٌ. هُناكَ بَرْنامَجٌ لِتَصْميمِ الأَثاثِ عَلَى الأَسْطُوانَةِ" تَقُولُ مُساعَدَةُ المَتْجَرِ.

shop assistant says to him.

"I really like it," Hiroshi says.

"You can see some textbooks on internet design there," the woman explains to him, "This book is about the computer program Microsoft Office. And these books are about the computer program Flash. Look at this red book. It is about Flash and it has some interesting lessons. Choose, please."

"How much is this red book?" Hiroshi asks her.

"This book, with two CDs, costs only 43 dollars," the shop assistant says to him.

"I want to buy this book by Palatino about

alathath 'ela alasetwanh" teqwel mesa'edh alemtejr.
"ahebh heqaan" yeqwel heyrewshey.
"yemkenk an tery b'ed alekteb alet'eleymeyh 'en tesmeym alenetrent henak". tesherh lh alemrah. "heda alektab 'en bernamej alekmebyewter mayekrewsewfet awefyes. whedh alekteb 'en bernamej felash. anezr ela heda alektab alahemr. enh 'en bernamej felash wefyh b'ed aledrews alesheyqh. akhetrh men fedlek."
"ma themn heda alektab alahemr?" yesalha heyrewshey.
"heda alektab, m' asetwanetyen, yeklef 43 dewlar feqt" teqwel mesa'edh alemtejr.
" areyd an ashetrey heda alektab leblateynew 'en

"أُحِبُّهُ حَقّاً" يَقُولُ هِيرُوشِي.
"يُمْكِنُكَ أَنْ تَرِي بَعْضَ الكُتُبِ التَعْلِيمِيَّةِ عَنْ تَصْمِيمِ الإِنْتَرْنِتْ هُناكَ". تَشْرَحُ لَهُ المَرْأَةُ. "هٰذا الكِتابُ عَنْ بَرْنامَجِ الكُمْبْيُوتَرِ مايكروسوفت أوفيس. وَهٰذِهِ الكُتُبُ عَنْ بَرْنامَجِ فلاش. أُنْظُرْ إِلَى هٰذا الكِتابِ الأَحْمَرِ. إِنَّهُ عَنْ بَرْنامَجِ فلاش وَفِيهِ بَعْضُ الدُرُوسِ الشَيِّقَةِ. اِخْتَرْهُ مِنْ فَضْلِكَ."

"ما ثَمَنُ هٰذا الكِتابِ الأَحْمَرِ؟" يَسْأَلُها هِيرُوشِي.

"هٰذا الكِتابُ، مَعَ أَسْطُوانَتَيْنِ، يُكَلِّفُ 43 دُولارٍ فَقَطْ" تَقُولُ مُساعَدَةُ المَتْجَرِ.

" أُرِيدُ أَنْ أَشْتَرِيَ هٰذا

furniture design and this red book about Flash. How much must I pay for them?" Hiroshi asks.

"You need to pay 95 dollars for these two books," the shop assistant says to him.

Hiroshi pays. Then he takes the books and the CDs.

"Bye," the shop assistant says to him.

"Bye," Hiroshi says to her and goes into the street.

tesmeym alathath wheda alektab alahemr 'en aleflash. kem yejb an adef' feyhem?" yesal heyrewshey.

"thetaj an tedf' 95 dewlar lhedyen alektabeyn," teqwel mesa'edh alemtejr.

yedf' heyrewshey. them yakhed alekteb walasetwanat.

"ela alelqa'" teqwel lh mesa'edh alemtejr.

"ela alelqa'" yeqwel lha heyrewshey weynetleq ela aleshar'e.

الكِتابَ لِبلاتينو عَنْ تَصْميمِ الأَثاثِ وَهذا الكِتابُ الأَحْمَرِ عَنْ الفْلاشِ. كَمْ يَجِبُ أَنْ أَدْفَعَ فِيهِمْ؟" يَسْأَلُ هِيرُوشِي.

"تَحْتاجُ أَنْ تَدْفَعَ 95 دُولارٍ لِهذَيْنِ الكِتابَيْنِ،" تَقُولُ مُساعَدَةُ المَتْجَرِ.

يَدْفَعُ هِيرُوشِي. ثُمَّ يَأْخُذُ الكُتُبَ وَالأَسْطُواناتِ.

"إلَى اللِقاءِ" تَقُولُ لَهُ مُساعَدَةُ المَتْجَرِ.

"إلَى اللِقاءِ" يَقُولُ لَها هِيرُوشِي وَيَنْطَلِقُ إلَى الشارِعِ.

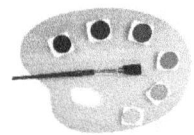

الفَصْلُ الحادِي عَشَرَ
Chapter 11

بروسّ يُرِيدُ أنْ يَكْسِبَ بَعْضَ المالِ
Bruce wants to earn some money

A

الكَلِمَاتُ
Words

1. يُجِيبُ - to answer, إجابَةُ - answer
2. إدارَةُ المُوَظِّفِينَ - personnel department
3. أَفْضَلُ - better
4. بِسُرْعَةٍ - quickly
5. بَعْدَ - after
6. جُزْءٌ - part
7. جَيِّداً ، حَسَناً - OK, well
8. رِسالَةٌ ، مُلاحَظَةٌ - note
9. بِاسْتِمْرارٍ - hourly; ساعَةُ - hour
10. ساعَةُ - o'clock; إنَّها الساعَةُ الثانِيَةُ - It is two o'clock.

11. سَرِيعٌ - quick
12. شاحِنَةٌ - truck
13. صَعْبٌ - hard
14. صُنْدُوقٌ ، عُلْبَةٌ - box
15. طاقَةٌ ، قُوَّةٌ - energy
16. عادِي ، مَأْلُوفٌ - usual
    عادَةً - usually
17. عَدَدٌ ، رَقْمٌ - number
18. قائِمَةٌ - list
19. لِأَنَّ - as, since
20. لِكُلِّ ، فِي - per;

I. أَكْسَبُ 10 دُولاراتٍ فِي الساعَةِ - earn 10 dollars per hour.

21. لِماذا - why
22. نَقْلٌ - transport
23. يُنْهِي - نِهايَةٌ - finish; to finish
24. هٰذا هُوَ السَبَبُ - that is why
25. واحِدٌ آخَرُ - one more
26. يُتْبَعُ - to be continued
27. حَمّالٌ - يَحْمِلُ - loader, to load
28. يَفْهَمُ - to understand
29. يَكْسِبُ - to earn
30. يَوْمَ - يَوْمِيّاً - day; daily

B

Bruce wants to earn some money (part 1)

berwes yeryed an yekseb b'ed alemal (alejz' alawel)

بْرُوس يُرِيدُ أَنْ يَكْسِبَ بَعْضَ المالِ (الجُزْءَ الأَوَّلَ)

Bruce has free time daily after college. He wants to earn some money. He heads to a job agency. They give him the address of a transport firm. The

berwes ledyh weqt feragh yewmeyaan b'ed alekleyh. yeryed an yekseb b'ed alemal. yetwejh ela wekalh tewzeyf. y'etewnh 'enewan sherkh lelneql.

بْرُوس لَدَيْهِ وَقْتُ فَراغٍ يَوْمِيّاً بَعْدَ الكُلِّيَّةِ. يُرِيدُ أَنْ يَكْسِبَ بَعْضَ المالِ. يَتَوَجَّهُ إِلَى وَكالَةِ تَوْظِيفٍ. يُعْطُونَهُ عُنْوانَ شَرِكَةٍ لِلنَقْلِ. تَحْتاجُ شَرِكَةُ النَقْلِ "رابيد" حَمّالاً.

transport firm Rapid needs a loader. This work is really hard. But they pay 11 dollars per hour. Bruce wants to take this job. So he goes to the office of the transport firm.

"Hello. I have a note for you from a job agency," Bruce says to a woman in the personnel department of the firm. He gives her the note.

"Hello," the woman says, "My name is Samira Hamdy. I am the head of the personnel department. What is your name?"

"My name is Bruce Smith," Bruce says.

"Are you Egyptian?" Samira asks.

"No. I am American," Bruce answers.

thetaj sherkh alenqel "rabeyd" hemalaan. heda al'emel s'eb heqaan. welkenhem yedf'ewen 11 dewlaraan fey alesa'eh. yeryed berwes an yhesl 'ela hedh alewzeyfh. ledlek yedheb ela mekteb sherkh alenqel. "ahelaan. m'ey resalh lek men wekalh aletwezyef", yeqwel berwes lesyedh fey edarh alemwezfeyn balesherkh. y'eteyha alersalh.
"ahelaan" teqwel alesyedh, "asemy semyerh hemdey. wana r'eyesh edarh alemwezfeyn. ma asemk?"
"asemy berwes", yeqwel berwes.
"hel anet mesrey?" semyerh tesal.
"la. ana ameryeky" yejyeb berwes.

هٰذا العَمَلُ صَعبٌ حَقّاً. وَلٰكِنَّهُمْ يَدفَعُونَ 11 دُولاراً فِي الساعَةِ. يُريدُ بروسُ أَنْ يَحصُلَ عَلَى هٰذِهِ الوَظيفَةِ. لِذٰلِكَ يَذهَبُ إلَى مَكتَبِ شَرِكَةِ النَقلِ.

"أَهلاً. مَعي رِسالَةٌ لَكَ مِنْ وَكالَةِ التَوظيفِ"، يَقُولُ بروسُ لِسَيِّدَةٍ في إدارَةِ المُوَظَّفينَ بِالشَرِكَةِ. يُعطيها الرِسالَةَ.

"أَهلاً" تَقُولُ السَيِّدَةُ، "اِسمي سَميرَةُ حَمدي. وَأَنا رَئيسَةُ إدارَةِ المُوَظَّفينَ. ما اِسمُكَ؟"

"اِسمي بروسُ"، يَقُولُ بروس.

"هَل أَنتَ مِصريٌّ؟" سَميرَة تَسأَلُ.

"لا. أَنا أَمريكِيٌّ" يُجيبُ بروسُ.

"Can you speak and read Arabic well?" she asks.

"Yes, I can" he says.

"How old are you, Bruce?" she asks.
"I am twenty years old," Bruce answers.

"You want to work at the transport firm as a loader. Why as a loader?" the head of the personnel department asks him.

Bruce is ashamed to say that he cannot have a better job because he cannot speak Arabic well. So he says: "I want to earn 11 dollars per hour."

"Well-well," Samira says, "Our transport firm usually does not have much loading work. But now we really need one

"hel testety' an tethedth wetqera al'erebyh jeydaan?" tesalh.
"n'em, asettey'e" yejyebha.
"ma 'emerk ya berwes?" tesalh.
"'emery 'esheryen senh" yejyeb berwes.
"teryed an t'emel fey sherkh alenqel khemal. lemada khemal?" tesalh r'eyesh edarh alemwezfeyn.
berwes khejl an yeqwel anh la yestety' alheswel 'ela wezyefh afedl lanh la yestety' alethedth bal'erebyh jeydaan. ledlek yeqwel: "areyd an akesb 11 dewlaraan fey alesa'eh."
"hesnaan - hesnaan" teqwel semyerh, 'eadhan la yewjed besherketna alektheyr men alethemyel. leknena alan nhetaj f'elaan lhemal akher. hel testety' an theml

"هَلْ تَسْتَطِيعُ أَنْ تَتَحَدَّثَ وَتَقْرَأَ العَرَبِيَّةَ جَيِّداً؟" تَسْأَلُهُ.

"نَعَمْ، أَسْتَطِيعُ" يُجِيبُها.

"ما عُمْرُكَ يا بْرُوسُ؟" تَسْأَلُهُ.

"عُمْرِي عِشْرِينَ سَنَةً" يُجِيبُ بْرُوسُ.

"تُرِيدُ أَنْ تَعْمَلَ فِي شَرِكَةِ النَقْلِ كَحَمَّالٍ. لِماذا كَحَمَّالٍ؟" تَسْأَلُهُ رَئِيسَةُ إِدَارَةِ المُوَظَّفِينَ.

بْرُوسُ خَجِلٌ أَنْ يَقُولَ أَنَّهُ لا يَسْتَطِيعُ الحُصُولَ عَلَى وَظِيفَةٍ أَفْضَلَ لِأَنَّهُ لا يَسْتَطِيعُ التَحَدُّثَ بِالعَرَبِيَّةِ جَيِّداً. لِذَلِكَ يَقُولُ: "أُرِيدُ أَنْ أَكْسِبَ 11 دُولاراً فِي الساعَةِ."

"حَسَناً - حَسَناً" تَقُولُ سَمِيرَة، عَادَةً لا يُوجَدُ بِشَرِكَتِنا الكَثِيرُ مِنَ التَحْمِيلِ. لَكِنَّنا الآنَ نَحْتاجُ فِعْلاً لِحَمَّالٍ

more loader. Can you load quickly boxes with 20 kilograms of load?"

"Yes, I can. I have a lot of energy," Bruce answers.

"We need a loader daily for three hours. Can you work from four to seven o'clock?" she asks.

"Yes, my lessons finish at one o'clock," the student answers to her.

"When can you begin the work?" the head of the personnel department asks him.

"I can begin now," Bruce answers.

"Well. Look at this loading list. There are some names of firms and shops in the list," Samira explains, "Every firm and shop has

senadeyq weznha 20 keylewjeramaan besr'eh?"
"n'em, asettey'e. 'enedy alektheyr men aleqwh," yejyeb berwes. "nhetaj lhemal yewmeyaan lemdh thelath sa'eat. hel yemkenk al'emel men alesa'eh alerab'eh ela alesab'eh?" tesalh. "n'em, tenthey derwesy fey alesa'eh alewahedh" yejyebha aletaleb. "meta yemkenk beda al'emel?" tesalh r'eyesh edarh alemwezfeyn. "yemkenney an abeda alan" yejyeb berwes. "hesnaan. anezr ela qa'emh alethemyel telk. henak b'ed asema' sherkat wemtajer fey aleqa'emh," tesherh semyerh, lekl sherkh wemtejr b'ed alareqam. whey areqam alesnadeyq. whedh areqam aleshahenat

آخَرَ. هَلْ تَسْتَطِيعُ أَنْ تَحْمِلَ صَنادِيقَ وَوَزْنِها 20 كيلوجراماً بِسُرْعَةٍ؟"

"نَعَمْ، أَسْتَطِيعُ. عِنْدِي الكَثِيرَ مِنَ القُوَّةِ،" يُجِيبُ بْروس.

"نَحْتاجُ لِحَمَّالٍ يَوْمِيّاً لِمُدَّةِ ثَلاثِ ساعاتٍ. هَلْ يُمْكِنُكَ العَمَلُ مِنَ الساعَةِ الرابِعَةِ إِلَى السابِعَةِ؟" تَسْأَلُهُ.

"نَعَمْ، تَنْتَهِي دُروسِي فِي الساعَةِ الواحِدَةِ" يُجِيبُها الطالِبُ.

"مَتَى يُمْكِنُكَ بَدَأَ العَمَلِ؟" تَسْأَلُهُ رَئِيسَةُ إِدارَةِ المُوَظَّفِينَ.

"يُمْكِنُنِي أَنْ أَبْدَأَ الآنَ" يُجِيبُ بْروس.

"حَسَناً. أُنْظُرْ إِلَى قائِمَةِ التَحْمِيلِ تِلْكَ. هُناكَ بَعْضُ أَسْماءِ شَرِكاتٍ وَمَتاجِرَ فِي القائِمَةِ،" تَشْرَحُ سَمِيرَة، لِكُلِّ

some numbers. They are numbers of the boxes. And these are numbers of the trucks where you must load these boxes. The trucks come and go hourly. So you need to work quickly. OK?"

"OK," Bruce answers, not understanding Samira well.

"Now take this loading list and go to the loading door number three," the head of the personnel department says to Bruce. Bruce takes the loading list and goes to work.

(to be continued)

heyth yejb themyel hedh alesnadeyq. tatey aleshahenat wetghader basetmerar. ledlek thetaj an t'emel besr'eh. hesnaan?"

"hesnaan, yejyeb berwes, whew la yefhem semyerh jeydaan.

"khed alan qa'emh alethemyel wadheb ela bab alethemyel reqm thelathh," teqwel r'eyesh edarh alemwezfeyn lebrews. yakhed berwes qa'emh alethemyel weydheb lel'emel.

(yetb'e)

شَرِكَةٍ وَمَتجَرٍ بَعضِ الأَرْقامِ. وَهِيَ أَرْقامُ الصَناديقِ. وَهٰذِهِ أَرْقامُ الشاحِناتِ حَيْثُ يَجِبُ تَحْميلُ هٰذِهِ الصَناديقِ. تَأْتي الشاحِناتُ وَتُغادِرُ بِاسْتِمْرارٍ. لِذلِكَ تَحْتاجُ أَنْ تَعْمَلَ بِسُرْعَةٍ. حَسَناً؟"

"حَسَناً، يُجيبُ بروس، وَهُوَ لا يَفْهَمُ سَميرَة جَيِّداً.

"خُذِ الآنَ قائِمَةَ التَحْميلِ وَاِذْهَبْ إِلى بابِ التَحْميلِ رَقْمَ ثَلاثَةٍ،" تَقولُ رَئيسَةُ إِدارَةِ المُوَظَّفينَ لِبروس. يَأْخُذُ بروس قائِمَةَ التَحْميلِ وَيَذْهَبُ لِلعَمَلِ.

(يتبع)

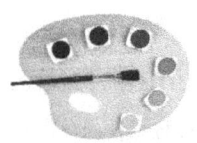

الفَصْلُ الثَانِي عَشَرَ
Chapter 12

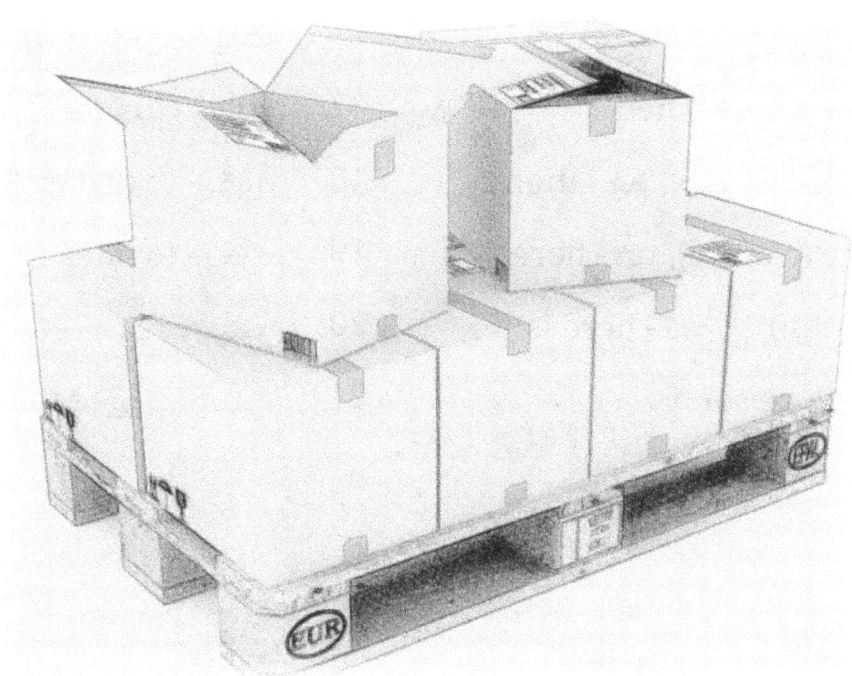

بروسّ يُرِيدُ أنْ يَكْسِبَ بَعْضَ المالِ (الجزء الثاني)

Bruce wants to earn some money (part 2)

A

الكَلِمَاتُ

Words

1. اِبنٌ - son
2. السَيِّدُ - mister
3. أمْ - mom, mother
4. بَدَلاً مِنْ - instead of
   بَدَلاً مِنْكَ - instead of you

5. سَبَبٌ - reason
6. سَيِّئٌ - bad
7. صَحِيحٌ - correct
   بِشَكْلٍ صَحِيحٍ - correctly
   بِشَكْلٍ غَيرِ صَحِيحٍ - incorrectly

7. يُصَحِّح - to correct
8. صِيغَةُ المَلَكِيَّةِ - your
9. ظَهَرَ ، خَلْفَ - back
10. مُبْتَهِجٌ ، مَسْرُورٌ - glad
11. مُدَرِّسٌ ، مُعَلِّمٌ - teacher
12. هُمْ ، ضَمِيرُ المَلَكِيَّةِ لِلجَمْعِ - their
13. هُنا - here (a place), هُنا - here (a direction), تَفَضَّلْ - here is
14. يَتَأَسَّفُ - to be sorry
    آسِفٌ - I am sorry.
15. يَجْلِبُ ، يَحْضُرُ - to bring
    جَلْب - bringing
16. يَسْتَيْقِظُ - to get up
    اِسْتَيْقَظْ - Get up!
17. يُقابِلُ - to meet
18. يَقُودُ - to drive; سائِقٌ - driver
19. يَكْرَهُ - to hate
20. يَمْشِي ، يَسِيرُ - to walk
21. يَوْمَ الاِثْنَيْنِ - Monday

B

Bruce wants to earn some money (part 2)

There are many trucks at the loading door number three. They come back bringing back their loads. The head of the personnel department and the head of the firm come there. They come to Bruce. Bruce loads

berwes yeryed an yekseb b'ed alemal (alejz' alethaney)

henak alektheyr men aleshahenat 'ened bab alethemyel reqm thelathh. enha t'ewed jalebhan ahemalha. tatey r'eyesh edarh alemwezfeyn wer'eyes alesherkh ela alemkan. yatewn ela berwes. berwes yheml senadeyq fey shahenh.

بروس يريد أن يكسب بعض المال (الجزء الثاني)
هُناكَ الكَثِيرُ مِن الشاحِناتِ عِندَ بابِ التَحْمِيلِ رَقْمِ ثَلاثَةٍ. إنَّها تَعُودُ جالِبَةَ أَحْمالِها. تَأْتِي رَئِيسَةُ إدارَةِ المُوَظَّفِينَ وَرَئِيسِ الشَرِكَةِ إلَى المَكانِ. يَأْتُونَ إلَى بروس. بروس يَحْمِلُ صَنادِيقَ فِي شاحِنَةٍ. وَهُوَ يَعْمَلُ بِسُرْعَةٍ.

boxes in a truck. He works quickly.

"Hey, Bruce! Please, come here," Samira calls him, "This is the head of the firm, Mr. Sami."

"I am glad to meet you," Bruce says coming to them.

"I too," Mr. Sami answers, "Where is your loading list?"

"It is here," Bruce gives him the loading list.

"Well-well," Mr. Sami says looking in the list, "Look at these trucks. They come back bringing back their loads because you load the boxes incorrectly. The boxes with books go to a furniture shop instead of the book shop, the boxes with videocassettes and DVDs go to a café instead of the video

whew y'emel besr'eh.
"ya berwes! men fedlek t'eal hena," semyerh tenadeyh "heda r'eyes alesherkh, alesyed samey."
"eneny mesrewr lemqabeltek" yeqwel berwes whew qademaan eleyhem.
"ana ayedaan," yejyeb alesyed samey, "ayen qa'emh themyelk?"
"enha hena," y'eteyh berwes qa'emh alethemyel.
"hesnaan - hesnaan", yeqwel alesd samey nazeraan fey aleqa'emh, "anezr ela hedh aleshahenat. enha t'ewed jalebhan hemweltha lanek hemlet alesnadeyq beshekl gheyr sheyh. senadeyq alekteb tedheb ela metjer athath bedlaan men alemketbh, senadeyq shera'et alefyedyew waledy fey dey tedheb ela meqha bedlaan men

"يَا بْرُوسْ! مِنْ فَضْلِكَ تَعَالَ هُنَا،" سَمِيرَةُ تُنَادِيهِ "هٰذَا رَئِيسُ الشَّرِكَةِ، السَّيِّدُ سَامِي."

"إِنَّنِي مَسْرُورٌ لِمُقَابَلَتِكَ" يَقُولُ بْرُوسْ وَهُوَ قَادِماً إِلَيْهِمْ.

"أَنَا أَيْضاً،" يُجِيبُ السَّيِّدُ سَامِي، "أَيْنَ قَائِمَةُ تَحْمِيلِكَ؟"

"إِنَّها هُنَا،" يُعْطِيهِ بْرُوسْ قَائِمَةَ التَحْمِيلِ.

"حَسَناً - حَسَناً"، يَقُولُ السَدُّ سَامِي نَاظِراً فِي القَائِمَةِ، "أُنْظُرْ إِلَى هٰذِهِ الشَاحِنَاتِ. إِنَّها تَعُودُ جَالِبَةً حُمُولَتِها لِأَنَّكَ حَمَلْتَ الصَنَادِيقَ بِشَكْلٍ غَيْرِ صَحِيحٍ. صَنَادِيقُ الكُتُبِ تَذْهَبُ إِلَى مَتْجَرِ أَثَاثٍ بَدَلاً مِنَ المَكْتَبَةِ، صَنَادِيقِ شَرَائِطِ الفِيدِيو وَالدِي فِي دِي تَذْهَبُ إِلَى مَقْهىً بَدَلاً مِنْ مَتْجَرِ الفِيدِيو،

75

shop, and the boxes with sandwiches go to a video shop instead of the café! It is bad work! Sorry but you cannot work at our firm," Mr. Sami says and walks back to the office.

Bruce cannot load boxes correctly because he can read and understand very few Arabic words. Samira looks at him. Bruce is ashamed.

"Bruce, you can learn Arabic better and then come again. OK?" Samira says.

"OK," Bruce answers, "Bye Samira."

"Bye Bruce," Samira answers.

Bruce walks home. He wants to learn Arabic

metjer alefyedyew, wesnadeyq alesheta'er tedheb ela metjer feydeyw bedlaan men alemqha! enh l'emel sey'e! asef welkenk la testety' an t'emel fey sherketna, " yeqwel alesyed samey weyseyr 'ea'edaan ela alemketb.
berwes la yestety' an yheml alesnadeyq beshekl sheyh lanh yeqra weyfhem kelmat 'erebyh qelyelh jedaan. tenzer eleyh semyerh. berwes yesh'er balekhejl.
"berwes, yemkenk an tet'elem al'erebyh beshekl afedl wet'ewed thaneyhan. hesnaan?" teqwel semyerh.
"hesnaan," yejyeb berwes, "ela alelqa' semyerh".
"ela alelqa' berwes," tejyeb semyerh.
yesyer berwes ela alebyet. alan yeryed an yet'elem al'erebyh beshekl afedl web'ed delk yhesl 'ela

وَصَنَادِيقِ الشَّطَائِرِ تَذْهَبُ إِلَى مَتْجَرِ فِيدِيو بَدَلاً مِنَ الْمَقْهَى! إِنَّهُ لَعَمَلٌ سَيِّئٌ! آسِفٌ وَلٰكِنَّكَ لا تَسْتَطِيعُ أَنْ تَعْمَلَ فِي شَرِكَتِنا،" يَقُولُ السَّيِّدُ سامي وَيَسِيرُ عائِداً إِلَى الْمَكْتَبِ.

بْرُوس لا يَسْتَطِيعُ أَنْ يَحْمِلَ الصَّنَادِيقَ بِشَكْلٍ صَحِيحٍ لِأَنَّهُ يَقْرَأُ وَيَفْهَمُ كَلِماتٍ عَرَبِيَّةً قَلِيلَةً جِدّاً. تَنْظُرُ إِلَيْهِ سَمِيرَة. بْرُوس يَشْعُرُ بِالْخَجَلِ.

"بْرُوس، يُمْكِنُكَ أَنْ تَتَعَلَّمَ الْعَرَبِيَّةَ بِشَكْلٍ أَفْضَلَ وَتَعُودَ ثانِيَةً. حَسَناً؟" تَقُولُ سَمِيرَة.

"حَسَناً،" يُجِيبُ بْرُوس، "إِلَى اللِقاءِ سَمِيرَة".

"إِلَى اللِقاءِ بْرُوس،" تُجِيبُ سَمِيرَة.

يَسِيرُ بْرُوس إِلَى الْبَيْتِ. الآنَ يُرِيدُ أَنْ يَتَعَلَّمَ الْعَرَبِيَّةَ بِشَكْلٍ أَفْضَلَ وَبَعْدَ ذٰلِكَ يَحْصُلَ عَلَى

better now and then take a new job.

It is time to go to college

Monday morning a mother comes into the room to wake up her son.

"Get up, it is seven o'clock. It is time to go to college!"

"But why, Mom? I don't want to go."

"Name me two reasons why you don't want to go," the mother says to the son.

"The students hate me for one and the teachers hate me too!"

"Oh, they are not reasons not to go to college. Get up!"

"OK. Name me two reasons why I must go

wezyefh jedyedh.

enh weqt aledhab ela alekleyh

tedkhel am fey sebah alathenyen ela alegherfh letweqz abenha.

"asetyeqz, enha alesa'eh alesab'eh. enh weqt aledhab ela alekleyh!"

"lekn lemada ya amey? la areyd an adheb."

"adekr ley sebbeyn lemada la teryed an tedheb," teqwel alam lebenha.

"aletlebh yekrhewneny awelaan walemdersewn yekrhewneny ayedaan!"

"yah, hedh leyset asebab tej'elek la tedheb ela alekleyh. asetyeqz!"

"hesnaan. adekrey ley sebbeyn lemada yejb an adheb ela alekleyh,"

وَظِيفَةٍ جَدِيدَةٍ.

إِنَّهُ وَقْتُ الذَهابِ إِلَى الكُلِّيَةِ

تَدَخَّلَ أُمٌّ فِي صَباحِ الاِثْنَيْنِ إِلَى الغُرْفَةِ لِتُوقِظَ اِبْنَها.

"اِسْتَيْقِظْ، إِنَّها الساعَةُ السابِعَةُ. إِنَّهُ وَقْتُ الذَهابِ إِلَى الكُلِّيَةِ!"

"لَكِنْ لِماذا يا أُمِّي؟ لا أُرِيدُ أَنْ أَذْهَبَ."

"أُذْكُرْ لِي سَبَبَيْنِ لِماذا لا تُرِيدُ أَنْ تَذْهَبَ،" تَقُولُ الأُمُّ لِإِبْنِها.

"الطَلَبَةُ يَكْرَهُونَنِي أَوَّلاً وَالمُدَرِّسُونَ يَكْرَهُونَنِي أَيْضاً!"

"ياه، هٰذِهِ لَيْسَتْ أَسْبابٌ تَجْعَلُكَ لا تَذْهَبَ إِلَى الكُلِّيَةِ. اِسْتَيْقِظْ!"

"حَسَناً. أُذْكُرِي لِي سَبَبَيْنِ لِماذا يَجِبُ أَنْ أَذْهَبَ إِلَى الكُلِّيَةِ،"

to college," he says to his mother.

 "Well, for one, you are 55 years old. And for two, you are the head of the college! Get up now!"

yeqwel lamh.

"hesnaan, alawel, an 'emerk 55 senh. walethaney, anek r'eyes alekleyh! asetyeqz alan!"

يَقُولُ لِأُمِّهِ.

"حَسَناً، الأَوَّلُ، أَنَّ عُمَرَكَ 55 سَنَةً. وَالثاني، أَنَّكَ رَئِيسُ الكُلِّيَةِ! اِسْتَيْقِظْ الآنَ!"

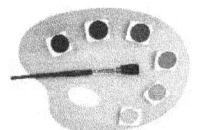

Elementary Course

الفَصْلُ الثالِثُ عَشَرَ
Chapter 13

اسْمُ الفُنْدُقِ

The name of the hotel

A

الكَلِمَاتُ

1. اِبْتِسامَةُ - يَبْتَسِمُ - smile; to smile
2. آخَرُ - another
3. إِعْلانُ - advert
4. أَفْضَلُ ، أَحْسَنُ - best
5. الآنَ - now
6. الآنَ ، بِالفِعْلِ - already
7. بُحَيْرَةُ - lake
8. بَعِيدٌ - away
9. بولندا - Poland
10. تَحْتَ ، أَسْفَلَ - down
11. ثُمَّ - then
12. جِسْرُ - bridge
13. حَوْلَ - round
14. خارِجاً إِلَى - outside to
15. خارِجاً مِنْ - out of
16. ساذَج - silly

17. سَيّارَةُ أُجْرَةٍ - taxi
    سائِقُ سَيّارَةِ أُجْرَةٍ - taxi driver
18. طَريقٌ - way
19. عَبْرَ ، نَحْوَ - through, across
20. غاضِبٌ - angry
21. فورد - Ford
22. فَوْقَ - over
23. عَلَى الأَقْدامِ - on foot; قَدَمَ - foot
24. كاسبر - Kasper
25. لَيْلَةَ لَيْلٍ ، - night
26. مارا بِ - past
27. مُتْعَبٌ - tired
28. مَرَّةً أُخْرَى ثانِيَةً ، - again

29. مَساءٌ - evening
30. مِصْعَدٌ - lift
31. مُفاجَأَةٌ - surprise
    يُفاجِئُ ، يُدْهَشُ - to surprise
    مُنْدَهِشٌ - surprised
32. يُبَيِّنُ ، يَظْهَرُ - to show
33. يَتَوَقَّفُ - to stop
34. يَجِدُ - to find
35. يَرَى - to see
36. يُفْتَحُ - to open
37. يَقِفُ - to stand
38. يَمْشِي ، يَسِيرُ - to walk
39. يَنامُ - to sleep

B

The name of the hotel

اِسْمُ الفُنْدُقِ

This is a student. His name is Kasper. Kasper is from Poland. He cannot speak Arabic. He wants to learn Arabic at a college in Egypt. Kasper lives in a hotel in Alexandria now.

إنَّهُ طالِبٌ. اِسْمُهُ كاسبَر. وَهُوَ مِنْ بولندا. وَلا يَتَحَدَّثُ العَرَبِيَّةَ. يُرِيدُ أَنْ يَتَعَلَّمَ العَرَبِيَّةَ فِي الكُلِّيَّةِ بِمِصْرَ. وَهُوَ يَعِيشُ الآنَ فِي فُنْدُقٍ بِالإسْكَنْدَرِيَّةِ.

He is in his room now. He looks at the map. This map is very good. Kasper sees streets, squares and shops on the map. He goes out of the room and through the long corridor to the lift. The lift takes him down. Kasper goes through the big hall and out of the hotel. He stops near the hotel and writes the name of the hotel into his notebook.

There is a round square and a lake at the hotel. Kasper goes across the square to the lake. He walks round the lake to the bridge. Many cars, trucks and people go over the bridge. Kasper goes under the bridge. Then he walks along a street to the city centre. He goes past many nice buildings.

It is evening already. Kasper is tired and he wants to go back to the hotel. He stops a taxi, then opens his notebook and shows the name of the hotel to the taxi driver. The taxi driver looks in the notebook, smiles and drives away. Kasper cannot

هُوَ فِي غُرْفَتِهِ الآنَ. يَنْظُرُ إِلَى الخَرِيطَةِ. هٰذِهِ الخَرِيطَةُ جَيِّدَةٌ جِدّاً. يَرَى كاسْبِر الشَوارِعَ وَالمَيادِينَ وَالمَتاجِرَ عَلَى الخَرِيطَةِ. يَخْرُجُ مِنْ الغُرْفَةِ عَبْرَ المَمَرِّ الطَوِيلِ إِلَى المِصْعَدِ. يَأْخُذُهُ المِصْعَدُ إِلَى أَسْفَلَ. يَخْرُجُ كاسْبِر عَبْرَ الصالَةِ الكَبِيرَةِ إِلَى خارِجِ الفُنْدُقِ. يَقِفُ قُرْبَ الفُنْدُقِ وَيَكْتُبُ اِسْمَهُ فِي مُفَكِّرَتِهِ.

هُناكَ مَيْدانٌ دائِرِيٌّ وَبُحَيْرَةٌ عِنْدَ الفُنْدُقِ. كاسْبِر يَعْبُرُ المَيْدانَ إِلَى البُحَيْرَةِ. يَسِيرُ حَوْلَ البُحَيْرَةِ إِلَى الجِسْرِ. الكَثِيرُ مِنَ السَيّاراتِ وَالشاحِناتِ وَالناسِ تَسِيرُ عَلَى الجِسْرِ. يَذْهَبُ كاسْبِر إِلَى أَسْفَلِ الجِسْرِ. ثُمَّ يَسِيرُ عَلَى طُولِ الشارِعِ إِلَى وَسَطِ المَدِينَةِ. وَيَسِيرُ ماراً بِالكَثِيرِ مِنَ المَبانِي الجَمِيلَةِ.

إِنَّهُ المَساءُ الآنَ. كاسْبِر مُتْعَبٌ وَيُرِيدُ أَنْ يَعُودَ إِلَى الفُنْدُقِ. يُوقِفُ سَيّارَةَ أُجْرَةٍ، ثُمَّ يَفْتَحُ مُفَكِّرَتَهُ وَيُبَيِّنُ اِسْمَ الفُنْدُقِ لِلسائِقِ. يَنْظُرُ السائِقُ فِي المُفَكِّرَةِ، يَبْتَسِمُ وَيَقُودُ مُبْتَعِداً. كاسْبِر لا يَسْتَطِيعُ أَنْ يَفْهَمَ ذٰلِكَ.

understand it. He stands and looks in his notebook. Then he stops another taxi and shows the name of the hotel to the taxi driver again. The driver looks in the notebook. Then he looks at Kasper, smiles and drives away too. Kasper is surprised. He stops another taxi. But this taxi drives away too. Kasper cannot understand it. He is surprised and angry. But he is not silly. He opens his map and finds the way to the hotel. He comes back to the hotel on foot.

It is night. Kasper is in his bed. He sleeps. The stars look in the room through the window. The notebook is on the table. It is open. "Ford is the best car". This is not the name of the hotel. This is an advert on the building of the hotel.

يَقِفُ وَيَنْظُرُ فِي مُفَكِّرَتِهِ. ثُمَّ يُوقِفُ سَيَّارَةَ أُجْرَةٍ أُخْرَى وَيُبَيِّنُ اِسْمَ الفُنْدُقِ لِلسائِقِ مَرَّةً أُخْرَى. يَنْظُرُ السائِقُ فِي المُفَكِّرَةِ. ثُمَّ يَنْظُرُ إِلَى كاسْبَر، يَبْتَسِمُ وَيَقُودُ مُبْتَعِداً أَيْضاً.

كاسْبَر مُنْدَهِشٌ. يُوقِفُ سَيَّارَةَ أُجْرَةٍ أُخْرَى. لَكِنَّها تَنْدَفِعُ مُبْتَعِدَةً أَيْضاً. كاسْبَر لا يَسْتَطِيعُ أَنْ يَفْهَمَ ذلِكَ. إِنَّهُ مُنْدَهِشٌ وَغاضِبٌ. لَكِنَّهُ لَيْسَ ساذِجاً. يَفْتَحُ خَرِيطَتَهُ وَيَجِدُ الطَّرِيقَ إِلَى الفُنْدُقِ. يَعُودُ إِلَى الفُنْدُقِ سَيْراً عَلَى الأَقْدامِ.

إِنَّهُ اللَيْلُ. كاسْبَر فِي فِراشِهِ. يَنامُ. تَظْهَرُ النُّجُومُ فِي الغُرْفَةِ مِنْ خِلالِ النافِذَةِ. المُفَكِّرَةُ عَلَى المِنْضَدَةِ. إِنَّها مَفْتُوحَةٌ. "فورد أَفْضَلُ سَيَّارَةٍ". هٰذا لَيْسَ اِسْمَ الفُنْدُقِ. إِنَّهُ إِعْلانٌ فَوْقَ مَبْنَى الفُنْدُقِ.

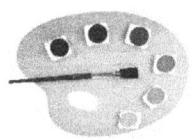

الفَصْلُ الرَّابِعُ عَشَرَ
Chapter 14

أسبرين

Aspirin

A

الكَلِمَاتُ

1. أَبْيَضُ - white
2. اِخْتِبارٌ ، اِمْتِحانٌ - test
   يَخْتَبِرُ ، يُمْتَحِنُ - to test
3. يَسْتَمِرُّ - to last; أَخِيرٌ - last;
   أَخِيراً ، فِي النِهايَةِ - at last
4. أَسْبِرين - aspirin
5. فِي الثامِنَةِ وَالنِصْفِ - past; بَعْدَ -
   at half past eight
6. بلور - crystal
7. حَبَّةُ دَواءٍ - pill
8. حَوالَيْ, بَعْضُ - some
9. ذَكِيٌّ - smart
10. ذٰلِكَ - that (conj)
11. رائِعٌ - wonderful
12. راحَةٌ قَصِيرَةٌ - break, pause
13. رَجُلٌ - guy
14. رَمادِي - grey
15. ساعَةُ اليَدِ - watch

16.	شَيْءٌ ما - something	28.	مَساكِنُ - dorms
17.	صَيْدَلِيَّةُ - pharmacy	29.	مَقْعَدٌ ، مَكْتَبٌ - desk
18.	طَبْعاً - of course	30.	مِنْ أَجْلِ ، لِمُدَّةِ - for
19.	عَشَرَةٌ - ten	31.	نِصْفُ - half
20.	فَصْلٌ دِراسِيٌّ - classroom	32.	واجِبٌ ، مُهِمَّةٌ - task
21.	خِلالَ ساعَةٍ - in; فِي ، خِلالَ - in; فِي الساعَةِ الواحِدَةِ - at one o'clock	33.	وَرَقَةٌ - paper
22.	كَثيراً ، غالِباً - often	34.	يَجْتازُ - to pass, اِجْتازَ الاِمْتِحانَ - passed exam
23.	كَريهُ الرائِحَةِ ، نَتِن - stinking	35.	يَجْلِسُ - to sit down
24.	كِيمْياءُ - chemistry	36.	يُحاوِلُ - to try
25.	كِيمْيائِيٌّ - chemical(adj)	37.	يَحْصُلُ عَلَى - to get (smth), يَصِلُ إلى - to get (smwh)
26.	كِيماوِيّاتٌ - chemicals	38.	يُفَكِّرُ - to think
27.	لِذَلِكَ ، جِدّاً - so		

B

Aspirin

This is Bruce's friend. His name is Hiroshi. Hiroshi is from Japan. He can speak Japanese very well. Japanese is his native language. Hiroshi lives in the dorms. Hiroshi is in his room now. Hiroshi has a chemistry test today. He

أسبرين

إنَّهُ صَديقٌ بروس. اِسْمُهُ هِيرُوشِي. إنَّهُ مِنْ اليابانِ. يَسْتَطيعُ التَحَدُّثَ باليابانِيَّةِ تَماماً جِدّاً. إنَّها لُغَتُهُ الأَصْلِيَّةُ. يَعيشُ هِيرُوشِي فِي مَساكِنِ الطُلّابِ. إنَّهُ فِي غُرْفَتِهِ الآنَ. لَدَيْهِ اِخْتِبارُ كِيمْياءِ اليَوْمَ. يَنْظُرُ فِي ساعَتِهِ.

looks at his watch. It is eight o'clock. It is time to go.

Hiroshi goes outside. He goes to the college. The college is near the dorms. It takes him about ten minutes to go to the college. Hiroshi comes to the chemical classroom. He opens the door and looks into the classroom. There are some students and the teacher there. Hiroshi comes into the classroom.

"Hello," he says.

"Hello," the teacher and the students answer.

Hiroshi comes to his desk and sits down. The chemistry test begins at half past eight. The teacher comes to Hiroshi's desk.

"Here is your task," the teacher says. Then he gives Hiroshi a sheet of paper with the task, "You must make aspirin. You can work from half past eight to twelve o'clock. Begin, please," the teacher says.

إنَّها السَّاعَةُ الثَّامِنَةُ. إنَّهُ وَقْتُ الذَّهابِ.

يَخْرُجُ هِيروشِي. يَذْهَبُ إلَى الكُلِّيَّةِ. وَهِيَ قُرْبَ مَساكِنِ الطُّلابِ. تَسْتَغْرِقُ مِنْهُ حَوالَي عَشْرِ دَقائِقَ لِيَذْهَبَ إلَى الكُلِّيَّةِ. يَصِلُ هِيروشِي إلَى فَصْلِ الدِّراسَةِ الكِيمِيائِيَّةِ. يَفْتَحُ البابَ وَيَنْظُرُ إلَى الفَصْلِ. يُوجَدُ هُناكَ بَعْضُ الطَّلَبَةِ وَالمُدَرِّسِ. يَدْخُلُ هِيروشِي إلَى الفَصْلِ.

"أهلاً،" هُوَ يَقُولُ.

"أهلاً،" يُجِيبُ المُدَرِّسُ وَالطَّلَبَةُ.

يَصِلُ هِيروشِي إلَى مَقْعَدِهِ وَيَجْلِسُ. يَبْدَأُ اِخْتِبارُ الكِيمِياءِ فِي الثَّامِنَةِ وَالنِّصْفِ. يَأْتِي المُدَرِّسُ إلَى مَقْعَدِ هِيروشِيِّ.

"تَفَضَّلْ واجِبَكَ" يَقُولُ المُدَرِّسُ. ثُمَّ يُعْطِي هِيروشِي وَرَقَةً بِالواجِبِ. "يَجِبُ أَنْ تَصْنَعَ أَسْبِرِين. تَسْتَطِيعُ أَنْ تَعْمَلَ مِنَ الثَّامِنَةِ وَالنِّصْفِ إلَى السَّاعَةِ الثَّانِيَةَ عَشْرَةَ. اِبْدَأْ مِنْ فَضْلِكَ،" يَقُولُ المُدَرِّسُ.

Hiroshi knows this task. He takes some chemicals and begins. He works for ten minutes. At last he gets something grey and stinking. This is not good aspirin. Hiroshi knows that he must get big white crystals of aspirin. Then he tries again and again. Hiroshi works for an hour but he gets something grey and stinking again.

Hiroshi is angry and tired. He cannot understand it. He stops and thinks a little. Hiroshi is a smart guy. He thinks for a minute and then finds the answer! He stands up.

"May I have a break for ten minutes?" Hiroshi asks the teacher.

"Of course, you may," the teacher answers.

Hiroshi goes outside. He finds a pharmacy near the college. He comes in and buys some pills of aspirin. In ten

يَعْرِفُ هِيرُوشِي هٰذا الواجِبَ. يَأْخُذُ بَعْضَ الكِيماوِيّاتِ وَيَبْدَأُ. يَعْمَلُ لِمُدَّةِ عَشْرِ دَقائِقٍ. فِي النِهايَةِ يَحْصُلُ عَلى شَيْءٍ رَمادِيٍّ وَكَرِيهِ الرائِحَةِ. هٰذا لَيْسَ أَسْبِرِينَ جَيِّدٌ. يَعْرِفُ هِيروشِي أَنَّهُ يَجِبُ أَنْ يَحْصُلَ عَلى بَلَوراتٍ بَيْضاءَ مِنَ الأَسْبِرِينِ. ثُمَّ يُحاوِلُ مَرَّةً بَعْدَ مَرَّةٍ. يَعْمَلُ هِيروشِي لِمُدَّةِ ساعَةٍ وَلٰكِنَّهُ يَحْصُلُ عَلى شَيْءٍ رَمادِيٍّ وَكَرِيهِ الرائِحَةِ مَرَّةً أُخْرى.

هِيرُوشِي غاضِبٌ وَمُتْعَبٌ. لا يَسْتَطِيعُ أَنْ يَفْهَمَ ذٰلِكَ. يَتَوَقَّفُ وَيُفَكِّرُ قَلِيلاً. إِنَّهُ رَجُلٌ ذَكِيٌّ. يُفَكِّرُ لِمُدَّةِ دَقِيقَةٍ ثُمَّ يَجِدُ الإِجابَةَ! وَيَقِفُ.

"أَيُمْكِنُنِي أَنْ آخُذَ راحَةً لِمُدَّةِ عَشْرِ دَقائِقَ؟" يَسْأَلُ هِيرُوشِي المُدَرِّسَ.

"طَبْعاً، يُمْكِنُكَ،" يُجِيبُ المُدَرِّسَ.

يَخْرُجُ هِيرُوشِي. يَجِدُ صَيْدَلِيَّةً قُرْبَ الكُلِّيَّةِ. يَدْخُلُ وَيَشْتَرِي بَعْضَ حُبُوبِ الأَسْبِرِينِ.

minutes he comes back to the classroom. The students sit and work. Hiroshi sits down.

"May I finish the test?" Hiroshi says to the teacher in five minutes.

The teacher comes to Hiroshi's desk. He sees big white crystals of aspirin. The teacher stops in surprise. He stands and looks at aspirin for a minute.

"It is wonderful! Your aspirin is so nice! But I cannot understand it! I often try to get aspirin and I get only something grey and stinking," the teacher says, "You passed the test," he says.

Hiroshi goes away after the test. The teacher sees something white at Hiroshi's desk. He comes to the desk and finds the paper from the aspirin pills.

"Smart guy. Ok, Hiroshi. Now you have a problem," the teacher says.

خِلالَ عَشرِ دَقائِقَ يَعُودُ إِلَى الفَصْلِ. الطَّلَبَةُ يَجْلِسُونَ وَيَعْمَلُونَ. يَجْلِسُ هِيرُوشِي.

"هَلْ لِي أَنْ أَنْتَهِيَ مِنَ الاِخْتِبارِ؟" يَقُولُ هِيرُوشِي لِلمُدَرِّسِ فِي خَمْسِ دَقائِقَ.

يَأْتِي المُدَرِّسُ إِلَى مَقْعَدِ هِيرُوشِيٍّ يَرَى بَلَّوراتٍ بَيضاءَ كَبِيرَةً مِنَ الأَسْبِرِينِ. يَتَوَقَّفُ المُدَرِّسُ مُنْدَهِشاً. يَقِفُ وَيَنْظُرُ إِلَى الأَسْبِرِينِ لِمُدَّةِ دَقِيقَةٍ.

"إِنَّهُ رائِعٌ! أَسْبَرِينَكَ جَمِيلٌ جِدّاً! وَلَكِنَّنِي لا أَسْتَطِيعُ أَنْ أَفْهَمَ ذَلِكَ. أُحاوِلُ كَثِيراً أَنْ أَحْصَلَ عَلَى أَسْبِرِينَ وَأَحْصَلَ فَقَط عَلَى شَيْءٍ رَمادِيٍّ وَكَرِيهِ الرائِحَةِ," يَقُولُ المُدَرِّسُ, "لَقَدْ اِجْتَزْتَ الاِخْتِبارَ," هُوَ يَقُولُ.

يَخْرُجُ هِيرُوشِي بَعْدَ الاِخْتِبارِ. يَرَى المُدَرِّسُ شَيْئاً أَبْيَضَ عِنْدَ مَقْعَدِ هِيرُوشِيٍّ. يَأْتِي إِلَى المَقْعَدِ وَيَجِدُ وَرَقَةَ حُبُوبِ الأَسْبِرِينِ.

"رَجُلٌ ذَكِيٌّ. حَسَناً, هِيرُوشِي. لَدَيْكَ الآنَ مُشْكِلَةٌ," يَقُولُ المُدَرِّسُ.

الفَصْلُ الخَامِسُ عَشَرَ
Chapter 15

مَرْيَمْ والكانجارو

Mariam and kangaroo

A

الكَلِمَاتُ

1. Oh! - أَداةُ نِداءٍ ، صَوْتٌ لِلدَهْشَةِ
2. أُذُنَ - ear
3. أَسَدٌ - lion
4. الآيس كريم - ice-cream
5. الكانجارو - kangaroo
6. أَوَّلُ - first
7. أوليمبيك - Olympic
8. بِقُوَّةٍ - strongly, قَوِيٌّ - strong
9. بِهُدُوءٍ - quietly
10. حَدِيقَةُ الحَيَوانِ - zoo
11. حَسَناً - okay, well
12. حِمارٌ وَحْشِيٌ - zebra
13. خِزانَةُ كُتُبٍ - bookcase
14. خُطَّةٌ - plan; يُخَطِّطُ - to plan
15. دَعْنا - let us
16. دَلْوٌ - pail
17. دُمْيَةٌ - doll
18. دُمْيَةٌ ، لُعْبَةٌ - toy

89

19. ذَيْلٌ - tail	32. مِبْتَلٌّ - wet
20. سَعِيدٌ، مُبْتَهِجٌ - happy	33. مَتِي، عِنْدَما - when
21. سَنَةٌ - year	34. مَعاً - together
22. شَعْرٌ - hair	35. مَلِئٌ، كامِلٌ - full
23. شَهْرٌ - month	36. نَمِرٌ - tiger
24. صِيغَةٌ مَلَكِيَّةٌ لِلمُفْرَدِ الغائِبِ - its	37. هُتافٌ لِلَفْتِ الاِنْتِباهِ - Hey!
25. ضَمِيرُ المُتَكَلِّمِ مَنْصُوبٌ - me	38. يَجْذِبُ - to pull
26. ضَمِيرُ المُتَكَلِّمِينَ مَنْصُوبٌ - us	39. يَدْرُسُ - to study
27. عَرِيضٌ، واسِعٌ - wide, عَرِيضاً، واسِعاً - widely	40. يُزْعِجُ - to bother
28. فَقِيرٌ، مِسْكِينٌ - poor	41. سُقُوطٌ - fall; يَسْقُطُ - to fall
29. قِرْدٌ - monkey	42. يُصْدَمُ، يَضْرِبُ - to hit, to beat
30. ماءٌ - water	43. يَصِيحُ؛ يَصْرُخُ - to cry
31. ما هٰذا؟ - What is this?; ماذا - what; أَيُّ مِنْضَدَةٍ؟ - What table?	44. يَطِيرُ - to fly

B

Mariam and kangaroo

Bruce is a student now. He studies at a college. He studies Arabic. Bruce lives at the dorms. He lives next door to Hiroshi's.

مَرْيَمُ وَالكانجارو

برُوس طالِبٌ الآنَ. يَدْرُسُ فِي كُلِّيَّةٍ. يَدْرُسُ اللَّغَةَ العَرَبِيَّةَ. يَسْكُنُ فِي مَساكِنِ الطُّلّابِ. يَسْكُنُ فِي البابِ التالي لِهيرُوشِي.

Bruce is in his room now. He takes the telephone and calls his friend Omar.

"Hello," Omar answers the call.

"Hello Omar. It is Bruce here. How are you?" Bruce says.

"Hello Bruce. I am fine. Thanks. And how are you?" Omar answers.

"I am fine too. Thanks. I will go for a walk. What are your plans for today?" Bruce says.

"My sister Mariam asks me to take her to the zoo. I will take her there now. Let us go together," Omar says.

"Okay. I will go with you. Where will we meet?" Bruce asks.

"Let us meet at the bus stop Olympic. And ask Hiroshi to come with us too," Omar says.

"Okay. Bye," Bruce answers.

"See you. Bye," Omar says.

بروسُ فِي غُرْفَتِهِ الآنَ. يَأْخُذُ الهاتِفَ وَيَتَّصِلُ بِصَدِيقِهِ عُمَرّ.

"أَلُو," يُجِيبُ عُمَرٌ عَلَى المُكالَمَةِ.

"أَلُو عُمَر. أَنا بروس. كَيْفَ حالكَ؟" يَقُولُ بروس.

"أَهلاً بروس. أَنا بِخَيْرٍ. شُكْراً. وَكَيْفَ حالكَ؟" يُجِيبُ عُمَرٌ.

"أَنا بِخَيْرٍ كَذَلِكَ. شُكْراً. سَأَذْهَبُ لِلتَنَزُّهِ. ما هِيَ خُطَطُكَ اليَوْمَ؟" يَقُولُ بروس.

"أُخْتِي مَرْيَمْ تَطْلُبُ مِنِّي أَنْ آخُذَها إِلَى حَدِيقَةِ الحَيَوانِ. سَآخُذُها هُناكَ الآنَ. فَلْنَذْهَبْ مَعاً" يَقُولُ عُمَرُ.

"حَسَناً. سَأَذْهَبُ مَعَكَ. أَيْنَ سَنَتَقابَلُ؟" يَسْأَلُ بروس.

"فَلْنَتَقابَلْ عِنْدَ مَحَطَّةِ الأوتوبيس أوليمبيك. وَأَطْلُبْ مِنْ هيروشي أَنْ يَأْتِيَ مَعَنا أَيْضاً," يَقُولُ عُمَرُ.

"حَسَناً. إِلَى اللِقاءِ," يُجِيبُ بروس.

"أَراكَ لاحِقاً. إِلَى اللِقاءِ," يَقُولُ عُمَرُ.

Then Bruce goes to Hiroshi's room. Hiroshi is in his room.

"Hello," Bruce says.

"Oh, hello Bruce. Come in, please," Hiroshi says. Bruce comes in.

"I, Omar and his sister will go to the zoo. Will you go together with us?" Bruce asks.

"Of course, I will go too!" Hiroshi says.

Bruce and Hiroshi walk to the bus stop Olympic. They see Omar and his sister Mariam there.

Omar's sister is only five years old. She is a little girl and she is full of energy. She likes animals very much. But Mariam thinks that animals are toys. The animals run away from her because she bothers them very much. She can pull tail or ear, hit with a hand or with a toy. Mariam has a dog and a cat at home. When Mariam is at home the dog is under a bed and the

بَعْدَ ذَلِكَ يَذْهَبُ بْرُوس إِلَى غُرْفَةِ هِيرُوشِي. هِيروشِي فِي غُرْفَتِهِ.

"أَهلاً،" يَقُولُ بْرُوس.

"أوهِ، أَهلاً بْرُوس. أدْخُلْ مِنْ فَضْلِكَ،" يَقُولُ هِيرُوشِي. يَدْخُلُ بْرُوس.

"أنَا وَعُمَرَ وَأُخْتُهُ سَنَذْهَبُ إِلَى حَدِيقَةِ الحَيَوانِ. هَلْ سَتَذْهَبُ مَعَنَا؟" يَسْأَلُ بْرُوس.

"طَبْعاً، سَأَذْهَبُ كَذَلِكَ!" يَقُولُ هِيرُوشِي.

بْرُوس وَهِيرُوشِي يَمَشِّيانِ إِلَى مَحَطَّةِ الأوتُوبِيس أولِيمبِيك. يَرَوْنَ عُمَرَ وَأُخْتَهُ مَرْيَمْ هُنَاكَ.

أُخْتُ عُمَرَ عُمْرُها خَمْسُ سَنَواتٍ فَقَطْ. إِنَّها فَتَاةٌ صَغِيرَةٌ وَمَلِيئَةٌ بِالنَشَاطِ. تُحِبُّ الحَيَواناتِ كَثِيراً جِدَّاً. لَكِنَّ مَرْيَمَ تَظُنُّ أَنَّ الحَيَواناتِ دُمىً. تَبْتَعِدُ الحَيَواناتُ عَنْها لِأَنَّها تُزعِجُهُم كَثِيراً جِدَّاً. يُمْكِنُها أَنْ تَجْذِبَ الذَيْلَ أَوِ الأُذَنَ، تَضْرِبُ بِاليَدِ أَوْ بِدُمْيَةٍ. مَرْيَمْ لَدَيْها كَلْباً وَقِطَّةً فِي البَيْتِ. عِنْدَما تَكُونُ بِالبَيْتِ يَكُونُ الكَلْبُ تَحْتَ السَرِيرِ وَتَجْلِسُ القِطَّةُ فَوْقَ خِزَانَةٍ

cat sits on the bookcase. So she cannot get them.

Mariam, Omar, Bruce and Hiroshi come into the zoo.

"I live in Egypt for five months but see big animals for the first time," Bruce says.

There are very many animals in the zoo. Mariam is very happy. She runs to the lion and to the tiger. She hits the zebra with her doll. She pulls the tail of a monkey so strong that all the monkeys run away crying. Then Mariam sees a kangaroo. The kangaroo drinks water from a pail. Mariam smiles and comes to the kangaroo very quietly. And then… "Hey!! Kangaroo-oo-oo!!" Mariam cries and pulls its tail. The kangaroo looks at Mariam with wide open eyes. It jumps in surprise so that the pail with water flies up and falls on Mariam. Water runs down her hair, her face and her dress. Mariam is all wet.

الكُتُبِ. لِذَلِكَ لا يُمْكِنُها أَنْ تَصِلَ إِلَيْهِمْ.

مَرْيَمُ وَعُمَرُ وَبْرُوس وَهِيرُوشِيّ يَصِلُونَ إِلَى الحَدِيقَةِ.

"أَعِيشُ فِي مِصْرَ مُنْذُ خَمْسَةِ شُهُورٍ لَكِنَّنِي أَرَى حَيَواناتٍ كَبِيرَةً لِأَوَّلِ مَرَّةٍ," يَقُولُ برُوس.

يُوجَدُ الكَثِيرُ جِدّاً مِنَ الحَيَواناتِ فِي حَدِيقَةِ الحَيَوانِ. مَرْيَمُ سَعِيدَةٌ جِدّاً. تَجْرِي إِلَى الأَسَدِ وَالنَّمِرِ. تَضْرِبُ الحِمَارَ الوَحْشِيَّ بِدُمْيَتِها. تَجْذِبُ ذَيْلَ قِرْدٍ بِقُوَّةٍ جِدّاً لِدَرَجَةِ أَنَّ كُلَّ القُرُودِ تَبْتَعِدُ وَهِيَ تَصْرُخُ. بَعْدَ ذَلِكَ تَرَى كانجارو. الكانجارو يَشْرَبُ ماءً مِنْ دَلْوٍ. تَبْتَسِمُ مَرْيَمُ وَتَأْتِي إِلَى الكانجارو بِهُدُوءٍ شَدِيدٍ.

"هاي!! كانجاروووو!!" تَصِيحُ مَرْيَمُ وَتَجْذِبُ ذَيْلَهُ. يَنْظُرُ الكانجارو إِلَى مَرْيَمَ بِعَيْنَيْنِ واسِعَتَيْنِ مَفْتُوحَتَيْنِ. يَقْفِزُ مُنْدَهِشاً حَتَّى أَنَّ دَلْوَ الماءِ يَطِيرُ وَيَسْقُطُ عَلَى مَرْيَمَ. يَنْزِلُ الماءُ مِنْ عَلَى شَعْرِها وَوَجْهِها وَفُسْتانِها. مَرْيَمُ كُلُّها مُبْتَلَّةٌ.

"You are a bad kangaroo! Bad!" she cries.

Some people smile and some people say: "Poor girl." Omar takes Mariam home.

"You must not bother the animals," Omar says and gives an ice-cream to her. Mariam eats the ice-cream.

"أَنْتَ كانجارو سَيِّئٌ! سَيِّئٌ!" مَرْيَمُ تَصِيحُ.

يَبْتَسِمُ بَعْضُ النّاسِ وَبَعْضُهُمْ يَقُولُ: "فَتاةٌ مِسْكِينَةٌ." عُمَرُ يَأْخُذُ مَرْيَمَ إِلَى البَيْتِ.

"لا يَجِبُ أَنْ تُزْعِجي الحَيَواناتِ،" يَقُولُ عُمَرُ وَيُعْطِيها آيس كِرِيم. تَأْكُلُ مَرْيَمُ الآيس كِرِيم.

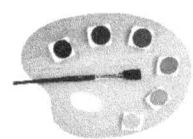

الفَصْلُ السَادِسُ عَشَرَ
Chapter 16

المِظَلِّيُـونَ
Parachutists

A

كلمات

1. أَبْ - daddy
2. أَحْمَرُ - red
3. آخَرُ - other
4. أَرْضٌ - land
5. يَهْبِطُ - to land
6. أَصْفَرُ - yellow
7. إِلَى الشَارِعِ - into the street, خَارِجَ - out of
8. بِالمُناسَبَةِ - by the way
9. بَعْدَ - after
10. بِغَضَبٍ - angrily
11. تِسْعَةُ - nine
12. جُزْءٌ - part

95

13. حَقيقِيٌّ - real
14. حِيلَةُ إنْقاذِ الحَياةِ - life-saving trick; حَياةُ - life
15. حِيلَةٌ ، خُدْعَةٌ - trick
16. خاصَّتَهُ ، مِلْكُهُ - own
17. داخِلَ - inside
18. سِروالٌ ، بنطلون - trousers
19. سَطْحٌ ، سَقْفٌ - roof
20. سُقوطٌ - falling
21. بِصَمْتٍ - silently; صامِتٌ - silent
22. آهِ ، صَوْتٌ اِنْفِعالي - ah..
23. طائِرَةٌ - airplane
24. طَيّار - pilot
25. عَرْضٌ جَوِيٌّ - airshow
26. عُضْوٌ - member
27. عَظيمٌ - great
28. عِماد - Emad
29. فَريقٌ - team
30. يَرْتَدي - to dress; فُسْتانٌ ، ثَوْبٌ - put on؛ مُرْتَدي - dressed
31. فَقَطْ ، بِالضَّبْطِ - just
32. فَوْقَ - over

33. لَوْ ، إذاً - if
34. مِظَلَّةٌ مَحْشُوَّةٍ - stuffed; مَحْشو - stuffed parachutist
35. مِظَلَّةُ هُبوطٍ - parachute
36. مِظَلّي - parachutist
37. مَعْدِن - metal
38. مِعْطَف - jacket
39. مِظَلَّةُ هُبوطٍ - parachute
40. مَقْعَدٌ - seat, يَجْلِسُ - to take a seat
41. نادِي - club
42. هَواءٌ ، جو - air
43. يُدَرَّبُ ، يَتَدَرَّبُ - to train
44. تَدَرَّبَ - trained
45. يَدْفَعُ - to push
46. يُعَدُّ ، يَسْتَعِدُّ - to prepare
47. يُغْلَقُ - to close
48. يَفْعَلُ - to do
49. يَكونُ - to be
50. يُمْسِكُ بِـ - to catch
51. يَنْزِلُ ، يَهْبِطُ - to get off
52. يُنْقِذُ - to save

B

Parachutists

It is morning. Bruce comes to Hiroshi's room. Hiroshi sits at the table and writes something. Hiroshi's cat Favorite is on Hiroshi's bed. It sleeps quietly.

"May I come in?" Bruce asks.

"Oh, Bruce. Come in please. How are you?" Hiroshi answers.

"Fine. Thanks. How are you?" Bruce says.

"I am fine. Thanks. Sit down, please," Hiroshi answers.

Bruce sits on a chair.

"You know I am a member of a parachute club. We will have an airshow today," Bruce says, "I will make some jumps there."

"It is very interesting," Hiroshi answers, "I may come to see the airshow."

المِظَلِّيُّونَ

فِي الصَباحِ، يَأْتِي بْرُوس إِلَى حُجْرَةِ هِيرُوشِيّ. يَجلِسُ هِيرُوشِي إِلَى المِنْضَدَةِ وَيَكْتُبُ شَيْئاً. قِطَّةُ هِيرُوشِي فَافُورِيَّتْ فَوْقَ سَرِيرِهِ. تَنامُ بِهُدُوءٍ.

"هَلْ لِي أَنْ أَدْخُلَ؟" يَسْأَلُ بْرُوس.

"أُوهِ، بْرُوس. أُدْخُلْ مِنْ فَضْلِكَ. كَيْفَ حالُكَ؟" يُجِيبُ هِيرُوشِي.

"بِخَيْرٍ. شُكْراً. كَيْفَ حالُكَ؟" يَقُولُ بْرُوس.

"أَنا بِخَيْرٍ. شُكْراً. اِجلِسْ مِنْ فَضْلِكَ،" يُجِيبُ هِيرُوشِي.

يَجلِسُ بْرُوس عَلَى كُرْسِيٍّ.

"تَعْلَمُ أَنَّنِي عُضْوٌ بِنادِي مِظَلّاتٍ. لَدَيْنا عَرْضٌ جَوِّيٌّ اليَوْمَ،" يَقُولُ بْرُوس. "سَأَقُومُ بِبَعْضِ القَفَزاتِ هُناكَ."

"هٰذا مُمْتِعٌ جِدّاً،" يُجِيبُ هِيرُوشِي، "رُبَّما أَحْضُرُ لِأَرَى العَرْضَ."

"If you want I can take you there and you can fly in an airplane," Bruce says.

"Really? That will be great!" Hiroshi cries, "What time is the airshow?"

"It begins at ten o'clock in the morning," Bruce answers, "Omar will come too. By the way we need help to push a stuffed parachutist out of the airplane. Will you help?"

"A stuffed parachutist? Why?" Hiroshi says in surprise.

"You see, it is a part of the show," Bruce says, "This is a life-saving trick. The stuffed parachutist falls down. At this time a real parachutist flies to it, catches it and opens his own parachute. The "man" is saved!"

"Great!" Hiroshi answers, "I will help. Let's go!"

Hiroshi and Bruce go outside. They come to the bus stop Olympic and take a bus. It takes only ten minutes

"إِذا تُريدُ فَإِنَّني أَسْتَطِيعُ أَنْ آخُذَكَ هُناكَ وَتَسْتَطِيعَ أَنْ تُحَلِّقَ فِي طائِرَةٍ،" يَقُولُ بروس.

"حَقّاً؟ سَيَكُونُ ذَلِكَ عَظِيماً!" يَصِيحُ هِيرُوشِي. "ما هُوَ مَوْعِدُ العَرْضِ؟"

"يَبْدَأُ فِي السّاعَةِ العاشِرَةِ صَباحاً،" يُجِيبُ بروس. "سَيَأْتِي عُمَرُ أَيْضاً. بِالمُناسَبَةِ نَحْتاجُ لِلْمُساعَدَةِ لِنَدْفَعَ مِظَلِّي مَحْشُوّ خارِجَ الطائِرَةِ. هَلْ سَتُساعِدُ؟"

"مِظَلِّي مَحْشُوٌّ؟ لِماذا؟" يَقُولُ هِيرُوشِي مُنْدَهِشاً.

"كَما تَرَى، إِنَّها جُزْءٌ مِنَ العَرْضِ،" يَقُولُ بروس، "هَذِهِ حِيلَةٌ إِنْقاذٍ لِلْحَياةِ. المِظَلِّي المَحْشُوّ يَسْقُطُ. فِي نَفْسِ الوَقْتِ يَطِيرُ إِلَيْهِ مِظَلِّيٌّ حَقِيقِيٌّ، يُمْسِكُهُ وَيَفْتَحُ مِظَلَّتَهُ. الرَّجُلُ يُنْقَذُ!"

"عَظِيمٌ!" يُجِيبُ هِيرُوشِي، "سَوْفَ أُساعِدُ. هَيّا نَذْهَبْ!"

هِيرُوشِي وَبروس يَخْرُجانِ. يَصِلانِ إِلَى مَحَطَّةِ الأُتوبيسِ أوليمبيك وَيَأْخُذانِ أُتوبيساً تَسْتَغْرِقُ عَشَرَ دَقائِقَ فَقَطْ لِيَصِلا لِلْعَرْضِ. عِنْدَ

to go to the airshow. When they get off the bus, they see Omar.

"Hello Omar," Bruce says, "Let's go to the airplane."

They see a parachute team at the airplane. They come to the head of the team. The head of the team is dressed in red trousers and a red jacket.

"Hello Emad," Bruce says, "Hiroshi and Omar will help with the life-saving trick."

"Okay. The stuffed parachutist is here," Emad says. He gives them the stuffed parachutist. The stuffed parachutist is dressed in red trousers and a red jacket.

"It is dressed like you," Omar says smiling to Emad.

"We have no time to talk about it," Emad says, "Take it into this airplane."

Hiroshi and Omar take the stuffed parachutist into the airplane. They take seats at the pilot. All the

النُزُولِ مِنْ الأتوبيس، يَرَيا عُمَرَ.

"أَهلاً عُمَرَ،" يَقُولُ بروس، "هَيّا نَذهَبُ إلَى الطَّائِرَةِ."

يَرَوْنَ فَرِيقَ المِظَلِّيِّينَ عِنْدَ الطَّائِرَةِ. يَأْتُونَ إلَى رَئِيسِ الفَرِيقِ. رَئِيسُ الفَرِيقِ يَرْتَدِي سِرْوالاً أَحْمَرَ وَمِعْطَفاً أَحْمَرَ.

"أَهلاً عِماد،" يَقُولُ بروس، "هِيرُوشِي وَعُمَرُ سَيُساعِدانِ فِي حِيلَةِ إنْقاذِ الحَياةِ."

"حَسَناً. المِظَلِّي المَحْشُوُّ هُنا،" يَقُولُ عِماد. يُعْطِيهِما المِظَلِّيَ المَحْشُوَّ. إنَّهُ مُرْتَدِياً سِرْوالاً أَحْمَرَ وَمِعْطَفاً أَحْمَرَ.

"إنَّهُ يَرْتَدِي مِثلَكَ،" يَقُولُ عُمَرُ مُبْتَسِماً إلَى عِمادٍ.

"لَيْسَ لَدَينا وَقتٌ لِنَتَحَدَّثَ عَنْ ذَلِكَ،" يَقُولُ عِماد، "خُذاهُ إلَى هَذِهِ الطَّائِرَةِ."

هِيرُوشِي وَعُمَرُ يَأْخُذانِ المِظَلِّيَ المَحْشُوَّ إلَى الطَّائِرَةِ. يَجْلِسانِ بِجِوارِ الطَيّارِ. كُلُّ فَرِيقٍ

parachute team but its head gets into the airplane. They close the door. In five minutes the airplane is in the air. When it flies over Alexandria Omar sees his own house.

"Look! My house is there!" Omar cries.

Hiroshi looks through the window at streets, squares, and parks of the city. It is wonderful to fly in an airplane.

"Prepare to jump!" the pilot cries. The parachutists stand up. They open the door.

"Ten, nine, eight, seven, six, five, four, three, two, one. Go!" the pilot cries.

The parachutists begin to jump out of the airplane. The audience down on the land sees red, green, white, blue, yellow parachutes. It looks very nice. Emad, the head of the parachute team looks up too. The parachutists fly down and some land already.

المِظَلِّيِّينَ ما عَدا رَئِيسَهُمْ يَدْخُلُونَ الطائِرَةَ. يُغْلِقُونَ البابَ. خِلالَ خَمْسِ دَقائِقٍ الطائِرَةُ تُحَلِّقُ فِي الجَوِّ. عِنْدَما تُحَلِّقُ فَوْقَ الإِسْكَنْدَرِيَّةِ يَرى عُمَرُ مَنْزِلَهُ.

"أُنْظُرْ! مَنْزِلِي هُناكَ!" يَصِيحُ عُمَرُ.

يَنْظُرُ هِيرُوشِي مِنْ خِلالِ النافِذَةِ إِلى الشَوارِعِ، وَالمَيادِينِ وَالمُتَنَزَّهاتِ فِي المَدِينَةِ. إِنَّهُ رائِعٌ أَنْ تُحَلِّقَ فِي طائِرَةٍ.

"مُسْتَعِدُّونَ لِلقَفْزِ!" يَصِيحُ الطَيّارُ. يَقِفُ المِظَلِّيُّونَ. يَفْتَحُونَ البابَ.

"عَشَرَةٌ، تِسْعَةٌ، ثَمانِيَةٌ، سَبْعَةٌ، سِتَّةٌ، خَمْسَةٌ، أَرْبَعَةٌ، ثَلاثَةٌ، إِثْنانِ، واحِدٌ. إِقْفِزُوا!" يَصِيحُ الطَيّارُ.

يَبْدَأُ المِظَلِّيُّونَ فِي القَفْزِ خارِجَ الطائِرَةِ. الجُمْهُورُ عَلَى الأَرْضِ يَرى مِظَلّاتٍ حَمْراءَ، وَخَضْراءَ، وَبَيْضاءَ، وَزَرْقاءَ وَصَفْراءَ. إِنَّها تَبْدُو جَمِيلَةً جِدّاً. عِماد، رَئِيسُ فِرَقِ المِظَلِّيِّينَ يَنْظُرُ إِلى أَعْلى أَيْضاً. يَطِيرُ المِظَلِّيُّونَ إِلى أَسْفَلَ وَبَعْضِهِمْ هَبَطَ بِالفِعْلِ.

"Okay. Good work guys," Emad says and goes to the nearby café to drink some coffee.

The airshow goes on.

"Prepare for the life-saving trick!" the pilot cries.

Omar and Hiroshi take the stuffed parachutist to the door.

"Ten, nine, eight, seven, six, five, four, three, two, one. Go!" the pilot cries.

Hiroshi and Omar push the stuffed parachutist through the door. It goes out but then stops. Its rubber "hand" catches on some metal part of the airplane.

"Go-go boys!" the pilot cries.

The boys push the stuffed parachutist very strongly but cannot get it out.

The audience down on the land sees a man dressed in red in the airplane door. Two other men try to push him

"حَسَناً. عَمَلٌ جَيِّدٌ أَيُّها الرِجالُ،" يَقولُ عِماد وَيَذهَبُ إِلى مَقهىً مُجاوِرٍ لِيَشرَبَ بَعضَ القَهوَةِ.

يَستَمِرُّ العَرضُ.

"اِستَعِدّوا لِحيلَةِ إِنقاذِ الحَياةِ!" يَصيحُ الطَيّارُ.

يَأخُذُ عُمَر وَهيروشي المِظَلّي المَحشوَّ إلى البابِ.

"عَشَرَةٌ، تِسعَةٌ، ثَمانِيَةٌ، سَبعَةٌ، سِتَّةٌ، خَمسَةٌ، أَربَعَةٌ، ثَلاثَةٌ، اِثنانِ، واحِدٌ. اِقفِزوا!" يَصيحُ الطَيّارُ.

يَدفَعُ هيروشي وَعُمَرُ المِظَلّي المَحشوَّ مِن خِلالِ البابِ. يَخرُجُ وَلَكِنَّهُ يَتَوَقَّفُ بَعدَ ذَلِكَ. يَدُهُ المَطّاطِيَّةُ تَقبِضُ عَلى جُزءٍ مَعدِنِيٍّ مِن الطائِرَةِ.

"اِقفِزوا - اِقفِزوا يا أَولادُ!" يَصيحُ الطَيّارُ.

يَدفَعُ الأَولادُ المِظَلّيَّ المَحشوَّ بِقُوَّةٍ جِدّاً وَلَكِنَّهُم لا يَستَطيعونَ إِخراجَهُ.

الجُمهورُ عَلى الأَرضِ يَرى رَجُلاً مُرتَدِياً مَلابِسَ حَمراءَ في بابِ الطائِرَةِ. يُحاوِلُ رَجُلانِ آخَرانِ

out. People cannot believe their eyes. It goes on about a minute. Then the parachutist in red falls down. Another parachutist jumps out of the airplane and tries to catch it. But he cannot do it. The parachutist in red falls down. It falls through the roof inside of the café. The audience looks silently. Then the people see a man dressed in red run outside of the café. This man in red is Emad, the head of the parachutist team. But the audience thinks that he is that falling parachutist. He looks up and cries angrily, "If you cannot catch a man then do not try it!"

The audience is silent.

"Daddy, this man is very strong," a little girl says to her dad.

"He is well trained," the dad answers.

After the airshow Hiroshi and Omar go to Bruce.

"How is our work?" Omar asks.

دَفَعَهُ إِلَى الخَارِجِ. لا يَسْتَطِيعُ النَاسُ تَصْدِيقَ عُيُونِهِم. يَسْتَمِرُّ هذا حَوَالَيْ دَقِيقَةٍ. ثُمَّ يَسْقُطُ المِظَلِّيُّ ذُو اللَوْنِ الأَحْمَرِ. يَقْفِزُ مِظَلِّيٌّ آخَرُ خَارِجَ الطَائِرَةِ وَيُحَاوِلُ اللَحَاقَ بِهِ. وَلَكِنَّهُ لا يَسْتَطِيعُ أَنْ يَفْعَلَها. يَسْقُطُ المِظَلِّيُّ ذُو اللَوْنِ الأَحْمَرِ. يَسْقُطُ مِنْ خِلَالِ السَقْفِ دَاخِلَ المَقْهَى. يَنْظُرُ الجُمْهُورُ بِصَمْتٍ. ثُمَّ يَرَى النَاسُ رَجُلاً مُرْتَدِياً مَلَابِسَ حَمْرَاءَ يَجْرِي خَارِجَ المَقْهَى. هذا الرَجُلُ ذُو اللَوْنِ الأَحْمَرِ هُوَ عِمَادٌ، رَئِيسُ فَرِيقِ المِظَلِّيِّينَ. لَكِنَّ الجُمْهُورَ يَظُنُّ أَنَّهُ المِظَلِّيُّ الَذِي سَقَطَ. يَنْظُرُ لِأَعْلَى وَيَصِيحُ بِغَضَبٍ، "إِذَا لَمْ تَسْتَطِعْ اللَحَاقَ بِرَجُلٍ لا تُحَاوِلْ بَعْدَ ذَلِكَ"!

الجُمْهُورُ صَامِتٌ.

"أَبِي، هذا الرَجُلُ قَوِيٌّ جِدّاً،" فَتَاةٌ صَغِيرَةٌ تَقُولُ لِأَبِيها.

"إِنَّهُ يُدَرَّبُ جَيِّداً،" يُجِيبُ الأَبُ.

بَعْدَ العَرْضِ يَذْهَبُ هِيرُوشِي وَعُمَرُ إِلَى بْرُوس.

"كَيْفَ عَمَلُنَا؟" يَسْأَلُ عُمَرُ.

"Ah... Oh, it is very good. Thank you," Bruce answers.

"If you need some help just say," Hiroshi says.

" آهِ... أوه، أَنَّهُ جَيِّدٌ جِدّاً. شُكراً لَكُمْ," يُجِيبُ بروس .

" إِذا كُنْتَ بِحاجَةٍ إِلَى بَعْضِ المُساعَدَةِ فَقَطْ أَخْبِرْنا," يَقُولُ هِيرُوشِي

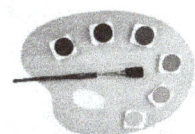

الفَصْلُ السَّابِعُ عَشَرَ
Chapter 17

أَغْلِقِ الغَازَ!

Turn the gas off!

A

كلمات

1. أَحَدَ عَشَرَ - eleven
2. إرادَة ، وَصِيَّةُ - will
3. أَرْبَعَةٌ وَأَرْبَعُونَ - forty-four
4. الَّذِي ؛ الَّذِينَ - who
5. بِطاقَةٌ ، تَذْكِرَةُ - ticket
6. جَلال - Galal
7. حالاً ، فَوْراً - immediately
8. حَذَّرَ ؛ مُعْتِنٍ - careful
9. حَيُّ - living
10. يُدَفِّئُ يَسْخُنُ ؛ دافِئُ - to warm; warm up
11. رَوْضَةُ أَطْفالِ - kindergarten
12. بِسُرْعَةٍ ؛ سَريعٌ - quick; quickly
13. سِكَّةٌ حَديدِيَّةٌ - railway

14. سكرتيرة ، سكرتير - secretary
15. سَمَاعَةُ الهاتِفِ - phone handset
16. سوْفَ - shall/will
17. شاحِبٌ - pale
18. شُعُورٌ - feeling
19. صُنْبُورٌ ، حَنَفِيَّةٌ - tap
20. صَوْتٌ - voice
21. عِشْرُونَ - twenty
22. غازٌ - gas
23. غَرِيبٌ - strange
24. غَلَّايَةٌ - kettle
25. فَجْأَةً - suddenly
26. فِي أَثْناءِ ذَلِكَ - meanwhile
27. عَلَى الأَقْدامِ - on foot; قَدَمٌ - foot
28. قِطارٌ - train
29. قِطَّةٌ صَغِيرَةٌ - pussycat
30. كُلُّ شَيْءٍ - everything
31. كيلومتر - kilometer
32. لا (تَفْعَلُ) - (do(-es) not

33. لَحْظَةٌ - moment
34. لِذَلِكَ - so
35. بِمَكْرٍ - sly; ماكِرٌ - slyly
36. مُجاوِرٌ ، قَرِيبٌ - nearby
37. مَحَطَّةٌ - station
38. نارٌ - fire
39. نَسِيَ - forgot
40. يَأْمُرُ - to order
41. يَتَجَمَّدُ ، يُجَمِّدُ - to freeze
42. يُحَوِّلُ ، يُدِيرُ - to turn; يَفْتَحُ - to turn on; يُغْلَقُ - to turn off
43. يُخْبِرُ ، يَقُولُ - to tell, to say
44. يَضَعُ رَأْسِيّاً - to put vertically
    يَضَعُ أُفُقِيّاً - to put horizontally
45. يُقْرَعُ أَوْ يَدُقُّ الجَرَس - to ring, رَنِين - ring
46. يَمْتَدُّ ، يَنْتَشِرُ - to spread
47. يَمْلَأُ - to fill up

B

أَغْلَقَ الغازَ!

إنَّها السَاعَةُ السَابِعَةُ صَبَاحاً. عُمَرْ وَمَرْيَمُ نَائِمانِ. أُمُّهما فِي المَطْبَخِ. الأُمُّ اِسْمُها حَنانٌ. عُمْرُها أَرْبَعُونَ سَنَةً. وَهِيَ اِمْرَأَةٌ مَعْنِيَّةٌ. تُنَظِّفُ حَنانُ المَطْبَخَ قَبْلَ أَنْ تَذْهَبَ إلَى العَمَلِ. إنَّها سكرتيرَةٌ. تَعْمَلُ عَلَى بُعْدِ عِشْرِينَ كِيلُومِترٍ مِنَ الإِسْكَنْدَرِيَّةِ. عَادَةً تَذْهَبُ إلَى العَمَلِ بِالقِطارِ.

تَخْرُجُ. مَحَطَّةُ السِكَّةِ الحَدِيدِيَّةِ قَرِيبَةٌ، لِذلِكَ تَذْهَبُ حَنانُ إِلَيْها سَيْراً عَلَى الأَقْدامِ. تَشْتَرِي تَذْكِرَةً وَتَصْعَدُ القِطارَ. تَسْتَغْرِقُ حَوالَيْ عِشْرينَ دَقِيقَةً لِتَصِلَ إلَى عَمَلِها. تَجْلِسُ حَنانُ فِي القِطارِ وَتَنْظُرُ خارِجَ النافِذَةِ.

فَجْأَةً تَتَجَمَّدُ. الغَلايَةُ! إنَّها عَلَى المَوْقِدِ وَنَسِيَتْ أَنْ تُغْلِقَ الغازَ. عُمَرْ وَمَرْيَمُ نائِمانِ. يُمْكِنُ أَنْ تَمْتَدَّ النارُ إلَى الأَثاثِ ثُمَّ ... حَنانُ تَبْدُو شاحِبَةً. لٰكِنَّها اِمْرَأَةٌ ذَكِيَّةٌ وَفِي لَحْظَةٍ تَعْرِفُ ماذا تَفْعَلُ. تَطْلُبُ مِنْ اِمْرَأَةٍ وَرَجُلٍ

Turn the gas off!

It is seven o'clock in the morning. Omar and Mariam sleep. Their mother is in the kitchen. The mother's name is Hanan. Hanan is forty-four years old. She is a careful woman. Hanan cleans the kitchen before she goes to work. She is a secretary. She works twenty kilometers away from Alexandria. Hanan usually goes to work by train.

She goes outside. The railway station is nearby, so Hanan goes there on foot. She buys a ticket and gets on a train. It takes about twenty minutes to go to work. Hanan sits in the train and looks out of the window.

Suddenly she freezes. The kettle! It stands on the cooker and she forgot to turn the gas off! Omar and Mariam sleep. The fire can spread on the furniture and then... Hanan turns pale. But she is a smart woman and in a minute she knows what to do. She asks a woman and a man, who sit nearby, to telephone her home and tell Omar about the kettle.

Meanwhile Omar gets up, washes and goes to the kitchen. He takes the kettle off the table, fills it up with water and puts it on the cooker. Then he takes bread and butter and makes sandwiches. Mariam comes into the kitchen.

"Where is my little pussycat?" she asks.

"I do not know," Omar answers, "Go to the bathroom and wash your face. We will drink some tea and eat some sandwiches now. Then I will take you to the kindergarten."

Mariam does not want to wash. "I cannot turn on the water tap," she says slyly.

"I will help you," her brother says. At this moment the telephone rings. Mariam runs quickly to the telephone and takes the handset.

"Hello, this is the zoo. And who are you?" she says. Omar takes the handset

يَجْلِسانِ بِجِوارِها أَنْ يَتَّصِلا هاتِفِيّاً بِبَيْتِها وَيُخْبِرا عُمَرَ عَنْ الغِلّايَةِ.

فِي أَثْناءِ ذَلِكَ يَسْتَيْقِظُ عُمَرُ، يَغْتَسِلُ وَيَذْهَبُ إِلَى المَطْبَخِ. يَضَعُ الغِلّايَةَ عَلَى المِنْضَدَةِ، يَمْلَؤُها بِالماءِ وَيَضَعُها عَلَى المَوْقِدِ. ثُمَّ يَأْخُذُ خُبْزاً وَزَبَداً وَيَصْنَعُ شَطائِرَ. تَأْتِي مَرْيَمُ إِلَى المَطْبَخِ.

"أَيْنَ قِطَّتِي الصَّغِيرَةُ؟" هِيَ تَسْأَلُ.

"لا أَعْرِفُ،" يُجِيبُ عُمَرُ،"اِذْهَبِي إِلَى الحَمّامِ وَاِغْسِلِي وَجْهَكِ. سَنَشْرَبُ بَعْضَ الشايِ وَنَأْكُلُ بَعْضَ الشَطائِرِ الآنَ. بَعْدَ ذَلِكَ سَوْفَ آخُذُكِ إِلَى رَوْضَةِ الأَطْفالِ.

مَرْيَمُ لا تُرِيدُ أَنْ تَغْتَسِلَ. "لا أَسْتَطِيعُ أَنْ أَفْتَحَ صُنْبُورَ الماءِ،" تَقُولُ بِمَكرٍ.

"سَأُساعِدُكِ،" يَقُولُ أَخُوها. فِي هَذِهِ اللَحْظَةِ يَدُقُّ جَرَسُ الهاتِفِ. تَجْرِي مَرْيَمُ بِسُرْعَةٍ لِلهاتِفِ وَتَأْخُذُ السَمّاعَةَ.

"أَلُوه، هُنا حَدِيقَةُ الحَيَوانِ. وَمَنْ أَنْتَ؟" هِيَ

from her and says, "Hello. This is Omar."

"Are you Omar Galal living at eleven Queen Street?" the voice of a strange woman asks.

"Yes," Omar answers.

"Go to the kitchen immediately and turn the gas off!" the woman's voice cries.

"Who are you? Why must I turn the gas off?" Omar says in surprise.

"Do it now!" the voice orders.

Omar turns the gas off. Mariam and Omar look at the kettle in surprise.

"I do not understand," Omar says, "How can this woman know that we will drink tea?"

"I am hungry," his sister says, "When will we eat?"

"I am hungry too," Omar says and turns the gas on again. At this minute the telephone rings again.

تَقُولُ. يَأْخُذُ عُمَرُ السَّمَّاعَةَ مِنْها وَيَقُولُ، "أَلُوه. أَنا عُمَرُ".

" هَلْ أَنْتَ عُمَرْ جَلالٍ تَسْكُنُ فِي 11 شارِعَ المَلِكَةِ؟" صَوْتُ اِمْرَأَةٍ غَرِيبَةٍ تَسْأَلُ.

" نَعَمْ،" يُجِيبُ عُمَرُ.

" اِذْهَبْ إِلَى المَطْبَخِ فَوْراً وَأَغْلِقْ الغازَ؟" صَوْتُ المَرْأَةِ يَصِيحُ.

" مَنْ أَنْتَ؟ لِماذا يَجِبُ أَنْ أُغْلِقَ الغازَ؟" يَقُولُ عُمَرُ مُنْدَهِشاً.

" اِفْعَلْها الآنَ!" الصَّوْتُ يَأْمُرُ.

يُغْلِقُ عُمَرُ الغازَ. مَرْيَمُ وَعُمَرُ يَنْظُرانِ إِلَى الغِلايَةِ فِي دَهْشَةٍ.

" أَنا لا أَفْهَمُ،" يَقُولُ عُمَرُ، كَيْفَ تَعْرِفُ هَذِهِ المَرْأَةُ أَنَّنا سَنَشْرَبُ شاياً؟"

" أَنا جائِعَةٌ،" تَقُولُ أُخْتُهُ، "مَتى سَنَأْكُلُ؟"

" أَنا جائِعٌ أَيْضاً،" يَقُولُ عُمَرُ وَيَفْتَحُ الغازَ ثانِيَةً. فِي هَذِهِ اللَّحْظَةِ يَدُقُّ جَرَسُ الهاتِفِ مَرَّةً أُخْرَى.

"Hello," Omar says.	" أَلُوهُ،" يَقُولُ عُمَرُ.
"Are you Omar galal who lives at eleven Queen Street?" the voice of a strange man asks.	" هَلْ أَنْتَ عُمَرْ جَلالِ الَّذِي يَسْكُنُ فِي 11 شَارِعَ المَلِكَةِ؟" صَوْتُ رَجُلٍ غَرِيبٍ يَسْأَلُ.
"Yes," Omar answers.	" نَعَمْ،" يُجِيبُ عُمَرُ.
"Turn off the cooker gas immediately! Be careful!" the voice orders.	" أَغْلِقْ غَازَ المَوْقِدِ حَالًا! كُنْ حَذِراً!" الصَوْتُ يَأْمُرُ.
"Okay," Omar says and turns the gas off again.	" حَسَناً،" يَقُولُ عُمَرُ وَيُغْلِقُ الغَازَ مَرَّةً أُخْرَى.
"Let's go to the kindergarten," Omar says to Mariam feeling that they will not drink tea today.	" فَلْنَذْهَبْ إِلَى رَوْضَةِ الأَطْفَالِ،" يَقُولُ عُمَرُ لِمَرْيَمَ شَاعِراً أَنَّهُمْ لَنْ يَشْرَبُوا شَاياً اليَوْمَ.
"No. I want some tea and bread with butter," Mariam says angrily.	" لا. أَنَا أُرِيدُ بَعْضَ الشاي وَالخُبْزِ بِالزُّبَدِ،" تَقُولُ مَرْيَمُ بِغَضَبٍ.
"Well, let's try to warm up the kettle again," her brother says and turns the gas on.	" حَسَناً، فَلْنُحَاوِلْ تَسْخِينَ الغَلّايَةِ ثَانِيَةً،" يَقُولُ أَخُوها وَيَفْتَحُ الغَازَ.
The telephone rings and this time their mother orders to turn the gas off. Then she explains everything. At last Mariam and Omar drink tea and go to the kindergarten.	يَدُقُّ جَرَسُ الهَاتِفِ وَفِي هٰذِهِ المَرَّةِ تَأْمُرُ أُمُّهُمْ أَنْ يُغْلِقا الغَازَ. ثُمَّ تَشْرَحُ كُلَّ شَيْءٍ. أَخِيراً مَرْيَمُ وَعُمَرُ يَشْرَبَانِ الشاي وَيَذْهَبا إِلَى رَوْضَةِ الأَطْفَالِ.

الفَصْلُ الثَامِنُ عَشَرَ
Chapter 18

وِكَالَةُ تَوْظِيفٍ
A job agency

A

كلمات

1. أَرْضِيَّةٌ - floor
2. أَكِيدٌ - sure
3. أوول راوند - all-round
4. بِحَذَرٍ , بِعِنايَةٍ - carefully
5. بِسَبَبٍ؛ لِأَنَّ - as
6. بَعْضُكُمْ البَعْضُ ، كُلُّ الآخَرِ - each other
7. تَنْظِيفُ - cleaning
8. تَيَّار - current
9. جِدِّيَّاً - seriously
10. خِبْرَةٌ ، تَجْرِبَةٌ - experience

11. خَمْسَةَ عَشَرَ - fifteen
12. ذِراعُ - arm, يُصارِعُ بالذِراع - to arm
13. رَمادِيُّ الشَعْرِ - gray-headed
14. زائِر - visitor
15. سِتُّونَ - sixty
16. سِلْك ، كابِل - cable
17. سِيِّدي سَيِّد ، - sir
18. عَدَد ، رَقْم - number
19. عَقْلِي ، ذِهْنِي - mental; ذِهْنِيّاً عَقْلِيّاً - mentally
20. عَمَل كِتابِيّ - writing work
21. عَمَل يَدَوِيّ - manual work
22. فِراش - mattress
23. فَرْدِيّاً - individually
24. في الساعَةِ - per hour
25. قِصَّة - story
26. قَوِيّ - strong; بِقُوَّةٍ - strongly
27. كانَ - was
28. كَذلِكَ, أيضاً - also
29. كَهْرَبائِيّ - electric
30. مَدِينَةُ ، بَلْدَةُ - town
31. مُرْتَبِك - confused
32. مُسْتَشار - consultant
33. مُعاوِن - helper
34. مُمْتاز - cool, great
35. مُمْتَدَّة - running
36. مُمِيت - deadly
37. نَشَرَ - publishing
38. نِصْف - half
39. نَفْس الشَيْءِ - the same; في نَفْسِ الوَقْتِ - at the same time
40. وَظِيفَة - position
41. يَدَعُ ، يَسْمَحُ - to let
42. يَسْتَشِير - to consult
43. يَسْتَلْقِي - to lie
44. يَقْلَقُ ، يُزْعِج - to worry
45. يَنْصَحُ - to recommend
46. يَهْتَزُّ - to shake
47. يُوافِقُ - to agree

A job agency

One day Hiroshi goes to Bruce's room and sees that his friend lies on the bed and shakes. Hiroshi sees some electrical cables running from Bruce to the electric kettle. Hiroshi believes that Bruce is under a deadly electric current. He quickly goes to the bed, takes the mattress and pulls it strongly. Bruce falls to the floor. Then he stands up and looks at Hiroshi in surprise.

"What was it?" Bruce asks.

"You were on electrical current," Hiroshi says.

"No, I listen to the music," Bruce says and shows his CD player.

"Oh, I am sorry," Hiroshi says. He is confused.

وَكَالَةُ تَوْظِيفٍ

ذاتِ يَوْمٍ يَذْهَبُ هِيرُوشِي إِلَى غُرْفَةِ بْرُوس ويرِي صَدِيقُهُ يَسْتَلقِي عَلَى السَرِيرِ وَيَهْتَزُّ. يَرِي هِيروشي بَعْضَ الأَسْلاكِ الكَهْرُبائِيَّةِ مُمْتَدَّةً مِنْ بْرُوس إِلَى الغَلّايَةِ الكَهْرَبائِيَّةِ. يَعْتَقِدُ هِيروشي أنَّ بْرُوس تَحْتَ تَأْثِيرِ تَيَّارٍ كَهْرَبائِيٍّ مُمِيتٍ. يَتَّجِهُ إِلَى السَرِيرِ، يُمْسِكُ الفِراشَ وَيَجْذِبُهُ بِقُوَّةٍ. يَسْقُطُ بْرُوس عَلَى الأَرْضِ. ثُمَّ يَقِفُ وَيَنْظُرُ إِلَى هِيرُوشِي مُنْدَهِشاً.

"ماذا كانَ ذٰلِكَ؟" يَسْأَلُ بْرُوس.

"كُنْتَ تَحْتَ تَأْثِيرِ تَيَّارٍ كَهْرَبائِيٍّ،" يَقُولُ هِيرُوشِي.

"لا، أنا أَسْتَمِعُ إِلَى المُوسِيقَى،" يَقُولُ بْرُوس وَيُظْهِرُ مَشْغَلَ أَسْطُواناتِهِ.

"أوهِ، أنا آسِفٌ،" يَقُولُ هِيرُوشِي. إنَّهُ مُرْتَبِكٌ.

"It's okay. Do not worry," Bruce answers quietly cleaning his trousers.

"Omar and I go to a job agency. Do you want to go with us?" Hiroshi asks.

"Sure. Let's go together," Bruce says.

They go outside and take the bus number seven. It takes them about fifteen minutes to go to the job agency. Omar is already there. They come into the building. There is a long queue to the office of the job agency. They stand in the queue. In half an hour they come into the office. There is a table and some bookcases in the room. At the table sits a gray-headed man. He is about sixty years old.

"Come in guys!" he says friendly, "Take seats, please."

Omar, Bruce and Hiroshi sit down.

"My name is Adel Hassan. I am a job consultant. Usually I speak with visitors individually. But as you are all students

"كُلُّ شَيْءٍ عَلَى ما يُرامُ. لا تَقْلَقْ،" يُجِيبُ بْرُوس بِهُدُوءٍ وَهُوَ يُنَظِّفُ سِرْوالَهُ.

"عُمَر وَأَنا ذاهِبانِ إِلَى وَكالَةِ تَوْظِيفٍ. هَلْ تُرِيدُ أَنْ تَأْتِيَ مَعَنا؟" يَسْأَلُ هِيرُوشِي.

"بِالتَّأْكِيدِ. فَلْنَذْهَبْ مَعاً،" يَقُولُ بْرُوس.

يَخْرُجانِ وَيَأْخُذا الأُتوبيس رَقْمَ سَبْعَةٍ. تَسْتَغْرِقُ حَوالَي خَمْسَةَ عَشَرَ دَقِيقَةً لِيَصِلا إِلَى وَكالَةِ التَّوْظِيفِ. عُمَر هُناكَ بِالفِعْلِ. يَدْخُلُونَ المَبْنَى. يُوجَدُ طابُورٌ طَوِيلٌ أَمامَ مَكْتَبِ وَكالَةِ التَّوْظِيفِ. يَقِفُونَ فِي الطابُورِ فِي خِلالِ نِصْفِ ساعَةٍ يَدْخُلُونَ المَكْتَبَ. هُناكَ مِنْضَدَةٌ وَبَعْضُ خَزائِنِ الكُتُبِ فِي الغُرْفَةِ. يَجْلِسُ إِلَى المِنْضَدَةِ رَجُلٌ رَمادِيُّ الشَّعْرِ. عُمْرُهُ حَوالَي سِتِّينَ سَنَةً.

"أُدْخُلُوا يا رِجالُ!" يَقُولُ بِوُدٍّ، "اِجْلِسُوا، مِنْ فَضْلِكُمْ."

يَجْلِسُ عُمَر، وَبْرُوس وَهِيرُوشِي.

"اِسْمِي عادِل حَسَن. مُسْتَشارُ تَوْظِيفٍ. عادَةً أَتَحَدَّثُ مَعَ الزائِرِينَ فَرْدِيّاً. لٰكِنْ لِأَنَّكُمْ جَمِيعاً طَلَبَةٌ وَتَعْرِفُونَ بَعْضَكُمُ البَعْضَ

and know each other I can consult you all together. Do you agree?"

"Yes, sir," Omar says, "We have three or four hours of free time every day. We need to find jobs for that time, sir."

"Well. I have some jobs for students. And you take off your player," Mr. Hassan says to Bruce.

"I can listen to you and to music at the same time," Bruce says.

"If you seriously want to get a job take the player off and listen carefully to what I say," Mr. Hassan says, "Now guys say what kind of job do you need? Do you need mental or manual work?"

"I can do any work," Hiroshi says, "I am strong. Want to arm?" he says and puts his arm on Mr. Hassan's table.

فَيُمْكِنُنِي أَنْ أُقَدِّمَ لَكُمُ الاِسْتِشَارَةَ كُلَّكُمْ مَعاً. هَلْ تُوافِقُونَ؟"

"نَعَمْ، سَيِّدِي،" يَقُولُ عُمَرُ، "لَدَيْنا ثَلاثُ أَوْ أَرْبَعُ ساعاتٍ مِنْ وَقْتِ الفَراغِ كُلَّ يَوْمٍ. نَحْتاجُ أَنْ نَجِدَ عَمَلاً لِهَذا الوَقْتِ، سَيِّدِي."

"حَسَناً. عِنْدِي بَعْضُ الوَظائِفِ لِلطَّلَبَةِ. وَأَنْتَ أَوْقِفْ مَشْغَلَ المُوسِيقَى،" يَقُولُ السَّيِّدُ/ حَسَن لِبرُوس.

"أَسْتَطِيعُ أَنْ اِسْتَمِعَ إِلَيْكَ وَلِلمُوسِيقَى فِي نَفْسِ الوَقْتِ،" يَقُولُ بروس.

"إِذا كُنْتَ تُرِيدُ جِدِّياً أَنْ تَحْصُلَ عَلَى وَظِيفَةٍ أَوْقِفِ المَشْغَلَ واِسْتَمِعْ بِعِنايَةٍ لِما أَقُولُ،" يَقُولُ السَّيِّدُ/ حَسَن، "وَالآنَ أَخْبِرُونِي يا رِجالُ ما نَوْعُ الوَظِيفَةِ الَّتِي تَحْتاجُونَها؟ هَلْ تَحْتاجُونَ إِلَى عَمَلٍ ذِهْنِيٍّ أَوْ يَدَوِيٍّ؟"

"أَسْتَطِيعُ أَنْ أَقُومَ بِأَيِّ عَمَلٍ،" يَقُولُ هِيرُوشِي. "أَنا قَوِيٌّ. هَلْ تُرِيدُ أَنْ تُصارِعَ بِالذِراعِ؟" يَقُولُ وَيَضَعُ ذِراعَهُ عَلَى مِنْضَدَةِ السَّيِّدِ/ حَسَن.

"It is not a sport club here but if you want..." Mr. Hassan says. He puts his arm on the table and quickly pushes down Hiroshi's arm, "As you see son, you must be not only strong but also smart."

"I can work mentally too, sir," Hiroshi says again. He wants to get a job very much. "I can write stories. I have some stories about my native town."

"This is very interesting," Mr. Hassan says. He takes a sheet of paper, "The publishing house "All-round" needs a young helper for a writing position. They pay nine dollars per hour."

"Cool!" Hiroshi says, "Can I try?"

"Sure. Here is their telephone number and their address," Mr. Hassan says and gives a sheet of paper to Hiroshi.

"إِنَّهُ لَيْسَ نادٍ رِياضِيٌّ هُنا لَكِنْ إِذا تُرِيدُ..." يَقُولُ السَّيِّدُ/ حَسَن. يَضَعُ ذِراعَهُ عَلَى المِنْضَدَةِ وَبِسُرْعَةٍ يَدْفَعُ لِأَسْفَلِ ذِراعِ هِيروشِي، "كَما تَرَى يا بُنَيَّ، لا يَنْبَغِي أَنْ تَكُونَ قَوِيّاً فَقَطْ لَكِنْ ذَكِيّاً أَيْضاً."

"أَسْتَطِيعُ أَنْ أَعْمَلَ ذِهْنِيّاً أَيْضاً، سَيِّدِي،" يَقُولُ هِيروشِي ثانِيَةً. يُرِيدُ أَنْ يَحْصُلَ عَلَى وَظِيفَةٍ بِدَرَجَةٍ كَبِيرَةٍ. "أَسْتَطِيعُ أَنْ أَكْتُبَ قِصَصاً. عِنْدِي بَعْضُ القِصَصِ عَنْ مَدِينَتِي الأَصْلِيَّةِ."

"هٰذا رائِعٌ جِدّاً" يَقُولُ السَّيِّدُ/ حَسَن. يَأْخُذُ وَرَقَةً، "دارُ النَّشْرِ "أوول راوْنْد" تَحْتاجُ مُعاوِنٌ شابٌّ لِوَظِيفَةِ كِتابَةٍ. إِنَّهُمْ يَدْفَعُونَ تِسْعَةَ دُولاراتٍ فِي الساعَةِ."

"مُمْتازٌ!" يَقُولُ هِيروشِي، "أَيُمْكِنُنِي أَنْ أُحاوِلَ؟"

"بِالتَأْكِيدِ. ها هُوَ رَقْمُ هاتِفِهِمْ وَعُنْوانُهُمْ،" يَقُولُ السَّيِّدُ/ حَسَن وَيُعْطِي وَرَقَةً لِهِيروشِي.

"And you guys can choose a job on a farm, in a computer firm, on a newspaper or in a supermarket. As you do not have any experience I recommend you to begin to work in a farm. They need two workers," Mr. Hassan says to Omar and Bruce.

"How much do they pay?" Omar asks.

"Let me see..." Mr. Hassan looks into the computer, "They need workers for three or four hours a day and they pay seven dollars per hour. Saturdays and Sundays are free. Do you agree?" he asks.

"I agree," Omar says.

"I agree too," Bruce says.

"Well. Take the telephone number and the address of the farm," Mr. Hassan says and gives a sheet of paper to them.

"Thank you, sir," the boys say and go outside.

"وَأَنْتُما يا رِجالُ تَسْتَطيعانِ اِخْتِيارَ وَظيفَةٍ فِي مَزْرَعَةٍ، فِي شَرِكَةِ كُمْبِيُوتَرٍ، فِي صَحيفَةٍ أَوْ فِي سوبَر ماركِت. وَلِأَنَّكُما لا تَمْتَلِكانِ أَيَّ خِبْرَةٍ، أَنْصَحُكُما أَنْ تَبْدَءا العَمَلَ فِي مَزْرَعَةٍ. إِنَّهُمْ يَحْتاجُونَ لِعامِلينِ،" يَقُولُ السَيِّدُ/ حَسَن لِعُمَر وَبْرُوس.

"كَمْ يَدْفَعُونَ؟" يَسْأَلُ عُمَر.

"اِسْمَحْ لِي أَنْ أَرَى..." يَنْظُرُ السَيِّدُ/ حَسَن إِلَى الكُمْبِيُوتَرِ، "يَحْتاجُونَ عُمّالاً لِمُدَّةِ ثَلاثِ أَوْ أَرْبَعِ ساعاتٍ يَوْمِيّاً وَيَدْفَعُونَ سَبْعَةَ دُولاراتٍ فِي الساعَةِ. السَبْتُ وَالأَحَدُ يَوْمَيْ عُطْلَةٍ. هَلْ تُوافِقانِ؟" هُوَ يَسْأَلُ.

"أَنا مُوافِقٌ،" يَقُولُ عُمَر.

"أَنا مُوافِقٌ أَيْضاً،" يَقُولُ بْرُوس.

"حَسَناً. خُذا رَقْمَ الهاتِفِ وَعُنْوانَ المَزْرَعَةِ،" يَقُولُ السَيِّدُ/ حَسَنْ وَيُعْطِيهِما وَرَقَةً.

"شُكْراً لَكَ، سَيِّدِي،" يَقُولُ الأَوْلادُ وَيَخْرُجُونَ.

الفَصْلُ التَاسِعُ عَشَرَ
Chapter 19

عُمَرُ وَبرُوس يَغْسِلَانِ الشَاحِنَةَ
Omar and Bruce wash the truck

A

كلمات

1. إِطلاقاً - not any
2. أَقْرَبُ - closer
3. أَكْبَرُ - bigger
4. التاسِعُ - ninth
5. الثالثُ - third
6. الثامِنُ - eighth
7. الخامِسُ - fifth
8. الرابِعُ - fourth
9. السابِعُ - seventh
10. السادِسُ - sixth
11. العاشِرُ - tenth
12. إِلَى مَسافَةٍ أَبْعَدَ - further

13. أَمامَ - front
14. أَوَّلاً - at first
15. بِبُطْءٍ - slowly
16. بَحْر - sea
17. بَذْرَةٌ - seed
18. بَعيدٌ - far
19. تَحْميلُ - loading
20. تَماماً ، جِدّاً- quite
21. تَنْظيفُ - cleaning
22. ثانٍ - second
23. كَبيرٌ جِدّاً ;too - too big
24. حَقْلٌ - field
25. رُخْصَةُ قِيادَةٍ - driving license
26. سَفينَةُ - ship
27. شاطِئُ البَحْرِ - seashore
28. صاحِبُ العَمَلِ - employer
29. صُنْدوقٌ ، عُلْبَةٌ - box
30. طَريقٌ - road
31. عَجَلَةٌ - wheel
32. عَلَى طولِ - along
33. غَسيلُ - washing
34. فَرْمَلَةٌ ، مَكْبَحٌ - brake, يُفَرْمِلُ ، يَكْبَحُ - to brake

35. فِناءٌ - yard
36. قَريبٌ - close
37. قُوَّةٌ - strength
38. كَثيرٌ - lot
39. ماكينَةٌ - machine
40. مالِك - owner
41. مُتَأَرْجِحٌ - pitching
42. مِتر - meter
43. مُحَرِّكٌ - engine
44. مُحْسِنٌ - Mohsen
45. مُناسِبٌ ، مُلائِمٌ - suitable
46. مَوْجَةٌ - wave
47. يَحْمِلُ - to carry in hands, يَنْقُلُ - to carry by transport
48. يُديرُ ، يَبْدَأُ - to start
49. يُسْتَخْدَمُ - to use
50. يَصِلُ - to arrive
51. يَضْغَطُ بِقَدَمِهِ - stepping
52. يَطْفو - to float
53. يَفْحَصُ ، يَخْتَبِرُ - to check
54. يُفْرِغُ - to unload
55. يَنْتَظِرُ - to wait

B

Omar and Bruce wash the truck

Omar and Bruce work on a farm now. They work three or four hours every day. The work is quite hard. They must do a lot of work every day. They clean the farm yard every second day. They wash the farm machines every third day. Every fourth day they work in the farm fields.

Their employer's name is Mohsen Zaki. Mr. Zaki is the owner of the farm and he does most of the work. Mr. Zaki works very hard. He also gives a lot of work to Omar and Bruce.

"Hey boys, finish cleaning the machines, take the truck and go to the transport firm Rapid," Mr. Zaki says, "They have a load for me. Load boxes with the seed in the truck, bring them to the farm, and unload in the farm yard. Do it quickly because I need to use the seed today. And do not forget to wash the truck".

عُمَر وَبرُوس يَغسِلانِ الشاحِنَةَ

عُمَر وَبرُوس يَعمَلانِ فِي مَزرَعَةٍ الآنَ. يَعمَلانِ ثَلاثَ أَو أَربَعَ ساعاتٍ يَومِيّاً. العَمَلُ شاقٌّ جِدّاً. يَجِبُ أَن يُنجِزا الكَثيرَ مِن العَمَلِ كُلَّ يَومٍ. يَنظُفانِ فِناءَ المَزرَعَةِ كُلَّ يَومَينِ. يَغسِلانِ آلاتِ المَزرَعَةِ كُلَّ ثَلاثَةِ أَيّامٍ. كُلَّ أَربَعَةِ أَيّامٍ يَعمَلانِ فِي حُقُولِ المَزرَعَةِ .

اِسمُ صاحِبِ العَمَلِ مُحسِن زَكِي. السَّيِّدُ زَكِيٌّ هُوَ مالِكُ المَزرَعَةِ وهُوَ يَقُومُ بِمُعظَمِ العَمَلِ. يَعمَلُ بِجِدٍّ تَماماً. أَيضاً يُعطِي الكَثيرَ مِن العَمَلِ لِعُمرٍ وَبرُوس .

" يا أَولادُ، اِنهِيا تَنظِيفَ الآلاتِ، خُذا الشاحِنَةَ وَاِذهَبا إِلى شَرِكَةِ النَقلِ رابِيد،" يَقُولُ السَّيِّدُ/ زَكِي، لَدَيهِم شُحنَةٌ مِن أَجلِي. حَمِّلا صَناديقَ البُذُورِ فِي الشاحِنَةِ، أَحضِرُوهُم إِلى المَزرَعَةِ وَأَنزِلُوهُم فِي فِناءِ المَزرَعَةِ. اِفعَلا ذَلِكَ بِسُرعَةٍ لِأَنَّني أَحتاجُ أَن أَستَخدِمَ البُذُورَ اليَومَ. وَلا تَنسَيا أَن تَغسِلا الشاحِنَةَ "

"Okay," Omar says. They finish cleaning and get into the truck. Omar has a driving license so he drives the truck. He starts the engine and drives at first slowly through the farm yard, then quickly along the road. The transport firm Rapid is not far from the farm. They arrive there in fifteen minutes. They look for the loading door number ten there.

Omar drives the truck carefully through the loading yard. They go past the first loading door, past the second loading door, past the third, past the fourth, past the fifth, past the sixth, past the seventh, past the eighth, then past the ninth loading door. Omar drives to the tenth loading door and stops.

"We must check the loading list first," Bruce says, who already has some experience with loading lists at this transport firm. He goes to the loader who works at the door and gives him the loading list. The loader loads

" حَسَناً، يَقُولُ عُمَرُ. يَنْتَهِيانِ مِنَ التَنْظِيفِ وَيَصْعَدانِ الشاحِنَةَ. عُمَرٌ لَدَيْهِ رُخْصَةُ قِيادَةٍ لِذَلِكَ يَقُودُ الشاحِنَةَ. يُدِيرُ المُحَرِّكَ وَيَقُودُ بِبُطْءٍ أَوَّلاً خِلالَ فِناءِ المَزْرَعَةِ، ثُمَّ بِسُرْعَةٍ عَلَى طُولِ الطَرِيقِ. شَرِكَةُ النَقْلِ رابِيد لَيْسَت بَعِيدَةً عَنِ المَزْرَعَةِ. يَصِلانِ إِلَى هُناكَ خِلالَ خَمْسَةَ عَشَرَ دَقِيقَةً. يَبْحَثانِ عَنْ بابِ التَحْمِيلِ رَقْمَ عَشَرَةٍ .

يَقُودُ عُمَرُ الشاحِنَةَ بِعِنايَةٍ خِلالَ فِناءِ التَحْمِيلِ. يَذْهَبانِ بَعْدَ بابِ التَحْمِيلِ الأَوَّلِ، بَعْدَ بابِ التَحْمِيلِ الثاني، بَعْدَ الثالِثِ، بَعْدَ الرابِعِ، بَعْدَ الخامِسِ، بَعْدَ السادِسِ، بَعْدَ السابِعِ، بَعْدَ الثامِنِ، ثُمَّ بَعْدَ بابِ التَحْمِيلِ التاسِعِ. يَقُودُ عُمَرُ حَتَّى بابِ التَحْمِيلِ العاشِرِ وَيَتَوَقَّفُ .

" يَجِبُ أَنْ نَفْحَصَ قائِمَةَ التَحْمِيلِ أَوَّلاً،" يَقُولُ بْرُوس الَّذِي لَدَيْهِ بِالْفِعْلِ بَعْضَ الخِبْرَةِ بِقَوائِمِ التَحْمِيلِ فِي شَرِكَةِ النَقْلِ هَذِهِ. يَذْهَبُ إِلَى المَحْمَلِ الَّذِي يَعْمَلُ عِنْدَ البابِ وَيُعْطِيهِ قائِمَةَ التَحْمِيلِ. يَحْمِلُ المَحْمَلُ بِسُرْعَةٍ

خَمْسَةَ صَنَادِيقَ إِلَى الشاحِنَةِ. يَفْحَصُ بْرُوس الصَنَادِيقِ بِعِنَايَةٍ. كُلُّ الأَرْقَامِ عَلَى الصَنَادِيقِ هِيَ أَرْقَامٌ مِنْ قَائِمَةِ التَحْمِيلِ.

"الأَرْقامُ صَحِيحَةٌ. نَسْتَطِيعُ أَنْ نَذْهَبَ الآنَ،" يَقُولُ بْرُوس.

" حَسَناً،" يَقُولُ عُمَر وَيُدِيرُ المُحَرِّكَ، "أَظُنُّ أَنَّنا نَسْتَطِيعُ أَنْ نَغْسِلَ الشاحِنَةَ الآنَ. هُناكَ مَكانٌ مُناسِبٌ لَيْسَ بَعِيدٌ عَنْ هُنا".

فِي خِلالِ خَمْسِ دَقائِقَ يَصِلانِ إِلَى شاطِئِ البَحْرِ.

" هَلْ تُرِيدُ أَنْ تَغْسِلَ الشاحِنَةُ هُنا؟" يَسْأَلُ بْرُوس مُنْدَهِشاً.

" نَعَمْ! إِنَّهُ مَكانٌ لَطِيفٌ، أَلَيْسَ كَذلِكَ؟" يَقُولُ عُمَرُ.

" وَأَيْنَ سَنَجِدُ دَلْواً؟" يَقُولُ بْرُوس.

" لا نَحْتاجُ إِلَى أَيِّ دَلْوٍ. سَأَقُودُ قَرِيبٌ جِدّاً مِنَ البَحْرِ. سَنَأْخُذُ الماءَ مِنَ البَحْرِ،" يَقُولُ عُمَر وَيَقُودُ قَرِيبٌ جِدّاً مِنَ الماءِ. تَذْهَبُ العَجَلاتُ الأَمامِيَّةُ فِي الماءِ وَالأَمْواجُ تَفِيضُ عَلَيْهِمْ.

quickly five boxes into their truck. Bruce checks the boxes carefully. All numbers on the boxes have numbers from the loading list.

"Numbers are correct. We can go now," Bruce says.

"Okay," Omar says and starts the engine, "I think we can wash the truck now. There is a suitable place not far from here".

In five minutes they arrive to the seashore.

"Do you want to wash the truck here?" Bruce asks in surprise.

"Yeah! It is a nice place, isn't it?" Omar says.

"And where will we take a pail?" Bruce asks.

"We do not need any pail. I will drive very close to the sea. We will take the water from the sea," Omar says and drives very close to the water. The front wheels go in the water and the waves run over them.

"Let's get out and begin washing," Bruce says.

"Wait a minute. I will drive a bit closer," Omar says and drives one or two meters further, "It is better now."

Then a bigger wave comes and the water lifts the truck a little and carries it slowly further into the sea.

"Stop! Omar, stop the truck!" Bruce cries, "We are in the water already! Please, stop!"

"It will not stop!!" Omar cries stepping on the brake with all his strength, "I cannot stop it!!"

The truck slowly floats further in the sea pitching on the waves like a little ship.

(to be continued)

" فَلْنَخْرُجْ وَنَبْدَأ الغَسيلَ،" يَقولُ بروس.

" اِنْتَظِرْ لَحْظَةً. سَأَقودُ أَقْرَبَ قَليلاً،" يَقولُ عُمَر وَيَقودُ مِتْرًا أَوْ مِتْرَيْنِ إِلَى مَسافَةٍ أَبْعَدَ، "إِنَّها أَفْضَلُ الآنَ".

بَعْدَ ذَلِكَ تَأْتي مَوْجَةٌ أَكْبَرُ وَيَرْفَعُ الماءُ الشاحِنَةَ قَليلاً وَيَحْمِلُها بِبُطْءٍ إِلَى مَسافَةٍ أَبْعَدَ بِاتِّجاهِ البَحْرِ.

" قِفْ! عُمَرُ، أَوْقِفِ الشاحِنَةَ!" بروس يَصْرُخُ، "نَحْنُ داخِلَ الماءِ بِالفِعْلِ مِنْ فَضْلِكَ، قِفْ"!

" لَنْ تَقِفَ!!" يَصْرُخُ عُمَرُ وَهُوَ يَضْغَطُ بِقَدَمِهِ عَلَى الفَرامِلِ بِكُلِّ قُوَّتِهِ، "لا أَسْتَطيعُ إيقافَها"!!

تَطْفو الشاحِنَةُ بِبُطْءٍ إِلَى مَسافَةٍ أَبْعَدَ داخِلَ البَحْرِ مُتَأَرْجِحَةً عَلَى الأَمْواجِ كَسَفينَةٍ صَغيرَةٍ.

(يُتْبَعُ)

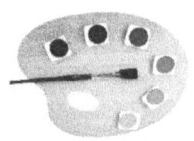

الفَصْلُ العِشْرُونَ
Chapter 20

عُمَرُ وبرُوس يَغُسِلَانِ الشَّاحِنَةَ (الجزء الثاني)
Omar and Bruce wash the truck (part 2)

A

كلمات

1. أَبَداً - never
2. أَتَساءَلُ - I wonder
3. إِحْتِفالُ - ceremony
4. أَرادَ - wanted
5. إِعادَةُ تَأْهيلٍ - rehabilitation
6. الَّذي ، الَّتي (لِغَيْرِ العاقِلِ) - which

7. بترولُ ، نَفْطٌ ، زَيْتٌ - oil
8. حادِثٌ - accident
9. حُوتٌ - whale,
   الحُوتُ القاتِلُ - killer whale
10. خِدْمَةُ الإِنْقاذِ - rescue service
11. خِطابٌ - speech

12.	خَمْسَةٌ وَعِشْرُونَ- twenty-five	32.	يَبْتَلِعُ - to swallow
13.	رائِعٌ - wonderful	33.	يَتَدَفَّقُ - to flow
14.	رِيحٌ - wind	34.	يَحْدُثُ - to happen, حَدَثَ - happened
15.	سَيْطَرَةُ ، تَحَكُّمُ - control	35.	يُخْبِرُ - to inform
16.	شاطِئُ - shore	36.	يُدِيرُ عَجَلَةَ القِيادَةِ - to steer
17.	صَحَفِيٌّ - journalist	37.	يَسارُ - left
18.	طائِر - bird	38.	يَسْبَحُ - to swim
19.	طافِياً - floating	39.	يَسْتَمْتِعُ بِ- enjoy
20.	عَزِيز - dear	40.	يُشْعِلُ - to fire
21.	غَداً - tomorrow	41.	يُصَوِّرُ - to photograph; مُصَوِّرُ - photographer
22.	قاتِل - killer	42.	يَضْحَكُ - to laugh
23.	كانُوا - were	43.	يُطْعَمُ ، يُغَذِّي - to feed
24.	مال - money	44.	يُطْلَقُ سَراح - to set free
25.	مِثالٌ - example; مَثَلاً - for example	45.	يُعِيدُ تَأْهِيلَ - to rehabilitate
26.	مُسْتَمِرٌّ ، ثابِتٌ - constant	46.	يَلَوِّثُ - to pollute بج بلوتكسون - Big Pollutexxon
27.	مِنْ أَجْلِ - for	47.	يَمِينُ - right
28.	مُنْذُ - ago; مُنْذُ سَنَةٍ - a year ago	48.	يُنْقِذُ - to rescue
29.	مَوْقِفُ ، حالَةُ - situation		
30.	ناقِلَةُ بترول - tanker		
31.	نَظَّفَ - cleaned		

B

Omar and Bruce wash the truck
(part 2)

The truck floats slowly further in the sea pitching on the waves like a little ship.

Omar steers to the left and to the right stepping on the brake and gas. But he cannot control the truck. A strong wind pushes it along the seashore. Omar and Bruce do not know what to do. They just sit and look out of the windows. The sea water begins to run inside.

"Let's go out and sit on the roof," Bruce says.

They sit on the roof.

"What will Mr. Zaki say, I wonder?" Bruce says.

The truck floats slowly about twenty meters away from the shore. Some

عُمَر وَبرُوس يَغْسِلانِ الشاحِنَة
(الجُزءُ الثاني)

تَطفُو الشاحِنَةُ بِبُطءٍ إلى مَسافةٍ أبْعَدَ داخِلَ البَحرِ مُتأرْجِحَةً عَلى الأمْواجِ كَسَفينةٍ صَغيرةٍ.

عُمرّ يُوَجِّهُ عَجَلَةَ القِيادَةِ لِليَسارِ وَلِليَمينِ ضاغِطاً عَلى الفَرامِلِ والبِنْزينِ. لكِنَّهُ لا يَسْتَطيعُ السَيْطَرَةَ عَلى الشاحِنَةِ. ريحٌ قَويَّةٌ تَدفَعُها عَلى طُولِ الشاطِئِ. عُمر وَبرُوس لا يَعرِفانِ ماذا يَفْعَلانِ. فَقَط يَجْلِسانِ وَيَنْظُرانِ إلى خارِجِ النَوافِذِ. مِياهُ البَحرِ تَبْدَأُ في الدُخُولِ.

"فَلْنَخْرُجْ وَنَجْلِسْ عَلى السَقْفِ،" يَقُولُ برُوس.

يَجْلِسانِ عَلى السَقْفِ.

"ماذا سَيَقُولُ السَيِّدُ/ زَكِي، أنا أتَساءَلُ؟" يَقُولُ برُوس.

تَطفُو الشاحِنَةُ بِبُطءٍ حَوالَي عِشْرينَ مِتراً

people on the shore stop and look at it in surprise.

"Mr. Zaki may fire us," Omar answers.

Meanwhile the head of the college Mr. Ibrahim comes to his office. The secretary says to him that there will be a ceremony today. They will set free two sea birds after rehabilitation. Workers of the rehabilitation centre cleaned oil off them after the accident with the tanker Big Pollutexxon. The accident happened one month ago. Mr. Ibrahim must make a speech there. The ceremony begins in twenty-five minutes.

Mr. Ibrahim and his secretary take a taxi and in ten minutes arrive to the place of the ceremony. These two birds are already there. Now they are not so white as usually. But they can swim and fly again now. There are many people, journalists, photographers there now. In two

بَعِيداً عَنِ الشَّاطِئِ. يَقِفُ بَعْضُ الناسِ عَلَى الشاطِئِ وَيَنْظُرُونَ إِلَيها فِي دَهْشَةٍ.

"السَّيِّدُ/ زَكِيٌّ رُبَّما يُطْلِقُ النارَ عَلَيْنا," يُجِيبُ عُمَرُ.

فِي أَثْناءِ ذلِكَ يَحْضُرُ مُدِيرُ الكُلِّيَّةِ السَّيِّدُ/ إِبْراهِيمُ إِلَى مَكْتَبِهِ. تَقُولُ لَهُ السكرتيرَةُ أَنَّ هُناكَ اِحْتِفالَ اليَوْمِ. سَيُطْلِقُونَ سَراحَ إِثْنانِ مِنْ طُيُورِ البَحْرِ بَعْدَ تَأْهِيلِهِما. العامِلُونَ بِمَرْكَزِ إِعادَةِ التَأْهِيلِ نَظَّفُوهُما مِنَ الزَيْتِ بَعْدَ حادِثِ ناقِلَةِ البترول بِج بلوتكسون. وَقَعَ الحادِثُ مُنْذُ شَهْرٍ واحِدٍ. يَجِبُ عَلَى السَّيِّدِ/ إِبْراهِيمُ أَنْ يُلْقِيَ خِطاباً هُناكَ. يَبْدَأُ الاحْتِفالُ فِي غُضُونِ خَمْسٍ وَعِشْرِينَ دَقِيقَةً.

يَسْتَقِلُّ السَّيِّدُ/ إِبْراهِيم وَسكرتيرتُهُ سَيّارَةَ أُجْرَةٍ وَفِي خِلالِ عَشْرِ دَقائِقَ يَصِلانِ إِلَى مَكانِ الاِحْتِفالِ. هذانِ الطائِرانِ مُتَواجِدانِ بِالفِعْلِ هُناكَ. لَوْنُهُما الآنَ لَيْسَ أَبْيَضاً ناصِعاً كَالْمُعْتادِ. وَلكِنْ الآنَ يُمكِنُهُما السِباحَةُ والطَيَرانُ مَرَّةً أُخْرَى. الآنَ هُناكَ الكَثيرُ مِنَ الناسِ، والصَحَفِيِّينَ والمُصَوِّرِينَ. يَبْدَأُ

minutes the ceremony begins. Mr. Ibrahim begins his speech.

"Dear friends!" he says, "The accident with the tanker Big Pollutexxon happened at this place a month ago. We must rehabilitate many birds and animals now. It costs a lot of money. For example the rehabilitation of each of these birds costs 5,000 dollars! And I am glad to inform you now that after one month of rehabilitation these two wonderful birds will be set free."

Two men take a box with the birds, bring it to the water and open it. The birds go out of the box and then jump in the water and swim. The photographers take pictures. The journalists ask workers of the rehabilitation centre about the animals.
Suddenly a big killer whale comes up, quickly swallows those two birds and goes down again. All the people look at the place where the birds were before.

الاِحْتِفالُ خِلالَ دَقِيقَتَيْنِ. السَّيِّدُ/ إِبْراهِيمُ يَبْدَأُ خِطابَهُ.

"الأَصْدِقاءُ الأَعِزّاءُ! هُوَ يَقُولُ، "وَقَعَ حادِثُ ناقِلَةِ البترولِ بِج بلوتكسون فِي هٰذا المَكانِ مُنْذُ شَهْرٍ. يَجِبُ أَنْ نُعِيدَ تَأْهِيلَ الكَثِيرِ مِنَ الطُّيُورِ وَالحَيَواناتِ الآنَ. وَهٰذا يُكَلِّفُ كَثِيراً مِنَ المالِ. فَمَثَلاً إِعادَةُ تَأْهِيلِ كُلاًّ مِنْ هٰذَيْنِ الطائِرَيْنِ يُكَلِّفُ 5000 دُولارٍ! وَيَسُرُّنِي أَنْ أُخْبِرَكُمُ الآنَ أَنَّهُ بَعْدَ شَهْرٍ واحِدٍ مِنْ إِعادَةِ تَأْهِيلِ هٰذَيْنِ الطائِرَيْنِ الرائِعَيْنِ سَيُطْلَقُ سَراحُهُما."

يَأْخُذُ رَجُلانِ صُنْدُوقاً بِهِ الطائِرَيْنِ، يُحْضِرانِهِ إِلَى الماءِ وَيَفْتَحانِهِ. يَخْرُجُ الطائِرانِ مِنَ الصُّنْدُوقِ ثُمَّ يَقْفِزانِ فِي الماءِ وَيَسْبَحانِ. المُصَوِّرُونَ يَلْتَقِطُونَ صُوَراً. يَسْأَلُ الصَّحَفِيُّونَ العامِلِينَ بِمَرْكَزِ إِعادَةِ التَأْهِيلِ عَنِ الحَيَواناتِ. فَجْأَةً يَصْعَدُ حُوتٌ قاتِلٌ ضَخْمٌ، يَبْتَلِعُ بِسُرْعَةٍ هٰذَيْنِ الطائِرَيْنِ وَيَنْزِلُ ثانِيَةً. يَنْظُرُ جَمِيعُ النّاسِ إِلَى المَكانِ حَيْثُ كانَ الطائِرانِ مِنْ

The head of the college does not believe his eyes. The killer whale comes up again looking for more birds. As there are no other birds there, it goes down again. Mr. Ibrahim must finish his speech now.

"Ah…," he chooses suitable words, "The wonderful constant flow of life never stops. Bigger animals eat smaller animals and so on… ah… what is that?" he says looking at the water. All the people look there and see a big truck floating along the shore pitching on the waves like a ship. Two guys sit on it looking at the place of the ceremony.

"Hello Mr. Ibrahim," Bruce says, "Why do you feed killer whales with birds?"

"Hello Bruce," Mr. Ibrahim answers, "What do you do there boys?"

"We wanted to wash the truck," Omar answers.

قَبْلُ. مُدِيرُ الكُلِّيَّةِ لا يُصَدِّقُ عَيْنَيْهِ. يَصْعَدُ الحُوتُ القاتِلُ مَرَّةً أُخْرَى باحِثاً عَنِ المَزِيدِ مِنَ الطُيُورِ. وَلِأَنَّهُ لا يُوجَدُ طُيُورٌ أُخْرَى هُناكَ، يَنْزِلُ الحُوتُ ثانِيَةً. يَجِبُ عَلَى السَيِّدِ/ إبْراهِيمُ أنْ يَنْتَهِيَ مِنْ خِطابِهِ الآنَ.

"آهِ…،" يَخْتارُ كَلِماتٍ مُناسِبَةً، "التَدَفُّقُ المُسْتَمِرُّ الرائِعُ لِلحَياةِ لا يَتَوَقَّفُ أَبَداً. الحَيَواناتُ الأَكْبَرُ تَأْكُلُ الحَيَواناتِ الأَصْغَرَ وَهَلُمَّ جَرّاً… آهِ… ما هٰذا؟" يَقُولُ وَهُوَ يَنْظُرُ إِلَى الماءِ. جَمِيعُ الناسِ يَنْظُرُونَ هُناكَ وَيَرَوْنَ شاحِنَةً كَبِيرَةً تَطْفُو بِمُحاذاةِ الشاطِئِ مُتَأَرْجِحَةً عَلَى الأَمْواجِ كَالسَفِينَةِ. يَجْلِسُ فَوْقَها رَجُلانِ يَنْظُرانِ إِلَى مَكانِ الاِحْتِفالِ.

"أَهْلاً السَيِّدُ/ إبْراهِيمُ،" يَقُولُ بْرُوس، لِماذا تُطْعِمُ الحِيتانُ القاتِلَةُ طُيُوراً؟"

"أَهْلاً بْرُوس،" يُجِيبُ السَيِّدُ/ إبْراهِيمُ، "ماذا تَفْعَلانِ هُناكَ يا أَوْلادُ؟"

"أَرَدْنا أنْ نَغْسِلَ الشاحِنَةَ،" يُجِيبُ عُمَرُ.

"أَرَى ذَلِكَ،" يَقُولُ السَّيِّدُ/ إِبْراهِيمُ. يَبْدَأُ بَعْضُ النّاسِ فِي الِاسْتِمْتاعِ بِهذا المَوْقِفِ. يَبْدِءانِ فِي الضَّحِكِ.

"حَسَناً، سَأَسْتَدْعِي خِدْمَةَ الإِنْقاذِ الآنَ. سَيَقُومُونَ بِإِخْراجِكُما مِنَ الماءِ. وَأُرِيدُ أَنْ أَراكُما بِمَكْتَبِي غَداً،" يَقُولُ مُدِيرُ الكُلِّيَّةِ وَيَسْتَدْعِي خِدْمَةَ الإِنْقاذِ.

"I see," Mr. Ibrahim says. Some of the people begin to enjoy this situation. They begin to laugh.

"Well, I will call the rescue service now. They will get you out of the water. And I want to see you in my office tomorrow," the head of the college says and calls the rescue service.

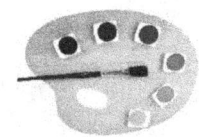

الفَصْلُ الحَادِي وَالعِشْرُونَ
Chapter 21

دَرْسّ

A lesson

A

كلمات

1. أَحَدُ الوالِدَيْنِ - parent
2. اِخْتِبارٌ ، اِمْتِحانٌ - test
3. آخَرُ - else
4. آخَرُ - less
5. أَطْفالٌ ، أَوْلادٌ - children
6. الَّذِي ، الَّتِي - which
7. اِنْتِباهُ - attention
8. بَدَلاً - instead
9. بِدُونِ - without
10. بِرِفْقٍ - slightly
11. بَيْنَ - between
12. تِليفِزيون - television
13. جَرَّةُ - jar
14. حَجَرٌ - stone

15.	حَقّاً - really	25.	طِبِّيّ - medical
16.	دائِماً - always	26.	فارِغٌ ، خالٍ - empty
17.	رَمْلٌ - sand	27.	فَصْلٌ - class
18.	سَعادَةُ - happiness	28.	مازالَ - still
19.	سَوْفَ (شَرْطِيَّة) - would (conditional) ... كُنْتُ سَأقْرَأُ إذاً - I would read if...	29.	هامٌّ - important
		30.	هٰذا الشَّيْءُ - this stuff
		31.	يُبَدِّدُ ، يُنْفِقُ - to spend
20.	شَيْءٌ- thing	32.	يَبْقَى - to remain
21.	صِحَّةُ - health	33.	يَسْكُبُ - to pour
22.	صَديقٌ - boyfriend	34.	يَعْتَني بِـ ، يَرْعَى - to care
23.	صَديقَةُ - girlfriend	35.	يَفْقِدُ - to lose
24.	صَغيرٌ - small		

B

A lesson

دَرْسٌ

The head of the college stands before the class. There are some boxes and other things on the table before him. When the lesson begins he takes a big empty jar and without a word fills it up with big stones.

يَقِفُ مُديرَ الكُلِّيَّةِ أمامَ الفَصْلِ. هُناكَ بَعْضُ العُلَبِ والأشياءِ الأُخْرَى عَلَى المِنْضَدَةِ أمامَهُ. عِنْدَما يَبْدَأُ الدَرْسُ، يَأْخُذُ جَرَّةً فارِغَةً وَبِدونِ كَلامٍ يَمْلَؤُها بِأحْجارٍ كَبيرَةٍ.

"Do you think the jar is already full?" Mr. Ibrahim asks students.

"هَلْ تَظُنُّونَ أنَّ الجَرَّةَ مَمْلوءَةٌ بِالفِعْلِ؟" السَّيِّدُ إبْراهيمُ يَسْأَلُ الطُّلّابَ.

"Yes, it is," agree students.

Then he takes a box with very small stones and pours them into the jar. He shakes the jar slightly. The little stones, of course, fill up the room between the big stones.

"What do you think now? The jar is already full, isn't it?" Mr. Ibrahim asks them again.

"Yes, it is. It is full now," the students agree again. They begin to enjoy this lesson. They begin to laugh.

Then Mr. Ibrahim takes a box of sand and pours it into the jar. Of course, the sand fills up all the other room.

"Now I want that you think about this jar like a man's life. The big stones are important things - your family, your girlfriend and boyfriend, your health, your children, your parents - things that if you lose everything and only they remain, your life still will be full. Little stones are other things which are

"نَعَم، إِنَّها كَذٰلِكَ،" الطُّلّابُ يُوافِقونَ.

بَعْدَ ذٰلِكَ يَأْخُذُ عُلْبَةً بِها أَحْجارٌ صَغيرَةٌ جِدّاً وَيَسْكُبُهُمْ فِي الجَرَّةِ. يَهُزُّ الجَرَّةَ بِرِفْقٍ. الأَحْجارُ الصَّغيرَةُ، طَبْعاً، تَمْلَأُ المِساحَةَ بَيْنَ الأَحْجارِ الكَبيرَةِ.

"ماذا تَعْتَقِدونَ الآنَ؟ الجَرَّةُ مُمْتَلِئَةٌ بِالفِعْلِ، أَلَيْسَ كَذٰلِكَ؟" يَسْأَلُهُمْ السَّيِّدُ/ إِبْراهيمُ مَرَّةً أُخْرى.

"نَعَم، إِنَّها كَذٰلِكَ. إِنَّها الآنَ مُمْتَلِئَةٌ،" الطُّلّابُ يُوافِقونَ مَرَّةً أُخْرى. يَبْدَءونَ فِي الاسْتِمْتاعِ بِهٰذا الدَّرْسِ. وَيَبْدَءونَ فِي الضَّحِكِ.

بَعْدَ ذٰلِكَ يَأْخُذُ عُلْبَةً بِها رَمْلٌ وَيَسْكُبُهُ فِي الجَرَّةِ. طَبْعاً، الرَّمْلُ يَمْلَأُ المِساحَةَ المُتَبَقِّيَةَ.

"الآنَ أُريدُكُمْ أَنْ تَعْتَبِروا هٰذِهِ الجَرَّةَ كَحَياةِ الإِنْسانِ. الأَحْجارُ الكَبيرَةُ هِيَ الأَشْياءُ الهامَّةُ - أُسَرُتُكُمْ، صَديقاتُكُمْ وَأَصْدِقائُكُمْ، صِحَّتُكُمْ، أَوْلادُكُمْ، وَوالِدَيْكُمْ - الأَشْياءُ الَّتى إِذا فَقَدْتُمْ كُلَّ شَيْءٍ وَبَقِيَتْ هِيَ فَقَطْ، سَتَظَلُّ حَياتُكُمْ مَليئَةً. الأَحْجارُ الصَّغيرَةُ هِيَ الأَشْياءُ الأُخْرى

less important. They are things like your house, your job, your car. Sand is everything else - small stuff. If you put sand in the jar at first, there will be no room for little or big stones. The same goes for life. If you spend all of your time and energy on the small stuff, you will never have room for things that are important to you. Pay attention to things that are most important to your happiness. Play with your children or parents. Take time to get medical tests. Take your girlfriend or boyfriend to a café. There will be always time to go to work, clean the house and watch television," Mr. Ibrahim says, "Take care of the big stones first - things that are really important. Everything else is just sand," he looks at the students, "Now Bruce and Omar, what is more important to you - washing a truck or your lives? You float on a truck in the sea full of killer whales like on a ship just because you wanted to wash the

الأَقَلُّ أَهَمِّيَّةً. إِنَّها الأَشْياءُ مِثْلُ مَنْزِلِكُمْ، وَوَظِيفَتِكُمْ، وَسَيّارَتِكُمْ. الرَمْلُ هُوَ كُلُّ شَيْءٍ آخَرَ - أَشْياءُ صَغيرَةٌ. إِذا وَضَعْتُمُ الرَمْلَ فِي الجَرَّةِ أَوَّلاً، لَنْ تَكونَ هُناكَ مِساحَةٌ لِلأَحْجارِ الصَغيرَةِ وَالكَبيرَةِ. يَنْطَبِقُ نَفْسُ الشَيْءِ عَلَى الحَياةِ. إِذا بَدَّدْتُمْ كُلَّ وَقْتِكُمْ وَطاقَتِكُمْ عَلَى الأَشْياءِ الصَغيرَةِ، لَنْ تَجِدوا مِساحَةً لِلأَشْياءِ الهامَّةِ لَكُمْ. أَعْطُوا اِنْتِباهَكُمْ لِلأَشْياءِ الهامَّةِ أَكْثَرَ لِسَعادَتِكُمْ. اِلْعَبُوا مَعَ أَوْلادِكُمْ أَوْ والِدَيْكُمْ. خَصِّصُوا وَقْتاً لِلقِيامِ بِفُحُوصٍ طِبِّيَّةٍ. خُذُوا صَديقَتَكُمْ أَوْ صَديقَكُمْ إِلَى مَقْهىً. سَيَكُونُ هُناكَ دائِماً وَقْتاً لِلذَهابِ إِلَى العَمَلِ، نَظِّفُوا المَنْزِلَ وشاهَدُوا التليفزيونَ،" يَقُولُ السَيِّدُ/ إِبْراهِيمُ، "اِعْتَنَوْا بِالأَحْجارِ الكَبيرَةِ أَوَّلاً - الأَشْياءُ الَّتي حَقّاً هامَّةٌ. كُلُّ شَيْءٍ آخَرَ هُوَ مُجَرَّدُ رَمْلٍ، " يَنْظُرُ إِلَى الطُلّابِ، "وَالآنَ يا بْرُوسَ وَعُمَرُ، ما الشَيْءُ الأَكْثَرُ أَهَمِّيَّةً لَكُما - غَسْلُ شاحِنَةٍ أَمْ حَياتُكُما؟ لَقَدْ طُفْتُما عَلَى شاحِنَةٍ فِي البَحْرِ المَلِيءِ بِالحِيتانِ القاتِلَةِ كَسَفينَةٍ فَقَطْ لِأَنَّكُما

truck. Do you think there is no other way to wash it?"

"No, we do not think so," Omar says.

"You can wash a truck in a washing station instead, can't you?" says Mr. Ibrahim.

"Yes, we can," say the students.

"You must always think before you do something. You must always take care of the big stones, right?"

"Yes, we must," answer the students.

أَرَدْتُما أَنْ تُغَسِّلا الشاحِنَةَ. هَلْ تَعْتَقِدانِ أَنَّهُ لا يُوجَدُ وَسِيلَةٌ أُخْرَى لِغَسْلِها؟"

"لا، لا نَعْتَقِدُ ذَلِكَ، يَقُولُ عُمَرُ.

"يُمْكِنُكُمْ أَنْ تَغْسِلا شاحِنَةً فِي مَحَطَّةِ غَسِيلٍ بَدَلاً مِنْ ذَلِكَ، أَلَيْسَ كَذَلِكَ؟" يَقُولُ السَّيِّدُ/ إِبْراهِيمُ.

"نَعَمْ، يُمْكِنُنا،" يَقُولُ الطُّلّابُ.

"يَجِبُ دائِماً أَنْ تُفَكِّروا قَبْلَ أَنْ تَفْعَلُوا شَيْءٍ ما. يَجِبُ دائِماً أَنْ تَعْتَنُوا بِالأَحْجارِ الكَبِيرَةِ، صَحِيحٌ؟"

"نَعَمْ، يَجِبُ عَلَيْنا،" يُجِيبُ الطُّلّابَ.

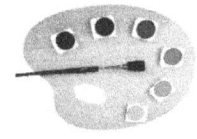

الفَصْلُ الثَانِي وَالعِشْرُونَ
Chapter 22

هيروشي يَعْمَلُ فِي دَارِ نَشْرٍ
Hiroshi works at a publishing house

A

كلمات

1. أَثْنَاءَ ، خِلَالَ - during
2. إِلَى آخِرِهِ - etc.
3. أَمامَ - in front
4. إِنْسانٌ - human
5. أَنْفٌ - nose
6. أَيُّ شَيْءٍ - nothing
7. بارِدٌ - cold (adj)
   بُرُودَةٌ ، بَرْدٌ - coldness
8. تَأْلِيفٌ ، إِنْشاءُ نَصٍّ - composition
9. تَسْجِيلُ الأَفْكارِ - thought-recording
10. تَنْسِيقٌ - co-ordination
11. ثَلاثُونَ - thirty
12. جِهازٌ لِلرَّدِّ عَلَى المُكالَماتِ - answering machine
13. حَزِينٌ - sad

14.	خُصُوصاً - especially	34.	مَرْحَباً - hi
15.	سَلالِمُ - stairs	35.	مُسْتَعِدٌّ ، جاهِزٌ - ready
16.	سَيْر - walking	36.	مُسْتَقْبَل - future
17.	شَرِكَةُ - company	37.	مُضْحِكٌ ، مُسِلٍّ - funny
18.	صَحِيفَةُ - newspaper	38.	مَطَر - rain
19.	صَعْبٌ - difficult	39.	مُظْلِم - dark
20.	صَفّارَةٌ ، نَغْمَةٌ عالِيَةٌ - beep	40.	مُمْكِنٌ - possible
21.	عادَةٌ ، قاعِدَةٌ - rule	41.	مَهارَةٌ - skill
22.	عالَمٌ - world	42.	مِهْنَةٌ - profession
23.	عَلَى الأَقَلِّ - at least	43.	نَصٌّ - text
24.	عَمِيلٌ - customer	44.	نَوْمٌ - sleeping
25.	فِي الخارِجِ - outdoors	45.	يُؤَلِّفُ - to compose
26.	قِصَّةٌ - story	46.	يَبِيعُ - to sell
27.	كُلَّما كانَ مُمْكِناً - as often as possible	47.	يَتَحَدَّثُ - to talk
28.	لا أَحَدَ - nobody	48.	يَتَّصِلُ هاتِفِيّاً - to call
29.	لِأَنَّ - since, as	49.	يَحْصُلُ عَلَى - to get
30.	لَعِبَ - playing	50.	يَرْفُضُ - to refuse
31.	مُبْدِعٌ - creative	51.	يُسَجِّلُ - to record
32.	مَجَلَّةٌ - magazine	52.	يَظْهَرُ ، يَطَوَّرُ - to develop
33.	مُخْتَلِفٌ - different	53.	يَعْنِي ، يَقْصِدُ - to mean
		54.	يُقَدِّمُ ، يُنْتِجُ - to produce

B

Hiroshi works at a publishing house

Hiroshi works as a young helper at the publishing house All-round. He does writing work.

"Hiroshi, our firm's name is All-round," the head of the firm Mr. Tharwat says, "And this means we can do any text composition and design work for any customer. We get many orders from newspapers, magazines and from other customers. All of the orders are different but we never refuse any."

Hiroshi likes this job a lot because he can develop creative skills. He enjoys creative works like writing compositions and design. Since he studies design at college it is a very suitable job for his future profession.

Mr. Tharwat has some new tasks for him today.

هِيرُوشِي يَعْمَلُ فِي دارِ نَشْرٍ

يَعْمَلُ هِيرُوشِي كَمُساعِدٍ شابٍّ فِي دارِ النَشْرِ أووَل راونْد. يَقُومُ بِعَمَلٍ كِتابِيٍّ.

" هيروشي، اِسْمُ شَرِكَتِنا هُوَ أوول راوند،" يَقُولُ السَيِّدُ/ ثَرْوَت رَئِيسُ الشَرِكَةِ، "وَهٰذا يَعْنِي أَنَّنا نَسْتَطِيعُ تَأْلِيفَ أَيِّ نَصٍّ وَعَمَلَ تَصْمِيمٍ لِأَيِّ عَمِيلٍ. نَحْصُلُ عَلَى طَلَباتٍ كَثِيرَةٍ مِنَ الصُحُفِ، وَالمَجَلّاتِ وَمِنْ عُمَلاءَ آخَرِينَ. كُلُّ الطَلَباتِ مُخْتَلِفَةٌ وَلٰكِنَّنا لا نَرْفُضُ أَيٍّ مِنها .

هيروشِي يُحِبُّ هٰذِهِ الوَظِيفَةَ كَثِيراً لِأَنَّهُ يَسْتَطِيعُ أَنْ يُظْهِرَ مَهاراتٍ إبْداعِيَّةً. فَهُوَ يَسْتَمْتِعُ بِالأَعْمالِ الإبْداعِيَّةِ مِثْلَ كِتابَةِ المَقالاتِ القَصِيرَةِ وَالتَصْمِيمِ. وَلِأَنَّهُ يَدْرُسُ التَصْمِيمَ فِي الجامِعَةِ، فَهِيَ وَظِيفَةٌ مُناسِبَةٌ جِدّاً لِمِهْنَتِهِ فِي المُسْتَقْبَلِ .

السَيِّدُ/ ثَرْوَت لَدَيْهِ بَعْضُ المَهامِّ الجَدِيدَةِ لِهيروشي اليَوْمَ.

"We have some orders. You can do two of them," Mr. Tharwat says, "The first order is from a telephone company. They produce telephones with answering machines. They need some funny texts for answering machines. Nothing sells better than funny things. Compose four or five texts, please."

"How long must they be?" Hiroshi asks.

"They can be from five to thirty words," Mr. Tharwat answers, "And the second order is from the magazine "Green world". This magazine writes about animals, birds, fish etc. They need a text about any home animal. It can be funny or sad, or just a story about your own animal. Do you have an animal?"

"Yes, I do. I have a cat. Its name is Favorite," Hiroshi answers, "And I think I can write a story about its tricks. When must it be ready?"

" لَدَيْنا بَعْضُ الطَّلَباتِ. تَسْتَطيعُ عَمَلَ اِثْنَيْنِ مِنْهُمْ," يَقولُ السَّيِّدُ/ ثَرْوَت, "الطَّلَبُ الأَوَّلُ مِنْ شَرِكَةِ هَواتِفَ. إِنَّهُمْ يُنْتِجونَ هَواتِفَ بِجِهازٍ لِلرَّدِّ عَلَى المُكالَماتِ. يَحْتاجونَ لِبَعْضِ النُّصوصِ المُضْحِكَةِ لِأَجْهِزَةِ الرَّدِّ عَلَى المُكالَماتِ. لا شَيْءَ يَبيعُ أَفْضَلَ مِنَ الأَشْياءِ المُضْحِكَةِ. أَكْتُبْ أَرْبَعَةَ أَوْ خَمْسَةَ نُصوصٍ مِنْ فَضْلِكَ" .

" ما طولُهُمْ؟" هيروشي يَسْأَلُ.

" يُمْكِنُ أَنْ يَكونوا مِنْ خَمْسَةٍ إِلَى ثَلاثينَ كَلِمَةً," يُجيبُ السَّيِّدُ/ ثَرْوَت, "وَالطَّلَبُ الثاني مِنْ مَجَلَّةِ "العالَمِ الأَخْضَرِ". هذِهِ المَجَلَّةُ تَكْتُبُ عَنِ الحَيَواناتِ, وَالطُّيورِ وَالأَسْماكِ إِلَى آخِرِهِ. يَحْتاجونَ إِلَى نَصٍّ عَنْ أَيِّ حَيَوانٍ مَنْزِلِيٍّ. يُمْكِنُ أَنْ يَكونَ مُضْحِكاً أَوْ حَزيناً أَوْ حَتَّى قِصَّةً عَنْ حَيَوانِكِ الخاصِّ. هَلْ عِنْدَكَ حَيَوانٌ؟"

" نَعَمْ, عِنْدي. عِنْدي قِطَّةٌ. اِسْمُها فافوريت," يُجيبُ هيروشي," وَأَعْتَقِدُ أَنَّني أَسْتَطيعُ كِتابَةَ قِصَّةٍ عَنْ أَعْمالِها البارِعَةِ. مَتَى يَجِبُ أَنْ تَكونَ جاهِزَةً؟"

"These two orders must be ready by tomorrow," Mr. Tharwat answers.

"Okay. May I begin now?" Hiroshi asks.

"Yes, Hiroshi," Mr. Tharwat says.

Hiroshi brings those texts the next day. He has five texts for the answering machines. Mr. Tharwat reads them:

1. "Hi. Now you say something."

2. "Hello. I am an answering machine. And what are you?"

3. "Hi. Nobody is at home now but my answering machine is. So you can talk to it instead of me. Wait for the beep."

4. "This is not an answering machine. This is a thought-recording machine. After the beep, think about your name, your reason for calling and a number which I can call you back. And I will think about calling you back."

" هٰذانِ الطَلَبانِ يَجِبُ أَنْ يَكُونا جاهِزَينِ غَداً،" يُجِيبُ السَيِّدُ/ ثَرْوَت.

" حَسَناً. هَلْ لِي أَنْ أَبدَأَ الآنَ؟" هيروشي يَسْأَل.

" نَعَم، هِيروشي،" يَقُولُ السَيِّدُ/ ثَرْوَت.

يَحْضُرُ هيروشي تِلكَ النُصُوصَ فِي اليَوْمِ التالي. لَدَيهِ خَمْسَةُ نُصُوصٍ لِجِهازِ الرَدِّ عَلَى المُكالَماتِ. السَيِّدُ/ ثَرْوَتْ يَقرَؤُهُمْ :

" 1. مَرْحَباً. قُلْ شَيئاً ما ".

" 2.أَهْلاً. أَنا جِهازُ الرَدِّ عَلَى المُكالَماتِ. وَماذا تَكُونُ أَنتَ؟"

" 3.مَرْحَباً. لا أَحَدَ فِي البَيتِ الآنَ وَلَكِنَّ جِهازَ الرَدِّ عَلَى المُكالَماتِ مَوجُودٌ. لِذلِكَ يُمكِنُكَ التَحَدُّث إِلَيهِ بَدَلاً مِنِّي. اِنتَظِرِ الصَفّارَةَ ".

" 4.هٰذا لَيسَ جِهازٍ لِلرَدِّ عَلَى المُكالَماتِ. إِنَّهُ جِهازُ تَسجِيلٍ لِلأَفكارِ. بَعدَ الصَفّارَةِ، فَكِّرْ فِي اِسمِكَ، وَسَبَبْ مُكالَمَتَكَ وَرَقَمٍ يُمكِنُنِي الاِتِّصالُ بِهِ عَلَيكَ. وَسَأَفَكَّرُ فِي الاِتِّصالِ بِكَ ".

5. "Speak after the beep! You have the right to be silent. I will record and use everything you say."

"It is not bad. And what about animals?" Mr. Tharwat asks. Hiroshi gives him another sheet of paper.

Mr. Tharwat reads:

Some rules for cats

Walking:

As often as possible, run quickly and as close as possible in front of a human, especially: on stairs, when they have something on their hands, in the dark, and when they get up in the morning. This will train their co-ordination.

In bed:

Always sleep on a human at night. So he or she cannot turn in the bed. Try to lie on his or her face. Make sure that your tail is right on their nose.

Sleeping:

To have a lot of energy for playing, a cat must sleep a lot (at least 16 hours

"5. تَكَلَّم بَعدَ الصَّفّارَةِ! لَدَيكَ الحَقُّ أَن تَظَلَّ صامِتاً. سَأُسَجِّلُ وَأَستَخدِمُ كُلَّ ما تَقولُهُ".

"هٰذا لَيسَ سَيِّئاً. ماذا عَن الحَيَواناتِ؟" السَّيِّدُ ثَروَت يَسأَل. يُعطيهِ هيروشي وَرَقَةً أُخرى. يَقرَأُ السَّيِّدَ/ ثَروَت:

بَعضُ عاداتِ القِطَطِ

السَّيرُ:

كُلَّما كانَ مُمكِنُنا، اِجري بِسُرعَةٍ وَأَقرَبَ ما يَكونُ أَمامَ إِنسانٍ، خُصوصاً: عَلَى السَّلالِمِ، عِندَما يوجَدُ شَيئاً ما بِأَيديهِم، وَفي الظَّلامِ وَعِندَما يَستَيقِظونَ في الصَّباحِ. هٰذا سَيُحَسِّنُ مِن تَنسيقِهِم.

فِي السَّريرِ:

نَم دائِماً فَوقَ الإِنسانِ لَيلاً. لِذٰلِكَ هُوَ أَو هِيَ لا يَستَطيعانِ الاِستِدارَةَ في السَّريرِ. حاوِلَ أَن تَرقُدَ عَلَى وَجهِهِ أَو وَجهِها. تَأَكَّدَ أَنَّ ذَيلَكَ عَلَى أُنوفِهِم تَماماً.

النَّومُ:

لِتَكتَسِبَ طاقَةً كَبيرَةً لِلَّعِبِ، يَجِبُ عَلَى القِطِّ أَن

per day). It is not difficult to find a suitable place to sleep. Any place where a human likes to sit is good. There are good places outdoors too. But you cannot use them when it rains or when it is cold. You can use open windows instead.

Mr. Tharwat laughs.

"Good work, Hiroshi! I think the magazine "Green world" will like your composition," he says.

يَنامَ كَثيراً (عَلى الأَقَلِّ 16 ساعَةً يَوميّاً). أَنَّهُ لَيسَ صَعباً أَنْ تَجِدَ المَكانَ المُناسِبَ لِتَنامَ. أَيُّ مَكانٍ حَيثُ يُحِبُّ الإِنسانُ أَنْ يَجلِسَ مُلائِمٌ. هُناكَ أَماكِنُ مُلائِمَةٌ في الخارِجِ أَيضاً. وَلكِنَّكَ لا تَستَطيعُ اِستِخدامَها عِندَ المَطَرِ أَو عِندَما يَكونُ الجَوُّ بارِداً. تَستَطيعُ اِستِخدامَ النَوافِذِ المَفتُوحَةِ بَدَلاً مِنْ ذلِكَ .

السَيِّدُ/تَروَت يَضحَكُ .

" عَمَلٌ جَيِّدٌ، يا هيروشي! أَعتَقِدُ أَنَّ مَجَلَّةَ "العالَمِ الأَخضَرِ" سَتُحِبُّ نَصَّكَ، " هُوَ يَقُولُ.

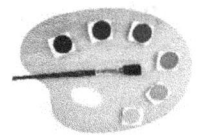

الفَصْلُ الثَّالِثُ وَالعِشْرُونَ
Chapter 23

عَادَاتُ القِطَطِ
Cat rules

A

كلمات

1. أَحْياناً - sometimes
2. أَيُّ شَيْءٍ - anything
3. بِالرَغْمِ مِنْ ، مَعَ أَنَّ - although
4. بَعُوضَةٌ ، نامُوسَةٌ - mosquito
5. تامٌّ ، غامِض - total
6. تَفْكيرُ - thinking
7. حُبٌّ - love, يُحِبُّ - to love
8. يَخْطُو ، يَدُوسُ ، خُطْوَةٌ - to step, step
9. خَلَفَ ، وَراءَ - behind
10. رَجُلٌ - leg
11. سِرٌّ - secret
12. ضَيْفٌ - guest
13. طَبِقٌ - plate
14. طِفْلٌ - child

15. طَقْسٌ - weather
16. طَهِي - cooking
17. فُرْصَةٌ - chance
18. قِراءةٌ - reading
19. قَلِيلٌ - few
20. كَوْكَبٌ - planet
21. لَذِيذُ المَذاقِ - tasty
22. لُغْزٌ ، سِرٌّ - mystery
23. لَوْحَةُ مَفاتِيحٍ - keyboard
24. مُتْعَةٌ - fun
25. مَدْرَسَةٌ - school
26. مِرْحاضٌ - toilet
27. مَوْسِمٌ ، فَصْلٌ - season
28. هَرَبَ - ran away
29. واجِبٌ مَنْزِلِي - homework
30. وَجْبَةٌ - meal
31. يَتَظاهَرُ بِـ - to pretend
32. يَحْتَكُّ بِـ - to rub
33. يَحْصُلُ عَلَى - to get
34. يَخْتَبِئُ - to hide
    اِخْتِباء - hiding, hide-n-seek
35. يُدَبِّرُ، يُدِيرُ - manage
36. يُرْعِبُ - to panic
37. يَسْرِقُ - to steal
38. يَعُضُّ - to bite
39. يُقْبِلُ - to kiss
40. يَنْسَى - to forget

B

Cat rules

عاداتُ القِطَطِ

"The magazine "Green world" places a new order," Mr. Tharwat says to Hiroshi next day, "And this order is for you, Hiroshi. They like

" مَجَلَّةُ "عالَمٌ أخْضَرُ" تَتَقَدَّمُ بِطَلَبٍ جَدِيدٍ،" السَّيِّدُ/ ثَرْوَتُ يَقُولُ لِهيروشي فِي اليَوْمِ التالِي، "وَهذا الطَلَبُ مِنْ أَجْلِكَ، يا هِيرُوشي. إنَّهُم يُحِبُّونَ نَصَّكَ وَيُرِيدُونَ نَصّاً أكْبَرَ عَنْ "عاداتِ

your composition and they want a bigger text about "Cat rules". It takes Hiroshi two days to compose this text. Here it is.

Some secret rules for cats

Although cats are the best and the most wonderful animals on this planet, they sometimes do very strange things. One of the humans managed to steal some cat secrets. They are some rules of life in order to take over the world! But how these rules will help cats is still a total mystery to the humans.

Bathrooms:

 Always go with guests to the bathroom and to the toilet. You do not need to do anything. Just sit, look and sometimes rub their legs.

Doors:

 All doors must be open. To get a door opened, stand looking sad at humans. When they open a door, you need not go through it. After you

القِطَطِ."

إِنَّهُ يَسْتَغْرِقُ يَوْمَيْنِ مِنْ هِيرُوشِي لِيُؤَلِّفَ هٰذا النَّصَّ. ها هُوَ.

بَعْضُ العاداتِ السِّرِّيَّةِ لِلقِطَطِ

مَعَ أَنَّ القِطَطَ هُمْ أَحْسَنُ وَأَرْوَعُ الحَيَواناتِ عَلَى هٰذا الكَوْكَبِ، فَإِنَّهُمْ أَحْياناً يَفْعَلُونَ أَشْياءَ غَرِيبَةً جِدّاً. أَحَدُ البَشَرِ دُبَّرَ لِيَسْرِقَ بَعْضَ أَسْرارِ القِطَطِ. إِنَّها بَعْضُ عاداتِ الحَياةِ لِكَيْ يَحْكُمَ العالَمُ! لٰكِنْ كَيْفَ هٰذِهِ العاداتُ الَّتِي سَتُساعِدُ القِطَطَ ما تَزالُ لُغْزٌ غامِضٌ لِلبَشَرِ.

الحَمّاماتُ.

اِذْهَبُوا دائِماً مَعَ الضُّيُوفِ إِلَى الحَمّامِ وَالمِرْحاضِ. إِنَّكُمْ لا تَحْتاجُونَ فِعْلَ أَيِّ شَيْءٍ. فَقَطْ اِجْلِسُوا، أَنْظُرُوا وَأَحْياناً اِحْتَكُّوا بِأَرْجُلِهِمْ.

الأَبْوابُ.

كُلُّ الأَبْوابِ يَجِبُ أَنْ تَكُونَ مَفْتُوحَةً. لِتَجْعَلُوا البابَ مَفْتُوحاً، قِفُوا فِي حُزْنٍ بِجِوارِ البَشَرِ. عِنْدَما يَفْتَحُونَ البابَ، لا يَجِبُ أَنْ تَخْرُجُوا مِنْهُ.

open in this way the outside door, stand in the door and think about something. This is especially important when the weather is very cold, or when it is a rainy day, or when it is the mosquito season.

Cooking:

Always sit just behind the right foot of cooking humans. So they cannot see you and you have a better chance that a human steps on you. When it happens, they take you in their hands and give something tasty to eat.

Reading books:

Try to get closer to the face of a reading human, between eyes and the book. The best is to lie on the book.

Children's school homework:

Lie on books and copy-books and pretend to sleep. But from time to time jump on the pen. Bite if a child tries to take you away from the table.

بَعْدَما تَفْتَحُوا بِهٰذِهِ الطَّرِيقَةِ البابَ الخارِجِيَّ، قَفُوا إِلَى داخِلِ البابِ وَفَكِّروا فِي شَيْءٍ ما. هٰذا مُهِمٌّ خُصُوصاً عِنْدَما يَكُونُ الطَّقْسُ بارِدٌ جِدّاً، أَوْ عِنْدَما يَكُونُ اليَوْمَ مُمْطِراً أَوْ عِنْدَما يَكُونُ مَوْسِماً لِلْبَعُوضِ.

الطَّهْيُ:

اِجْلِسُوا دائِماً بِالضَّبْطِ خَلْفَ القَدَمِ اليُمْنَى لِمَنْ يَطْبُخُ مِنَ البَشَرِ. لِذٰلِكَ فَهُمْ لَنْ يَتَمَكَّنُوا مِنْ رُؤْيَتِكُمْ وَلَدَيْكُمْ فُرْصَةٌ أَفْضَلُ أَنْ يَخْطُوَ إِنْسانٌ عَلَيْكُمْ. عِنْدَما يَحْدُثُ ذٰلِكَ، يَأْخُذُونَكُمْ بِأَيْدِيهِمْ وَيُعْطُونَكُمْ شَيْئاً ما لَذيذَ المَذاقِ لِتَأْكُلُوهُ.

قِراءَةُ الكُتُبِ:

حاوَلُوا أَنْ تَكونُوا أَقْرَبَ إِلَى وَجْهِ إِنْسانٍ يَقْرَأُ، بَيْنَ العَيْنِ وَالكِتابِ. وَالأَفْضَلُ أَنْ تَرْقُدُوا فَوْقَ الكِتابِ.

الواجِباتُ المَدْرَسِيَّةُ لِلْأَطْفالِ:

أَرْقُدُوا فَوْقَ الكُتُبِ وَالمُذَكِّراتِ وَتَظاهَرُوا بِالنَّوْمِ. لٰكِنْ مَنْ وَقْتٍ لِآخَرَ اِقْفِزُوا عَلَى القَلَمِ. عُضُّوا إِذا حاوَلَ طِفْلٌ أَنْ يَأْخُذَكُمْ بَعِيداً عَنْ

Computer:

If a human works with a computer, jump up on the desk and walk over the keyboard.

Food:

Cats need to eat a lot. But eating is only half of the fun. The other half is getting the food. When humans eat, put your tail in their plate when they do not look. It will give you a better chance to get a full plate of food. Never eat from your own plate if you can take some food from the table. Never drink from your own water plate if you can drink from a human's cup.

Hiding:

Hide in places where humans cannot find you for a few days. This will make humans panic (which they love) thinking that you ran away. When you come out of the hiding place, the humans will kiss you and show their love. And you may get

المِنْضَدَةِ.

الكُمْبِيُوتَرُ:

إِذاً الإِنْسانُ يَعْمَلُ عَلَى كُمْبِيُوتَرٍ، اِقْفِزُوا عَلَى المَكْتَبِ وَسِيرُوا فَوْقَ لَوْحَةِ المَفاتِيحِ.

الطَعامُ:

تَحْتاجُ القِطَطُ أَنْ تَأْكُلَ كَثيراً. وَلكِنَّ الطَعامَ فَقَطْ هُوَ نِصْفُ المُتْعَةِ. النِصْفُ الآخَرُ هُوَ الحُصُولُ عَلَى الطَعامِ. عِنْدَما يَأْكُلَ البَشَرُ، ضَعُوا ذُيُولَكُمْ فِي أَطْباقِهِمْ عِنْدَما لا يَنْظُرُونَ. هذا سَيُعْطِيكُمْ فُرْصَةً أَفْضَلَ لِتَحْصُلُوا عَلَى طَبَقٍ كامِلٍ مِنَ الطَعامِ. لا تَأْكُلُوا مِنْ طَبَقِكُمْ لَوْ يُمْكِنُكُمْ أَخْذُ بَعْضِ الطَعامِ مِنَ المِنْضَدَةِ. لا تَشْرَبُوا مِنْ طَبَقِ الماءِ الخاصِّ بِكُمْ لَوْ يُمْكِنُكُمْ الشُرْبُ مِنْ كُوبِ إِنْسانٍ.

الإِخْتِباءُ:

اِخْتَبِئُوا فِي أَماكِنَ حَيْثُ لا يَسْتَطِيعُ البَشَرُ أَنْ يَعْثُرُوا عَلَيْكُمْ لِأَيَّامٍ قَلِيلَةٍ. هذا سَيَجْعَلُ البَشَرَ مَذْعُورُونَ (الَّذِينَ يُحِبُّونَ) يَظُنُّونَ أَنَّكُمْ هَرَبْتُمْ. عِنْدَما تَعُودُونَ مِنْ مَكانِ اِخْتِبائِكُمْ، سَيُقَبِّلُكُمْ البَشَرُ وَيُظْهِرُونَ حُبَّهُمْ. وَرُبَّما تَحْصُلُونَ عَلَى شَيْءٍ ما لَذِيذِ المَذاقِ.

something tasty.

Humans:

Tasks of humans are to feed us, to play with us, and to clean our box. It is important that they do not forget who the head of the house is.

البَشَرُ:

مَهامُّ البَشَرِ هِيَ إِطْعامُنا، اللَعِبُ مَعَنا وَتَنْظِيفُ صُنْدُوقِنا. إِنَّهُ مُهِمٌّ أَلّا يَنْسَوْا مَنْ هُوَ رَئِيسُ المَنْزِلِ.

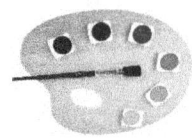

الفَصْلُ الرَّابِعُ والعِشْرُونَ
Chapter 24

فَرِيقُ العَمَلِ
Team work

A

كلمات

1. مَلِكَ (الماضي مِنْ فِعْلِ To have) - had
2. اِبْتَسَمَ - smiled
3. اِبْتَعِدْ - went away
4. أَتَى ، حَضَرَ - came
5. أُحِبُّ - loved
6. أَخْبِرْ - informed
7. الأَرْضُ - earth
8. الراديو - radio
9. أَلْفُ - thousand
10. اللَّيْزَرُ - laser
11. أَنْهَى - finished
12. أَيٌّ مِنْ - either
13. بَدَأَ - began
14. بِلِيون - billion

15. تَحَرَّكَ - moved
16. تَدَفَّقَ - flew away
17. تَذَكَّرَ - remembered
18. تَوَقَّفَ - stopped
19. جَمِيلٌ - beautiful
20. جِهازُ التليفزيون - TV-set
21. حالاً ، قَرِيباً - soon
22. حَتَّى - until
23. حَدِيقَةٌ - garden
24. حَرْبٌ - war
25. رَئِيسِي - central
26. رائِدٌ ، قائِدٌ - captain
27. رادار - radar
28. زَمِيلٌ - colleague
29. زَهْرَةٌ - flower
30. سَفِينَةُ فَضاءٍ - spaceship
31. سَمِعَ - heard
32. ضِدَّ - against
33. عامِلٌ ، عَمَلَ - working
34. عُرَفَ - knew
35. غَرِيبٌ ، أَجْنَبِيٌّ - alien

36. فَتَحَ ، أَدارَ - switched on
37. قَصِيرَ - short
38. فَضاءٌ - space
39. قالَ - said
40. قُتِلَ - killed
41. مُسْتَدِيرٌ - turning
42. مُسَلْسَلٌ - serial
43. نَظَرَ - looked
44. هَزَّ - shook
45. وَجَّهَ - pointed
46. يَدْرُسُ ، يَعْلَمُ - to teach
47. يُدَمِّرُ - destroy
48. يَرْقُصُ - to dance
    رَقْصَ - danced
    الرَقْصُ - dancing
49. يَسْتَمِرُّ - to continue;
    اسْتَمَرَّ - continued
50. يَسْقُطُ - to fall; سَقَطَ - fell
51. يَشْتَرِكُ - to take part
52. يَمُوتُ - to die; ماتَ - died

B

| Team work | فَرِيقُ العَمَلِ |

Omar wants to be a journalist. He studies at a college. He has a composition lesson today. Mr. Ibrahim teaches students to write compositions.

"Dear friends," he says, "some of you will work for publishing houses, newspapers or magazines, the radio or television. This means you will work in a team. Working in a team is not simple. Now I want that you try to make a journalistic composition in a team. I need a boy and a girl."

Many students want to take part in the team work. Mr. Ibrahim chooses Omar and Carol. Carol is from Spain but she can speak English very well.

"Please, sit at this table. Now you are colleagues," Mr. Ibrahim says to them, "You will write a short composition. Either of you will begin the composition and then give it to your

يُرِيدُ عُمَرُ أَنْ يُصْبِحَ صَحَفِيّاً. يَدْرُسُ فِي الجامِعَةِ. لَدَيْهِ دَرْسٌ فِي كِتابَةِ النَّصِّ اليَوْمَ. السَّيِّدُ/ إِبْراهِيم يَعْلَمُ الطَّلَبَةَ كِتابَةَ النُّصُوصِ.

"أَصْدِقائِي الأَعِزّاءُ،" هُوَ يَقُولُ، "بَعْضُكُمْ سَوْفَ يَعْمَلُ فِي دَوْرِ النَّشْرِ، وَالصُّحُفِ أَوِ المَجَلّاتِ، وَالإِذاعَةِ وَالتليفزيونِ. هٰذا يَعْنِي أَنَّكُمْ سَتَعْمَلُونَ فِي فَرِيقٍ. العَمَلُ فِي فَرِيقٍ لَيْسَ بَسِيطاً. الآنَ أُرِيدُ مِنْكُمْ مُحاوَلَةَ عَمَلِ نَصٍّ صَحَفِيٍّ فِي فَرِيقٍ. أَحْتاجُ لِفَتىً وَفَتاةٍ."

يُرِيدُ كَثِيرٌ مِنَ الطَّلَبَةِ المُشارِكَةِ فِي فَرِيقِ العَمَلِ. السَّيِّدُ/ إِبْراهِيم يَخْتارُ عُمَر وَكارول. كارول مِنْ أَسْبانِيا لٰكِنْ يُمْكِنُها التَّحَدُّثُ بِالإنجليزِيَّةِ جَيِّداً جِدّاً.

"مِنْ فَضْلِكُمْ، اِجْلِسا إِلَى هٰذِهِ المِنْضَدَةِ. الآنَ أَنْتُمْ زُمَلاءُ،" السَّيِّدُ/ إِبْراهِيم يَقُولُ لَهُما، "سَتَكْتُبانِ نَصّاً قَصِيراً. أَيّاً مِنْكُما سَيَبْدَأُ النَّصَّ

colleague. Your colleague will read the composition and continue it. Then your colleague will give it back and the first one will read and continue it. And so on until your time is over. I give you twenty minutes."

Mr. Ibrahim gives them paper and Carol begins. She thinks a little and then writes.

Team composition

Carol:

Julia looked through the window. The flowers in her garden moved in the wind as if dancing. She remembered that evening when she danced with Billy. It was a year ago but she remembered everything - his blue eyes, his smile and his voice. It was a happy time for her but it was over now. Why was not he with her?

Omar: At this moment space captain Billy Brisk was at the spaceship White Star. He had an important task and he did not have time to think about that silly girl who he danced with a year

وَبَعْدَ ذٰلِكَ يُعْطِيهِ لِزَمِيلِهِ. سَيَقْرَأُ زَمِيلُكَ النَّصَّ وَيَسْتَمِرُّ فِيهِ. ثُمَّ سَيُعِيدُهُ زَمِيلُكَ وَسَيَقْرَأُهُ الزَّمِيلُ الأَوَّلُ وَيَسْتَمِرُّ فِيهِ. وَهَلُمَّ جَرّاً حَتَّى يَنْتَهِيَ وَقْتُكُمْ. أُعْطِيكُمْ عِشْرِينَ دَقِيقَةً."

يُعْطِيهِما السَّيِّدُ/ إِبْراهِيمُ وَرَقَةً وَتَبْدَأُ كارول. تُفَكِّرُ قَلِيلاً ثُمَّ تَكْتُبُ.

نَصٌّ جَماعِيٌّ

كارول:

نَظَرَتْ جُولِيا مِنَ النافِذَةِ. الزُّهُورُ فِي حَدِيقَتِها تَحَرَّكَتْ فِي الرِّيحِ كَما لَوْ كانَتْ تَرْقُصُ. تَذَكَّرَتْ تِلْكَ المَساءَ عِنْدَما رَقَصَتْ مَعَ بيللي. كانَ ذٰلِكَ مُنْذُ سَنَةٍ لٰكِنَّها تَتَذَكَّرُ كُلَّ شَيْءٍ - عُيُونَهُ الزَّرْقاءَ، إِبْتِسامَتَهُ وَصَوْتَهُ. كانَ وَقْتاً سَعِيداً بِالنِّسْبَةِ لَها لٰكِنَّهُ إِنْتَهَى الآنَ. لِماذا لَمْ يَكُنْ مَعَها؟

عُمَر: فِي هٰذِهِ اللَّحْظَةِ كانَ رائِدُ الفَضاءِ بيللي بريسك فِي سَفِينَةِ الفَضاءِ النَّجْمَةِ البَيْضاءِ. كانَ لَدَيْهِ مُهِمَّةٌ هامَّةٌ وَلَمْ يَكُنْ عِنْدَهُ وَقْتٌ

ago. He quickly pointed the lasers of White Star at alien spaceships. Then he switched on the radio and talked to the aliens: "I give you an hour to give up. If in one hour you do not give up I will destroy you." But before he finished an alien laser hit the left engine of the White Star. Billy's laser began to hit alien spaceships and at the same time he switched on the central and the right engines. The alien laser destroyed the working right engine and the White Star shook badly. Billy fell on the floor thinking during the fall which of the alien spaceships he must destroy first.

Carol: But he hit his head on the metal floor and died at the same moment. But before he died he remembered the poor beautiful girl who loved him and he was very sorry that he went away from her. Soon people stopped this silly war on poor aliens. They destroyed all of their own spaceships

لِيُفَكِّرَ فِي تِلْكَ الفَتاةِ السّاذَجَةِ الَّتِي رَقَصَ مَعَها مُنْذُ عامٍ. وَجَّهَ بِسُرْعَةٍ أَشِعَّةَ لَيْزَرِ النَّجْمَةِ البَيْضاءِ إِلى سُفُنِ فَضاءٍ غَرِيبَةٍ. ثُمَّ فَتَحَ جِهازَ الراديو وَتَحَدَّثَ إِلى الغُرَباءِ: "أُعْطِيكُمْ ساعَةً لِتَتَوَقَّفُوا. إذا لَمْ تَتَوَقَّفُوا خِلالَ ساعَةٍ سَوْفَ أُدَمِّرُكُمْ." لٰكِنْ قَبْلَ أَنْ يَنْتَهِيَ ضَرَبَ لَيْزَرُ الغُرَباءِ المُحَرِّكِ الأَيْسَرِ لِلنَّجْمَةِ البَيْضاءِ. لَيْزَرُ بِيلِّي بَدَأَ يَضْرِبُ سُفُنَ الفَضاءِ الغَرِيبَةِ وَفِي نَفْسِ الوَقْتِ قامَ بِتَشْغِيلِ المُحَرِّكَينِ الرَّئِيسِيِّ وَالأَيْمَنِ. لَيْزَرُ الغُرَباءِ دَمَّرَ المُحَرِّكَ الأَيْمَنَ العامِلَ وَاِهْتَزَّتْ النَّجْمَةُ البَيْضاءُ بِعُنْفٍ. سَقَطَ بِيلِّي عَلى الأَرْضِ وَهُوَ يُفَكِّرُ أَثْناءَ السُّقُوطِ أَيٌّ مِنْ سُفُنِ الفَضاءِ الغَرِيبَةِ يَجِبُ أَنْ يُدَمِّرَها أَوَّلاً.

كارول: لٰكِنْ اِصْطَدَمَتْ رَأْسُهُ عَلَى الأَرْضِيَّةِ المَعْدِنِيَّةِ وَماتَ فِي نَفْسِ اللَّحْظَةِ. وَلٰكِنْ قَبْلَ أَنْ يَمُوتَ تَذَكَّرَ الفَتاةَ الجَمِيلَةَ المِسْكِينَةَ الَّتِي أَحَبَّتْهُ وَكانَ حَزِيناً جِدّاً أَنَّهُ اِبْتَعَدَ عَنْها. حالاً أَوْقَفَ النّاسُ هٰذِهِ الحَرْبَ السّاذَجَةَ عَلَى الغُرَباءِ المَساكِينِ. دَمَّرُوا سُفُنَهُم الفَضائِيَّةَ

and lasers and informed the aliens that people would never start a war against them again. People said that they wanted to be friends with the aliens. Julia was very glad when she heard about it. Then she switched on the TV-set and continued to watch a wonderful Mexican serial.

Omar: Because people destroyed their own radars and lasers, nobody knew that spaceships of aliens came very close to the Earth. Thousands of aliens' lasers hit the Earth and killed poor silly Julia and five billion people in a second. The Earth was destroyed and its turning parts flew away in space.

"I see you came to the finish before your time is over," Mr. Ibrahim smiled, "Well, the lesson is over. Let us read and speak about this team composition during the next lesson."

وَاللَّيْزَرَ وَأَخْبَرُوا الغُرَباءَ أَنَّهُمْ لَنْ يَبْدَؤُوا حَرْباً ضِدَّهُمْ مَرَّةً أُخْرَى. قالَ النّاسُ أَنَّهُمْ يُرِيدُونَ أَنْ يَكُونُوا أَصْدِقاءَ مَعَ الغُرَباءِ. جُولْيا كانَتْ سَعِيدَةً جِدّاً عِنْدَنا سَمِعْتْ عَنْ ذَلِكَ. ثُمَّ فَتَحَتْ جِهازَ التِّلِفِزْيُونِ وَاسْتَمَرَّتْ فِي مُشاهَدَةِ مُسَلْسَلٍ مَكْسِيكِيٍّ رائِعٍ.

عُمَر: وَلِأَنَّ النّاسَ دَمَّرُوا رادارا تَهُمْ وَلَيْزَرَهُمْ، لا أَحَدَ عَرَفَ أَنَّ السُّفُنَ الفَضائِيَّةَ الخاصَّةَ بِالغُرَباءِ أَصْبَحَتْ قَرِيبَةً جِدّاً لِلأَرْضِ. آلافٌ مِنْ أَشِعَّةِ اللَّيْزَرِ الخاصَّةِ بِالغُرَباءِ ضَرَبَتْ الأَرْضَ وَقُتِلَتْ المِسْكِينَةُ السّاذَجَةُ جُولْيا وَخَمْسَةَ بليونِ شَخْصٍ فِي ثانِيَةٍ واحِدَةٍ. دَمَّرْتْ الأَرْضَ وَأَجْزائُها المُسْتَدِيرَةَ تَدَفَّقَتْ بَعِيداً فِي الفَضاءِ.

"أَرَى أَنَّكُمْ وَصَلْتُمْ إِلَى النِّهايَةِ قَبْلَ أَنْ يَنْتَهِيَ وَقْتُكُمْ،" اِبْتَسَمَ السَّيِّدُ/ إِبْراهِيمُ، "حَسَناً، الدَّرْسُ اِنْتَهَى. فَلْنَقْرَأْ وَنَتَحَدَّثْ عَنْ هَذا النَّصِّ الجَماعِيِّ خِلالَ الدَّرْسِ القادِمِ."

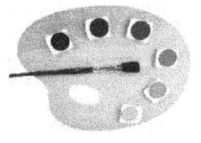

الفَصْلُ الخَامِسُ وَالعِشْرُونَ
Chapter 25

بروس وَعُمَر يَبْحَثَانِ عَنْ وَظِيفَةٍ جَدِيدَةٍ
Bruce and Omar are looking for a new job

A

كلمات

1. اِسْتِبْيانٌ ، اِسْتِطْلاعُ رَأْيٍ - questionnaire
2. اِسْتِشاراتٌ - consultancy
3. إعْلانٌ - ad
4. أَلْمانِيٌّ ، اللَّغَةُ الأَلْمانِيَّةُ - German
5. بابٌ ، عُنْوانٌ - rubric
6. بارِعٌ - sly
7. بِصَوْتٍ مُرْتَفِعٍ - aloud
8. بَيْنَما ، أَثْناءَ - while
9. جارٌ - neighbour
10. جَرْوٌ ، كَلْبٌ صَغِيرٌ - puppy
11. حَقِيرٌ - dirty
12. يَحْلُمُ ؛ حُلْمٌ - dream; to dream
13. حَيَوانٌ أَلِيفٌ - pet
14. سبانيل (نَوْعٌ مِنَ الكِلابِ) - spaniel
15. سميث - Smith
16. سِنٌّ ، عُمَرٌ - age

17. شَخْصِيٌّ - personal
18. طَبِيبٌ - doctor
19. طَبِيبٌ بَيْطَرِيٌّ - vet
20. طَبِيعَةٌ - nature
21. طَرِيفَةٌ - method
22. طَعامٌ - food
23. عَثَرَ عَلَى ، وَجَدَ - found
24. فَأْرٌ - rat
25. فِكْرَةٌ - idea
26. فَنٌّ - art
27. فَنَّانٌ - artist
28. قائِدٌ - leader
29. قِطَّةٌ صَغِيرَةٌ - kitten
30. كاتِبٌ - writer

31. مُبَرْمِجٌ - programmer
32. مُتَرْجِمٌ - translator
33. مُزارِعٌ - farmer
34. مَمِلٌّ ، رَتِيبٌ - monotonous
35. مُهَنْدِسٌ - engineer
36. مَوْهِبَةٌ - gift
37. يَخْدُمُ - to serve
38. يُسافِرُ - to travel
39. يُقِيمُ ، يُثْمِنُ - to estimate
40. يَكْرَهُ - to mind (to be against something)
41. يَنْصَحُ - to recommend; نَصِيحَةٌ - recommendation

B

Bruce and Omar are looking for a new job

Bruce and Omar are at Omar's home. Omar is cleaning the table after breakfast and Bruce is reading adverts and ads in a newspaper. He is reading the rubric "Animals". Omar's sister

بْروس وَعُمَرُ يَبْحَثانِ عَنْ وَظِيفَةٍ جَدِيدَةٍ

بْروس وَعُمَرَ فِي بَيْتِ عُمَرَ. عُمَرُ يُنَظِّفُ المِنْضَدَةَ بَعْدَ الفُطورِ وَبْروس يَقْرَأُ إِعْلاناتٍ وَإِعْلاناتٍ مُبَوَّبَةً فِي صَحِيفَةٍ. يَقْرَأُ بابَ "الحَيَواناتِ". مَرْيَمُ أُخْتُ عُمَرَ فِي الغُرْفَةِ

Mariam is in the room too. She is trying to catch the cat hiding under the bed.

"There are so many pets for free in the newspaper. I think I will choose a cat or a dog. Omar, what do you think?" Bruce asks Omar.

"Mariam, do not bother the cat!", Omar says angrily, "Well Bruce, it is not a bad idea. Your pet will always wait for you at home and will be so happy when you come back home and give some food. And do not forget that you will have to walk with your pet in mornings and evenings or clean its box. Sometimes you will have to clean the floor or take your pet to a vet. So think carefully before you get an animal."

"Well, there are some ads here. Listen," Bruce says and begins to read aloud:

أَيْضاً. تُحاوِلُ أَنْ تُمْسِكَ القِطَّةَ المُخْتَبِئَةَ تَحْتَ السَرِيرِ.

" هُناكَ الكَثيرُ جِدّاً مِنَ الحَيَواناتِ الأَليفَةِ مَجّاناً فِي الصَحِيفَةِ. أَعْتَقِدُ أَنَّني سَأَخْتارُ قِطَّةً أَوْ كَلْباً. ما رَأْيُكِ يا عُمَرُ؟ بروس يَسْأَلُ عُمَرَ.

" يا مَرْيَمُ، لا تُزْعِجِي القِطَّةَ!"، يَقُولُ عُمَرُ بِغَضَبٍ، "حَسَناً يا روس، إِنَّها لَيْسَتْ فِكْرَةً سَيِّئَةً. حَيَوانُكَ سَوْفَ يَنْتَظِرُكَ دائِماً فِي البَيْتِ وَسَيَكُونُ سَعِيدٌ جِدّاً عِنْدَما تَعُودُ لِلبَيْتِ وَتُعْطِيهِ بَعْضَ الطَعامِ. وَلا تَنْسَ أَنَّهُ سَيَجِبُ عَلَيْكَ أَنْ تَتَنَزَّهَ مَعَ حَيَوانِكَ فِي الصَباحِ وَالمَساءِ أَوْ تُنَظِّفَ صُنْدُوقَهُ. وَأَحْياناً سَيَجِبُ عَلَيْكَ تَنْظِيفُ الأَرْضِيَّةِ أَوْ تَأْخُذَ حَيَوانَكَ إِلَى طَبِيبٍ بَيْطَرِيٍّ. لِذَلِكَ فَكِّرْ بِعِنايَةٍ قَبْلَ أَنْ تَقْتَنِيَ حَيَواناً ".

" حَسَناً، تُوجَدُ بَعْضُ الإِعْلاناتِ هُنا. اِسْتَمِعْ،" يَقُولُ بروس وَيَبْدَأُ القِراءَةَ بِصَوْتٍ مُرْتَفِعٍ.

"Found dirty white dog, looks like a rat. It may live outside for a long time. I will give it away for money."

Here is one more:

"German dog, speaks German. Give away for free. And free puppies half spaniel half sly neighbor's dog,"

Bruce looks at Omar, "How can a dog speak German?"

"A dog may understand German. Can you understand German?" Omar asks smiling.

"I cannot understand German. Listen, here is one more ad:

"Give away free farm kittens. Ready to eat. They will eat anything,"

Bruce turns the newspaper, "Well, I think pets can wait. I will better look for a job," he finds the rubric about jobs and reads aloud,

"عَثَرَ عَلَى كَلْبٍ أَبْيَضَ قَذِرٍ، يُشْبِهُ الفَأْرَ. رُبَّما عاشَ فِي الخارِجِ لِمُدَّةٍ طَويلَةٍ. سَأَتَخَلَّى عَنْهُ مِنْ أَجْلِ المالِ".

ها هُوَ إِعْلانٌ آخَرُ:

"كَلْبٌ أَلْمانِيٌّ، يَتَكَلَّمُ الأَلْمانِيَّةَ. أَسْتَغْنِي عَنْهُ بِلا مُقابِلٍ. وَمَجّاناً جِراءٌ لِكَلْبِ الجارِ النِصْفِ سبانيل وَالنِصْفِ بارِعٌ.

بْروس يَنْظُرُ إِلَى عُمَرٍ، "كَيْفَ يَسْتَطيعُ كَلْبٌ أَنْ يَتَكَلَّمَ الأَلْمانِيَّةَ؟"

"الكَلْبُ رُبَّما يَفْهَمُ الأَلْمانِيَّةَ. هَلْ تَفْهَمُ الأَلْمانِيَّةَ؟" عُمَرٌ يَسْأَلُ مُبْتَسِماً.

"لا أَسْتَطيعُ أَنْ أَفْهَمَ الأَلْمانِيَّةَ. اِسْتَمِعْ، ها هُوَ إِعْلانٌ آخَرُ:

"أَسْتَغْنِي مَجّاناً عَنْ قِطَطٍ صَغيرَةٍ بِمَزْرَعَةٍ. مُسْتَعِدَّةٌ أَنْ تَأْكُلَ. سَوْفَ تَأْكُلُ أَيَّ شَيْءٍ،"

بْروس يُقَلِّبُ الصَحيفَةَ، "حَسَناً، أَعْتَقِدُ أَنَّ الحَيَواناتِ الأَليفَةَ يُمْكِنُها أَنْ تَنْتَظِرَ. سَأَبْحَثُ أَفْضَلَ عَنْ وَظيفَةٍ،" يَجِدُ البابَ الخاصَّ بِالوَظائِفِ وَيَقْرَأُ بِصَوْتٍ مُرْتَفِعٍ،

"Are you looking for a suitable job? The job consultancy "Suitable personnel" can help you. Our consultants will estimate your personal gifts and will give you a recommendation about the most suitable profession,"

Bruce looks up and says: "Omar what do you think?"

"The best job for you is washing a truck in the sea and let it float," Mariam says and quickly runs out of the room.

"It is not a bad idea. Let's go now," Omar answers and takes carefully the cat out of the kettle, where Mariam put the animal a minute ago.

Bruce and Omar arrive to the job consultancy "Suitable personnel" by their bikes. There is no queue, so they go inside. There are two women there. One of them is speaking on the telephone. Another woman is writing something. She asks Bruce and Omar to take seats. Her name is Mrs. Madiha.

" هَلْ تَبْحَثُ عَنْ وَظِيفَةٍ مُنَاسِبَةٍ؟ الاِسْتِشَارَاتُ الوَظِيفِيَّةُ "المُوَظَّفُونَ الأَكْفَاءُ" يُمْكِنُها مُساعَدَتُكَ. سَوْفَ يُقِيمُ مُسْتَشَارُونا مَواهِبَكَ الشَخْصِيَّةَ وَسَيُعْطُونَكَ نَصِيحَةً عَنْ أَفْضَلِ مِهْنَةٍ مُنَاسِبَةٍ،"

يَنْظُرُ بُرُوس إِلَى أَعْلَى وَيَقُولُ: "ما رَأْيُكَ يا عُمَرُ؟"

" أَفْضَلُ وَظِيفَةٍ تُنَاسِبُكَ هِيَ غَسْلَ شاحِنَةٍ فِي البَحْرِ وَتَرْكُها تَعُومُ،" تَقُولُ مَرْيَمُ وَبِسُرْعَةٍ تَجْرِي إِلَى خارِجِ الغُرْفَةِ .

" إِنَّها لَيْسَتْ فِكْرَةً سَيِّئَةً. فَلْنَذْهَبِ الآنَ،" يُجِيبُ عُمَرُ وَيَأْخُذُ القِطَّةَ بِحَذَرٍ بَعِيداً عَنِ الغَلَّايَةِ، حَيْثُ وَضَعَتْ مَرْيَمُ الحَيْوانَ مُنْذُ دَقِيقَةٍ .

يَصِلُ بُرُوس وَعُمَرُ إِلَى الاِسْتِشَارَاتِ الوَظِيفِيَّةِ "المُوَظَّفُونَ الأَكْفَاءُ" بِدَرَّاجاتِهِما. لا يُوجَدُ طابُورٌ، لِذَلِكَ يَدْخُلانِ. هُناكَ تُوجَدُ اِمْرَأَتانِ. واحِدَةٌ مِنْهُما تَتَحَدَّثُ عَلَى الهاتِفِ. وَالأُخْرَى تَكْتُبُ شَيْئاً ما. تَطْلُبُ مِنْ بُرُوس وَعُمَرِ أَنْ يَجْلِسا. اِسْمُها السَيِّدَةُ/ مَدِيحَةُ.

She asks them their names and their age.

"Well, let me explain the method which we use. Look, there are five kinds of professions.

1. The first kind is man - nature. Professions: farmer, zoo worker etc.

2. The second kind is man - machine. Professions: pilot, taxi driver, truck driver etc.

3. The third kind is man - man. Professions: doctor, teacher, journalist etc.

4. The fourth kind is man - computer. Professions: translator, engineer, programmer etc.

5. The fifth kind is man - art. Professions: writer, artist, singer etc.

We give recommendations about a suitable profession only when we learn about you more. First let me estimate your personal gifts. I must know what you like and what you dislike. Then we will know which kind of profession is

تَسْأَلُهُما عَنْ اِسْمِهِما وَعُمرِهِما.

" حَسَناً، سَأَشْرَحُ الطَّرِيقَةَ الَّتِي نَسْتَخْدِمُها. أُنْظُرا، هُناكَ خَمْسَةُ أَنْواعٍ مِنَ المِهَنِ.

1. النَّوْعُ الأَوَّلُ هُوَ الإِنْسانُ - الطَّبِيعَةُ. المِهَنُ: مُزارِعٌ، عامِلُ حَدِيقَةِ حَيَوانٍ إِلَى آخِرِهِ.

2. النَّوْعُ الثانِي هُوَ الإِنْسانُ - الآلَةُ. المِهَنُ: طَيّارٌ، سائِقُ سَيّارَةِ أُجرَةٍ، سائِقُ شاحِنَةٍ إِلَى آخِرِهِ.

3. النَّوْعُ الثالِثُ هُوَ الإِنْسانُ - الإِنْسانُ. المِهَنُ: طَبِيبٌ، مُدَرِّسٌ، صَحَفِيٌّ إِلَى آخِرِهِ.

4. النَّوْعُ الرابِعُ هُوَ الإِنْسانُ - الكَمْبْيُوتَرُ. المِهَنُ: مُتَرْجِمٌ، مُهَنْدِسٌ، مُبَرْمِجٌ إِلَى آخِرِهِ.

5. النَّوْعُ الخامِسُ هُوَ الإِنْسانُ - الفَنُّ. المِهَنُ: كاتِبٌ، فَنّانٌ، مُغَنٍّ إِلَى آخِرِهِ.

نُعْطِي نَصائِحَ عَنِ المِهْنَةِ المُناسِبَةِ فَقَطْ عِنْدَما نَعْلَمُ عَنْكُما المَزِيدَ. أَوَّلاً اِسْمَحا لِي أَنْ أُقِيمَ مَواهِبَكُما الشَّخْصِيَّةَ. يَجِبُ أَنْ أَعْرِفَ ما تُحِبّانِهِ وَما تَكْرِهانِهِ. بَعْدَ ذٰلِكَ سَنَعْرِفُ أَيَّ

the most suitable for you. Please, fill up the questionnaire now," Mrs. Madiha says and gives them the questionnaires. Omar and Bruce fill up the questionnaires.

نَوْعٍ مِنَ المِهَنِ يُناسِبُكُما أَكْثَرَ. مِنْ فَضْلِكُما، اِمْلِئا الاِسْتِبْيانَ الآنَ،" تَقولُ السَّيِّدَةُ/ مَديحَةٌ وَتُعْطِيهِما الاِسْتِبْيانانِ. عُمَر وَبْروس يَمْلآنِ الاِسْتِبْيانانِ.

Questionnaire
Name: Omar Galal

استبيان
الاسم: عمر جلال

	أَكْرَهُ	لا أَكْرَهُ	أُحِبُّ		
	I hate	I do not mind	I like		
1.		√		مُراقَبَةُ الآلاتِ	Watch machines
2.			√	التَحَدُّثُ مَعَ الناسِ	Speak with people
3.		√		خِدْمَةُ العُمَلاءِ	Serve customers
4.			√	قِيادَةُ السَّيّاراتِ، الشاحِناتِ	Drive cars, trucks
5.			√	العَمَلُ الداخِلِيُّ	Work inside
6.			√	العَمَلُ الخارِجِيُّ	Work outside
7.		√		التَذَكُّرُ بِكَثْرَةٍ	

#					
	Remember a lot				
8.	السَفَرُ Travel	√			
9.	التَقْيِيمُ، الاِخْتِبارُ Estimate, check				√
10.	العَمَلُ الحَقِيرُ Dirty work		√		
11.	المُمِلّ العَمَل Monotonous work				√
12.	العَمَلُ الشاقُّ Hard work		√		
13.	تَكُونُ قائِدا Be leader		√		
14.	العَمَلُ فِي فَرِيقٍ Work in team		√		
15.	الحُلْمُ أَثْناءَ العَمَلِ Dream while working	√			
16.	التَدْرِيبُ Train		√		
17.	القِيامُ بِعَمَلٍ إِبْداعِيٍّ Do creative work	√			
18.	العَمَلُ مَعَ النُصُوصِ Work with texts	√			

	Questionnaire			استبيان
	Name: Bruce Smith			الاسم: بْرُوس سميث

		أُحِبّ I like	لا أَكْرَهُ I do not mind	أَكْرَهُ I hate
1.	مُراقَبَةُ الآلاتِ Watch machines		√	
2.	التَحَدُّثُ مَعَ الناسِ Speak with people	√		
3.	خِدْمَةُ العُمَلاءِ Serve customers		√	
4.	قِيادَةُ السَيّاراتِ، الشاحِناتُ Drive cars, trucks		√	
5.	العَمَلُ الداخِلِيُّ Work inside	√		
6.	العَمَلُ الخارِجِيُّ Work outside	√		
7.	التَذَكُّرُ بِكَثْرَةِ Remember a lot		√	
8.	السَفَرُ Travel	√		
9.	التَقْييمُ، الاِخْتِبارُ Estimate, check		√	

10.	العَمَلُ الحَقيرُ Dirty work		√	
11.	المُمِلّ العَمَل Monotonous work			√
12.	العَمَلُ الشاقُّ Hard work		√	
13.	تَكُونُ قائِدا Be leader			√
14.	العَمَلُ فِي فَريقٍ Work in team	√		
15.	الحُلْمُ أثناءَ العَمَلِ Dream while working	√		
16.	التَدْريبُ Train		√	
17.	القِيامُ بِعَمَلٍ إبداعِيٍّ Do creative work	√		
18.	العَمَلُ مَعَ النُصوصِ Work with texts	√		

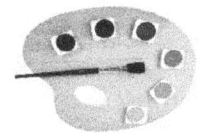

الفَصْلُ السادِسُ وَالعِشْرُونَ
Chapter 26

" تَقْدِيمُ طَلَبِ تَوْظِيفٍ لِصَحِيفَةِ "الإسْكَنْدَرِيَّةِ اليَوْمَ "

Applying to "Alexandria today"

A

كلمات

1. إِجْرامِي - criminal (adj), مُجْرِمٌ - criminal
2. أَخَذَ - took
3. أُسْبُوعٌ - week
4. اِسْتَطاعَ - could
5. اِسْتِمارَةٌ, نَمُوذَجٌ - form
6. أَعْزَبُ - single
7. أَعْطَى - gave
8. الاِسْمُ الأَوْسَطُ - middle name
9. الجِنْسُ - sex
10. الشُرْطَةُ - police
11. إِلَى اللِقاءِ - goodbye
12. أُنْثَى - female
13. آنِسَةُ - miss
14. بِطَلاقَةٍ - fluently
15. بيل - Bill

164

16. تَعْلِيم - education
17. جِنْسِيَّةٌ - nationality
18. حالَةٌ - status,
    الحالَةُ العائِلِيَّةُ - family status
19. دَوْرِيَّةٌ - patrol
20. ذَكَرَ - male
21. سَأَلَ - asked
22. سَبْعَةَ عَشَرَ - seventeen
23. عَلامَةُ النَّجْمَةِ - asterisk
24. عِلْمُ المالِيَّةِ - finance
25. عَلِمَ عَنْ - learned about
26. عَمَلَ - worked
27. غادَة - Ghada
28. فارِغ - blank, empty

29. قَيَّمَ - estimated
30. مَجالٌ, حَقْلٌ - field
31. مُحَرِّرٌ - editor
32. مَعْلُوماتٌ - information
33. نَصَحَ - recommended
34. واحِدٌ وَعِشْرونَ - twenty-one
35. وَصَلَ - arrived
36. يَتْرُكُ - to leave
37. يُرافِقُ، يُصاحِبُ - to accompany
38. يَضَعُ خَطٌّ تَحْتَ كَلِمَةِ - to underline
39. صَحَفِيٌّ، يُقَدِّمُ تَقْرِيرٌ - to report; مُراسِلٌ صَحَفِيٌّ - reporter
40. يُقَدِّمُ طَلَبٌ - to apply

B

Applying to "Alexandria today"

تَقْدِيمُ طَلَبِ تَوْظِيفٍ لِصَحِيفَةِ "الإِسْكَنْدَرِيَّةِ اليَوْمَ"

Mrs. Madiha estimated Omar's and Bruce's answers in the questionnaires. When she learned about their personal gifts she could give them some recommendations

قَيَّمَتِ السَّيِّدَةُ/ مَدِيحَةَ إِجاباتِ عُمَرَ وَبْروسَ فِي الاسْتِبْيانَيْنِ. عِنْدَما عَلِمَتْ عَنْ مَواهِبِهِما الشَّخْصِيَّةِ اسْتَطاعَتْ أَنْ تُعْطِيَهُما بَعْضَ

النَصَائِحِ عَنِ المِهَنِ المُنَاسِبَةِ. قَالَتْ أَنَّ النَوْعَ الثَالِثَ لِلمِهَنِ مُنَاسِبٌ أَكْثَرَ لَهُمَا. فَيُمْكِنُهُمَا أَنْ يَعْمَلَا كَأَطِبَّاءَ، وَمُدَرِّسِينَ أَوْ صَحَفِيِّينَ إِلَى آخِرِهِ. نَصَحَتْهُمَا السَيِّدَةُ/ مَدِيحَةَ أَنْ يَتَقَدَّمَا لِوَظِيفَةٍ فِي صَحِيفَةِ "الإِسْكَنْدَرِيَّةِ اليَوْمَ". فَقَدْ أَعْطَوْا وَظِيفَةً لِنِصْفِ الوَقْتِ لِلطَلَبَةِ الَّذِينَ يُمْكِنُهُمْ كِتَابَةُ مَوْضُوعَاتٍ شُرْطِيَّةٍ لِبَابِ الجَرِيمَةِ. لِذَلِكَ جَاءَ بْرُوس وَعُمَرُ إِلَى إِدَارَةِ المُوَظَّفِينَ بِصَحِيفَةِ "الإِسْكَنْدَرِيَّةِ اليَوْمَ" وَتَقَدَّمُوا لِهَذِهِ الوَظِيفَةِ.

"لَقَدْ كُنَّا فِي مَكْتَبِ الاِسْتِشَارَاتِ الوَظِيفِيَّةِ "المُوَظَّفُونَ الأَكْفَاءَ" اليَوْمَ،" قَالَ عُمَرُ لِلآنِسَةِ/ غَادَةَ، الَّتِي كَانَتْ رَئِيسَةَ إِدَارَةِ المُوَظَّفِينَ، "لَقَدْ نَصَحَانَا بِتَقْدِيمِ طَلَبِ تَوْظِيفٍ لِصَحِيفَتِكُمْ."

"حَسَنًا، هَلْ عَمِلْتُمَا كَمُرَاسِلِينَ صَحَفِيِّينَ مِنْ قَبْلُ؟" الآنِسَةُ/ غَادَةَ سَأَلَتْ.

"لَا، لَمْ نَعْمَلَا،" أَجَابَ عُمَرُ.

"مِنْ فَضْلِكُمَا، اِمْلَأَا هَذَانِ النَمُوذَجَانِ لِلبَيَانَاتِ الشَخْصِيَّةِ،" قَالَتِ الآنِسَةُ/ غَادَةَ وَأَعْطَتْهُمَا

about suitable professions. She said that the third profession kind is the most suitable for them. They could work as a doctor, a teacher or a journalist etc. Mrs. Madiha recommended them to apply for a job with the newspaper "Alexandria today". They gave a part time job to students who could compose police reports for the criminal rubric. So Bruce and Omar arrived at the personnel department of the newspaper "Alexandria today" and applied for this job.

"We have been to the job consultancy "Suitable personnel" today," Omar said to Miss Ghada, who was the head of the personnel department, "They have recommended us to apply to your newspaper."

"Well, have you worked as a reporter before?" Miss Ghada asked.

"No, we have not," Omar answered.

"Please, fill up these personal information forms," Miss Ghada said and gave them two forms. Bruce and Omar filled up the personal information forms.

نَموذَجانِ. مَلَأَ بْروس وَعُمَرُ نَموذَجاً البَياناتِ الشَخْصِيَّةَ.

نَموذَجُ بَياناتٍ شَخْصِيَّةٍ يَجِبُ مِلْءُ الحُقولِ ذاتِ عَلامَةِ النَجْمَةِ *. يُمْكِنُكَ تَرْكُ الحُقولِ الأُخْرى فارِغَةً.	Personal information form You must fill up fields with asterisk *. You can leave other fields blank.
الاِسْمُ الأَوَّلُ * First name *	عُمَر Omar
الاِسْمُ الأَوْسَطُ Middle name	
الاِسْمُ الثاني * Second name *	جَلال Galal
الجِنْسُ * Sex *	أُنْثى ذِكْرٍ (ضَعْ خَطّاً تَحْتَ الاِخْتِيارِ) (underline) Male Female
العُمْرُ * Age *	عِشْرونَ سَنَةً Twenty years old
الجِنْسِيَّةُ * Nationality *	مِصْرِيٌّ Egyptian
الحالَةُ العائِلِيَّةُ Family status	مُتَزَوِّج أَعْزَبٌ (ضَعْ خَطّاً تَحْتَ الاِخْتِيارِ) (underline) Single Married
العُنوانُ * Address *	11 شارِعُ المَلِكَةِ، الإِسْكَنْدَرِيَّةُ Queen street 11, Alexandria

أدرُسُ عِلْمَ المالِيَّةِ فِي السَّنَةِ الثالِثَةِ بِالجامِعَةِ I study finance in the third year at a college	التَّعْلِيمُ Education	
عَمِلْتُ لِمُدَّةِ شَهْرَيْنِ كَعامِلِ مَزْرَعَةٍ I worked for two months as a farm worker	أَيْنَ عَمِلْتَ سابِقاً؟ Where have you worked before?	
أَسْتَطِيعُ أَنْ أَقُودَ سَيّارَةً، شاحِنَةً وَأَسْتَطِيعُ اِسْتِخْدامَ الكُمْبِيُوتَرِ I can drive a car, a truck and I can use a computer	ما هِيَ الخِبْرَةُ وَالمَهاراتُ الَّتِي اِكْتَسَبْتَها؟* What experience and skills have you had?*	
اللُّغَةُ العَرَبِيَّةُ - 10، اللُّغَةُ الإنجليزِيَّةُ - 8 Arabic - 10, English - 8	اللُّغاتُ* 0 - لا، 10 - بِطَلاقة Languages* 0 - no, 10 - fluently	
لا نعم النَّوعُ: ب ج، أَسْتَطِيعُ قِيادَةَ شاحِناتٍ (ضَعْ خَطّاً تَحْتَ الاِخْتِيارِ) (underline) No Yes Kind: BC, I can drive trucks	رُخْصَةُ القِيادَةِ* Driving license*	
كُلُّ الوَقْتِ نِصْفُ الوَقْتِ: 15 ساعَةً أُسْبُوعِيّاً (ضَعْ خَطّاً تَحْتَ الاِخْتِيارِ) (underline) Full time Part time: 15 hours a week	تَحْتاجُ لِوَظِيفَةٍ* You need a job*	
15 دُولاراً فِي الساعَةِ 15 dollars per hour	تُرِيدُ أَنْ تَكْسِبَ You want to earn	

Personal information form You must fill up fields with asterisk *. You can leave other fields blank.	نَموذَجُ بَياناتٍ شَخْصِيَّةٍ يَجِبُ مِلْءُ الحُقُولِ ذاتِ عَلامَةِ النَّجْمَةِ *. يُمْكِنُكَ تَرْكُ الحُقُولِ الأُخْرَى فارِغَةً.
الاِسْمُ الأَوَّلُ * First name * بروس Bruce	
الاِسْمُ الأَوْسَطُ Middle name بيل Bill	
الاِسْمُ الثاني * Second name * سميث Smith	
الجِنْسُ * Sex * أُنْثَى ذِكْرٍ (ضَعْ خَطّاً تَحْتَ الاِخْتِيارِ) (underline) Male Female	
العُمْرُ * Age * واحِد وعِشْرُونَ سَنَةً Twenty-one years old	
الجِنْسِيَّةُ * Nationality * أَمَرِكي American	
الحالَةُ العائِلِيَّةُ Family status مُتَزَوِّجٌ أَعْزَبٌ (ضَعْ خَطّاً تَحْتَ الاِخْتِيارِ) (underline) Single Married	
العُنْوانُ * Address * غرفة 218، مساكن الطلبة، 5 شارع الجامعة، الإسكندرية Room 218, student dorms, College street 5, Alexandria	
التَّعْلِيمُ أدرس التصميم بالكمبيوتر في السنة الثانية	

Education	بالجامعة I study computer design in the second year at a college
أَيْنَ عَمِلْتَ سابِقاً؟ Where have you worked before?	عَمِلَتْ لِمُدَّةِ شَهْرَيْنِ كَعامِلِ مَزْرَعَةِ I worked for two months as a farm worker
ما هِيَ الخِبْرَةُ وَالمَهاراتُ الَّتِي اِكْتَسَبْتها؟* What experience and skills have you had?*	أستطيع استخدام الكمبيوتر I can use a computer
اللُغاتِ* 0 - لا، 10 - بطلاقة Languages* 0 - no, 10 - fluently	اللُغَةُ العَرَبِيَّةُ - 10، اللُغَةُ الإنجليزِيَّةُ - 8 Arabic - 10, English - 8
رُخْصَةُ القِيادَةِ* Driving license*	لا نعم النوع: (ضَعْ خَطّاً تَحْتَ الاِخْتِيارِ) (underline) <u>No</u> Yes Kind:
تَحْتاج لِوَظيفَةٍ* You need a job*	كُلُّ الوَقْتِ نِصْفُ الوَقْتِ: 15 ساعَةً أسْبُوعِيّاً (ضَعْ خَطّاً تَحْتَ الاِخْتِيارِ) (underline) Full time <u>Part time</u>: 15 hours a week
تُريدُ أنْ تَكْسِبَ You want to earn	15 دُولاراً فِي الساعَةِ 15 dollars per hour

Miss Ghada took their personal information forms to the editor of "Alexandria today".	أَخَذَتْ الآنِسَةُ/ غادَةْ نَموذَجاً بَياناتِهِما الشَخْصِيَّة إلى رَئِيسِ تَحْريرِ "الإسْكَنْدَرِيَّةِ اليَوْمَ".
"The editor has agreed," Miss Ghada said when she came back, "You will accompany a police patrol and then compose reports for the criminal rubric. A police car will come tomorrow at seventeen o'clock to take you. Be here at this time, will you?"	"وافَقَ رَئِيسُ التَحْريرِ, قالَتْ الآنِسَةُ غادَةْ عِنْدَما عادَتْ, "سَتُرافِقانِ دَوْرِيَّةَ شُرْطَةٍ ثُمَّ تَكْتُبانِ تَقاريرَ لِبابِ الجَريمَةِ. سَتَأْتي سَيَّارَةُ الشُرْطَةِ غَداً في الساعَةِ سَبْعَةَ عَشَرَ لِتَأْخَذَكُما. كُونا هُنا في هٰذا الوَقْتِ, هَلْ سَتَفْعَلانِ؟"
"Sure," Bruce answered.	"بِالتَأْكيدِ," أَجابَ بُروس.
"Yes, we will," Omar said, "Goodbye."	"نَعَمْ, سَنَفْعَلُ," قالَ عُمَرُ, "إلى اللِقاءِ."
"Goodbye," Miss Ghada answered.	"إلى اللِقاءِ," أَجابَتْ الآنِسَةُ/ غادَةُ.

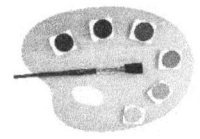

الفَصْلُ السابِعُ وَالعِشْرُونَ
Chapter 27

دَوْرِيَّةُ الشُرْطَةِ (الجُزْءُ الأَوَّلُ)
The police patrol (part 1)

A

كلمات

1. P07, P11 - numbers of patrol cars
2. اِثْنا عَشَرَ - twelve
3. أَحْزِمَةُ الأَمانِ - seat belts
4. اِخْتَبَأَ - hid
5. أَدارَ - started (the engine); بَدَأَ، اِنْطَلَقَ - started (to drive)
6. أَظْهَرَ - showed
7. أَمْرٌ، شَأْنٌ - matter, business
8. اِنْتَظِرْ - waited
9. اِنْدَفَعَ - rushed
10. إِنْذارُ - alarm
11. حاوَلَ - tried
12. حَدُّ - limit
13. حَوْلَ - around

#	Arabic	English
14.	خائِفٌ	afraid
15.	رافِقَ ، صاحِبُ	accompanied
16.	رَجُلُ شُرْطَةٍ	policeman
17.	رَقيب	sergeant
18.	سُرْعَةٌ - speed; المُسْرِعُ - speeder, مُسْرِعَةٌ - speeding	
19.	سِعْرٌ	price
20.	صاحَ	cried
21.	صارِخَ ، زاعِقٌ	howling
22.	صَفّارَةُ الإنْذارِ	siren
23.	ضابِطٌ	officer
24.	ضَغَطَ	stepped
25.	عالٍ	high
26.	فَتَحَ	opened
27.	فَعَلَ	did
28.	فَهِمَ	understood
29.	قابَلَ	met
30.	قادَ	drove
31.	قُيُودٌ	handcuffs
32.	كُلُّ شَخْصٍ	everybody
33.	سَرِقَةٌ ، سَطو - robber; لِص - robbery	
34.	لُصُوصٌ، thief, لِصُّ - thieves	
35.	مِائَةٌ	hundred
36.	مُسَدَّسٌ	gun
37.	مُطارَدَةً	pursuit
38.	مُغْلَقٌ ؛ أَغْلِقَ	closed
39.	مِفْتاحٌ	key
40.	مُكَبِّرُ الصَّوْتِ	microphone
41.	نَبَحَ	barked
42.	يَثْبِتُ	fasten
43.	يُجَفِّفُ	to dry,
44.	جاف	dry (adj)

B

The police patrol (part 1)

دَوْرِيَّةُ الشُرْطَةِ (الجُزْءُ الأَوَّلُ)

Bruce and Omar arrived at the building of the newspaper

وَصَلَ بروس وَعُمَرُ إِلَى مَبْنَى صَحيفَةِ "الإِسْكَنْدَرِيَّةِ اليَوْمَ" فِي الساعَةِ سَبْعَةَ عَشَرَ

"Alexandria today" at seventeen o'clock next day. The police car was waiting for them already. A policeman got out of the car.

"Hello. I am sergeant Osama Mamdouh," he said when Omar and Bruce came to the car.

"Hello. Glad to meet you. My name is Bruce. We must accompany you," Bruce answered.

"Hello. I am Omar. Were you waiting long for us?" Omar asked.

"No. I have just arrived here. Let us get into the car. We begin city patrolling now," the policeman said. They all got into the police car.

"Are you accompanying a police patrol for the first time?" sergeant Mamdouh asked starting the engine.

"We have never accompanied a police patrol before," Omar answered.

At this moment the police radio began to talk: "Attention P11 and P07! A blue car is speeding along College street."

فِي اليَوْمِ التَّالِي. سَيَّارَةُ الشُّرْطَةِ كانَتْ بِإِنْتِظارِهِما بِالفِعْلِ. خَرَجَ رَجُلُ شُرْطَةٍ مِنَ السَّيَّارَةِ.

"أَهْلاً. أَنا الرَّقِيبُ أسامَة مَمْدوح," قالَ عِنْدَما أتى عُمَرُ وبرُوس إلى السَّيَّارَةِ.

"أَهْلاً. مَسْرُورٌ لِمُقابَلَتِكَ. اِسْمِي برُوس. يَجِبُ عَلَيْنا مُرافَقَتُكَ," أَجابَ برُوس.

"أَهْلاً. أَنا عُمَرُ. هَلِ اِنْتَظَرْتَنا طَوِيلاً؟" عُمَرُ سَأَلَ.

"لا. لَقَدْ وَصَلْتُ لِلتَّوِّ. فَلْنَدْخُلْ إلى السَّيَّارَةِ. نَحْنُ نَبْدَأُ حِراسَةَ المَدِينَةِ الآنَ," قالَ رَجُلُ الشُّرْطَةِ. دَخَلُوا جَمِيعاً إلى سَيَّارَةِ الشُّرْطَةِ.

"هَلْ تُصاحِبانِ دَوْرِيَّةَ شُرْطَةٍ لِلمَرَّةِ الأُولى؟" سَأَلَ الرَّقِيبُ مَمْدوح وهُوَ يُدِيرُ المُحَرِّكَ.

"لَمْ نُصاحِبا دَوْرِيَّةَ شُرْطَةٍ مِنْ قَبْلُ," أجابَ عُمَرُ.

فِي هذِهِ اللَّحْظَةِ بَدَأَ جِهازُ راديو الشُّرْطَةِ يَتَكَلَّمُ: "اِنْتِباهُ P11 وP07! سَيَّارَةٌ زَرْقاءُ مُسْرِعَةٌ فِي مُوازاةِ شارِعِ الجامِعَةِ."

"P07 وَجَدَّتُها،" قالَ الرَّقيبُ أسامةُ مَمْدوحٌ في مُكَبِّرِ الصَّوتِ. ثُمَّ قالَ لِلشَّبابِ: "رَقْمُ سَيّارَتِنا P07." سَيّارَةٌ زَرْقاءُ كَبيرَةٌ تَجاوَزَتْهُمْ بِسُرْعَةٍ عالِيَةٍ جِدّاً. أَخَذَ أسامةُ مَمْدوحٌ مُكَبِّرَ الصَّوتِ مَرَّةً أُخْرى وَقالَ: "P07 تَتَحَدَّثُ. أَرى السَّيّارَةَ الزَّرْقاءَ المُسْرِعَةَ. أَبدَأُ المُطارَدَةَ،" ثُمَّ قالَ لِلشَّبابِ، "ثَبِّتا أَحْزِمَةَ الأَمانِ." اِنْطَلَقَتْ سَيّارَةُ الشُّرْطَةِ بِسُرْعَةٍ. ضَغَطَ الرَّقيبُ عَلى البِنْزينِ حَتّى النِّهايَةِ وَأدارَ صَفّارَةَ الإنذارِ. اِنْدَفَعوا مَعَ صَفّارَةِ الإنذارِ الصّارِخَةِ مارّينَ بِالمَباني، وَالسَّيّاراتِ وَالحافِلاتِ. أسامةُ مَمْدوحٌ جَعَلَ السَّيّارَةَ الزَّرْقاءَ تَتَوَقَّفُ. خَرَجَ الرَّقيبُ مِنَ السَّيّارَةِ وَذَهَبَ إِلى السّائِقِ المُسْرِعِ. ذَهَبَ عُمَرُ وَبروس خَلْفَهُ.

"أَنا ضابِطُ الشُّرْطَةِ أسامةُ مَمْدوحٌ. أَظْهِرْ رُخْصَةَ قِيادَتِكِ، مِنْ فَضْلِكَ،" قالَ رَجُلُ الشُّرْطَةِ لِلسّائِقِ المُسْرِعِ.

"ها هِيَ رُخْصَةُ قِيادَتي،" أَظْهَرَ السّائِقُ رُخْصَتَهُ، "ما الأَمْرُ؟" قالَ بِغَضَبٍ.

"P07 got it," sergeant Mamdouh said in the microphone. Then he said to the boys: "The number of our car is P07." A big blue car rushed past them with very high speed. Osama Mamdouh took the mic again and said: "P07 is speaking. I see the speeding blue car. Begin pursuit," then he said to the boys, "Fasten your seat belts." The police car started quickly. The sergeant stepped on the gas up to the stop and switched on the siren. They rushed with the howling siren past buildings, cars and buses. Osama Mamdouh made the blue car stop. Sergeant got out of the car and went to the speeder. Omar and Bruce went after him.

"I am police officer Osama Mamdouh. Show your driving license, please," the policeman said to the speeder.

"Here is my driving license," the driver showed his driving license, "What is the matter?" he said angrily.

"كُنْتَ تَقُودُ خِلالَ المَدِينَةِ بِسُرْعَةِ مِائَةٍ وَعِشْرِينَ كِيلُومِتراً فِي الساعَةِ. والحَدُّ الأَقْصَى لِلسُرْعَةِ سِتِّينَ،" قالَ الرَقِيبُ.

"آهٍ، هٰكَذا. كَما تَرَى، لَقَدْ غَسَلْتُ سَيَّارَتي لِلتَوِّ. لِذٰلِكَ كُنْتُ أَقُودُ أَسْرعُ قَلِيلاً لِأُجَفِّفَها،" قالَ الرَجُلُ بِابْتِسامَةٍ ماكِرَةٍ.

"هَلْ يُكَلِّفُ غَسْلَ السَيَّارَةِ كَثِيراً؟" رَجُلُ الشُرْطَةِ سَأَلَ.

"لَيْسَ كَثِيراً. إِنَّها تُكَلِّفُ اثْنا عَشَرَ دُولاراً،" قالَ السائِقُ المُسْرِعُ.

"أَنْتَ لا تَعْرِفُ الأَسْعارَ." قالَ الرَقِيبُ مَمْدُوح، "إِنَّها تُكَلِّفُكِ حَقِيقَةَ مِائَتَيْنِ وَاثْنا عَشَرَ دُولاراً لِأَنَّكَ سَتَدْفَعُ مِائَتَيْ دُولارٍ لِتَجْفِيفِ السَيَّارَةِ. ها هِيَ بِطاقَةُ المُخالَفَةِ. أَتَمَنَّى لَكَ يَوْماً لَطِيفاً،" قالَ رَجُلُ الشُرْطَةِ. أَعْطَى بِطاقَةَ مُخالَفَةِ السُرْعَةِ بِقِيمَةِ مِائَتَيْ دُولارٍ وَرُخْصَةِ القِيادَةِ لِلسائِقِ المُسْرِعِ وَعادَ إِلَى سَيَّارَةِ الشُرْطَةِ.

"You were driving through the city with a speed of one hundred and twenty kilometers an hour. The speed limit is sixty," the sergeant said.

"Ah, this. You see, I have just washed my car. So I was driving a little faster to dry it up," the man said with a sly smile.

"Does it cost much to wash the car?" the policeman asked.

"Not much. It cost twelve dollars," the speeder said.

"You do not know the prices," sergeant Mamdouh said, "It really cost you two hundred and twelve dollars because you will pay two hundred dollars for drying the car. Here is the ticket. Have a nice day," the policeman said. He gave a speeding ticket for two hundred dollars and the driving license to the speeder and went back to the police car.

"Osama, I think you have lots of experiences with speeders, haven't you?" Omar asked the policeman.

"I have met many of them," Osama said starting the engine, "At first they look like angry tigers or sly foxes. But after I speak with them, they look like afraid kittens or silly monkeys. Like that one in the blue car."

Meanwhile a little white car was slowly driving along a street not far from the city park. The car stopped near a shop. A man and a woman got out of the car and went up to the shop. It was closed. The man looked around. Then he quickly took out some keys and tried to open the door. At last he opened it and they went inside.

"Look! There are so many dresses here!" the woman said. She took out a big bag and began to put in everything there. When the bag was

"أُسَامَة، أَعْتَقِدُ أَنَّ لَدَيْكَ الكَثِيرَ مِنَ التَجارِبِ مَعَ السائِقينَ المُسرِعينَ، أَلَيسَ كَذَلِكَ؟" عُمَرُ سَأَلَ رَجُلَ الشُرْطَةِ.

"لَقَدْ قابَلْتُ الكَثيرَ مِنهُمْ،" قالَ أُسَامَةُ وَهُوَ يُدِيرُ المُحَرِّكَ، "فِي البِدايَةِ يَبدونَ كَالنُمورِ الغاضِبَةِ أَو الثَعالِبِ الماكِرَةِ. لكِنْ بَعدَ التَحَدُّثِ مَعَهُمْ، يَبدونَ كَالقِطَطِ الصَغيرَةِ الخائِفَةِ أَو القُرودِ الساذَجَةِ. مِثلُ ذَلِكَ السائِقِ فِي السَيّارَةِ الزَرقاءِ."

فِي أَثناءِ ذَلِكَ كانَتْ هُناكَ سَيّارَةٌ بَيضاءُ صَغيرَةٌ تَسيرُ بِبُطءٍ فِي شارِعٍ لَيسَ بِبَعيدٍ عَنْ مُنتَزَهِ المَدينَةِ. تَوَقَّفَتْ السَيّارَةُ قُربَ مَتجَرٍ. خَرَجَ رَجُلٌ وَامْرَأَةٌ مِنَ السَيّارَةِ وَذَهَبا إِلَى المَتجَرِ. كانَ مُغلَقاً. نَظَرَ الرَجُلُ حَولَهُ. ثُمَّ أَخَذَ بِسُرعَةٍ بَعضَ المَفاتيحِ وَحاوَلَ أَنْ يَفتَحَ البابَ. أَخيراً فَتَحَهُ وَدَخَلا.

"أُنْظُرا! يوجَدُ الكَثيرُ جِدّاً مِنَ الفَساتينِ هُنا!" قالَتِ المَرأَةُ. أَخَذَتْ حَقيبَةً كَبيرَةً وَبَدَأَتْ فِي وَضعِ كُلِّ شَيءٍ بِها. عِندَما امْتَلَأَتِ الحَقيبَةُ،

full, she took it to the car and came back.

"Take everything quickly! Oh! What a wonderful hat!" the man said. He took from the shop window a big black hat and put it on.

"Look at this red dress! I like it so much!" the woman said and quickly put on the red dress. She did not have more bags. So she took more things in her hands, ran outside and put them on the car. Then she ran inside to bring more things.

The police car P07 was slowly driving along the city park when the radio began to talk: "Attention all patrols. We have got a robbery alarm from a shop near the city park. The address of the shop is 72 Park street."

"P07 got it," Osama said in the mic, "I am very close to this place. Drive there." They found the shop very quickly and drove up to the white car. Then they got out of the car and hid behind it. The woman in new red

أَخَذَتْها إِلَى السَّيَّارَةِ وَعادَتْ.

"خُذِي كُلَّ شَيْءٍ بِسُرْعَةٍ! أوه! يا لَها مِن قُبَّعَةٍ رائِعَةٍ!" قالَ الرَّجُلُ. أَخَذَ مِن نافِذَةِ العَرْضِ بِالمَتْجَرِ قُبَّعَةً سَوْداءَ كَبيرَةً وَارْتَداها.

"أُنْظُرْ إِلَى هذا الفُسْتانِ الأَحْمَرِ! أُحِبُّهُ كَثيراً جِدّاً!" قالَتِ المَرْأَةُ وَبِسُرْعَةٍ ارْتَدَتِ الفُسْتانَ الأَحْمَرَ. لَيْسَ مَعَها المَزيدُ مِنَ الحَقائِبِ. لِذلِكَ أَخَذَتِ المَزيدَ مِنَ الأَشْياءِ في يَدَيْها، جَرَتْ إِلَى الخارِجِ وَوَضَعَتْها عَلَى السَّيَّارَةِ. ثُمَّ جَرَتْ إِلَى الداخِلِ لِتُحْضِرَ المَزيدَ مِنَ الأَشْياءِ.

سَيَّارَةُ الشُّرْطَةِ P07 كانَتْ تَسيرُ بِبُطْءٍ عِنْدَ مُنْتَزَهِ المَدينَةِ عِنْدَما بَدَأَ الراديو التَحَدُّثَ: "اِنْتِباهُ كُلِّ الدَّوْرِيّاتِ. لَدَيْنا إِنْذارُ سَرِقَةٍ مِن مَتْجَرٍ قُرْبَ مُنْتَزَهِ المَدينَةِ. عُنْوانُ المَتْجَرِ 72 شارِعُ المُنْتَزَهِ."

"P07 وَجَدْتُهُ،" قالَ أسامَةُ في مُكَبِّرِ الصَّوْتِ، "أنا قَريبٌ جِدّاً مِن هذا المَكانِ. أَسيرُ إِلَى هُناكَ." وَجَدوا المَتْجَرَ بِسُرْعَةٍ جِدّاً وَساروا إِلَى السَّيَّارَةِ البَيْضاءِ. ثُمَّ خَرَجوا مِنَ السَّيَّارَةِ

dress ran out of the shop. She put some dresses on the police car and ran back in the shop. The woman did it very quickly. She did not see that it was a police car!

"Damn it! I forgot my gun in the police station!" Osama said. Bruce and Omar looked at the sergeant Mamdouh and then surprised at each other. The policeman was so confused that Omar and Bruce understood they must help him. The woman ran out of the shop again, put some dresses on the police car and ran back. Then Omar said to Osama: "We can pretend that we have guns."

"Let's do it," Osama answered, "But you do not get up. The thieves may have guns," he said and then cried, "This is the police speaking! Everybody who is inside the shop! Put your hands up and come slowly one by one out of the shop!"

They waited for a minute. Nobody came out. Then Bruce had an idea.

وَاخْتَبَؤُوا خَلْفَها. المَرأَةُ فِي الفُسْتانِ الأَحْمَرِ الجَديدِ خَرَجَتْ مُسْرِعَةً مِنَ المَتْجَرِ. وَضَعَتْ بَعْضَ الفَساتِينِ عَلَى سَيّارَةِ الشُّرْطَةِ وَعادَتْ مُسْرِعَةً إِلَى المَتْجَرِ. المَرأَةُ فَعَلَتْ ذَلِكَ بِسُرْعَةٍ جِدّاً. لَمْ تُلاحِظْ أَنَّها سَيّارَةُ شُرْطَةٍ!

"اللَعْنَةُ! نَسِيتُ مُسَدَّسِي فِي قِسْمِ الشُّرْطَةِ!" قالَ أُسامَةُ. بْروس وَعُمَرُ نَظَرا إِلَى الرَقيبِ مَمْدُوح ثُمَّ نَظَرا بِدَهْشَةٍ لِبَعْضِهِما. رَجُلُ الشُّرْطَةِ كانَ مُرْتَبِكاً جِدّاً حَتَّى أَنَّ عُمَر وَبْروس فَهِما أَنَّ عَلَيْهِما مُساعَدَتَهُ. خَرَجَتِ المَرأَةُ مُسْرِعَةً مِنَ المَتْجَرِ ثانِيَةً وَعادَتْ مُسْرِعَةً. ثُمَّ قالَ عُمَرُ لِأُسامَةَ: "يُمْكِنُنا أَنْ نَتَظاهَرَ بِامْتِلاكِ مُسَدَّساتٍ."

"فَلْنَفْعَلْ ذَلِكَ،" أَجابَ أُسامَة، لَكِنْ لا تَنْهَضا. رُبَّما يَمْتَلِكُ اللُصُوصَ مُسَدَّساتٍ،" قالَ ذَلِكَ ثُمَّ صاحَ، "ها هِيَ الشُّرْطَةُ تَتَحَدَّثُ! إِلَى كُلِّ شَخْصٍ بِداخِلِ المَتْجَرِ! اِرْفَعُوا أَيْدِيكُمْ وَاخْرُجُوا بِبُطْءٍ واحِداً تِلْوَ الآخَرِ مِنَ المَتْجَرِ!"

اِنْتَظِرُوا لِمُدَّةِ دَقيقَةٍ. لَمْ يَخْرُجْ أَحَدٌ. حِينَئِذٍ

كَانَ لَدَى برُوس فِكْرَةٍ.

"إِنْ لَمْ تَخْرُجُوا الآنَ، سَنُطْلِقُ كَلْبَ الشُّرْطَةِ عَلَيْكُمْ" صَاحَ ثُمَّ نَبَحَ مِثْلَ كَلْبٍ غَاضِبٍ كَبِيرٍ. خَرَجَ اللِّصَانِ مُسْرِعَانِ رَافِعَانِ أَيْدِيَهُما فِي الحَالِ. وَضَعَ مَمْدُوحٌ بِسُرْعَةٍ القُيُودَ بِيَدَيْهِما وَأَخَذَهُما إِلَى سَيَّارَةِ الشُّرْطَةِ. ثُمَّ قَالَ لِبرُوس: "لَقَدْ كَانَتْ فِكْرَةً عَظِيمَةً التَّظَاهُرِ بِأَنَّ مَعَنا كَلْباً! كَما تَرَيْنَ، لَقَدْ نَسِيتُ مُسَدَّسِي مَرَّتَيْنِ مِنْ قَبْلُ. لَوْ عَلِمُوا أَنَّنِي نَسِيتُهُ لِلْمَرَّةِ الثَّالِثَةِ، رُبَّما يَفْصِلُونَنِي أَوْ يَجْعَلُونِي أَعْمَلُ عَمَلاً مَكْتَبِيّاً. لَنْ تُخْبِرا أَحَداً عَنْ ذَلِكَ، أَلَيْسَ كَذَلِكَ؟"

"بِالتَّأْكِيدِ، لَنْ نَفْعَلَ!" قَالَ برُوس.

"أَبَداً" قَالَ عُمَرُ.

"شُكْراً جَزِيلاً لِمُساعَدَتِي، يَا رِجَالُ!" صَافَحَهُما أُسَامَةُ بِقُوَّةٍ.

"If you will not come out now, we will set the police dog on you!" he cried and then barked like a big angry dog. The thieves ran out with hands up immediately. Osama quickly put handcuffs on them and got them to the police car. Then he said to Bruce: "It was a great idea pretending that we have a dog! You see, I have forgotten my gun two times already. If they learn that I have forgotten it for the third time, they may fire me or make me do office work. You will not tell anybody about it, will you?"

"Sure, not!" Bruce said.

"Never," Omar said.

"Thank you very much for helping me, guys!" Osama shook their hands strongly.

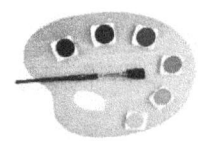

الفَصْلُ الثامِنُ وَالعِشْرُونَ
Chapter 28

دَوْرِيَّةُ الشُرْطَةِ (الجُزْءُ الثاني)
The police patrol (part 2)

A

كلمات

1. أجابَ - answered
2. أدارَ ، حَوْلَ - turned
3. اِرْتدادُ - ricochet
4. أطْلَقَ النارُ - shot
5. أَمْسِ - yesterday
6. أَيْضاً - either, too, also
7. بِإخْلاصٍ - sincerely
8. بَنْكُ اكسبريس - Express Bank
9. جيب - pocket
10. حَتَّى الآنَ - yet
11. خَزِينَةٌ - safe
12. رامي - Ramy
13. رَأى - saw
14. رِجالٌ - men
15. رَمْزي - Ramzy
16. رَنَّ - rang
17. زُجاجٌ - glass
18. زِرٌ - button

19.	سِرّاً ، خَفيَّةً - secretly	31.	مَسرُوقٌ - stolen
20.	سَيِّدَةُ - madam	32.	مَفقُودٌ - gone
21.	شَخْصٌ ما - somebody	33.	مَلِكي - mine
22.	عادِي ، مَألُوفٌ - usual	34.	نادِراً - seldom
23.	فاقِدٌ لِلوَعي - unconscious	35.	نُقُودٌ ، مال - cash,
24.	فَتَحَ - opened		مُسَجِّلَةُ النُقود - cash register,
25.	لَكَ, لَكُمْ ، لَكُما - yours		صَرّافٌ - cashier, teller
26.	لِمَنْ ، الَّذي ، الَّتي ، الَّذينَ - whose	36.	هاتِفٌ - phone,
27.	مَأخُوذٌ - taken		يَتَّصِلُ هاتِفِيّاً - to phone
28.	ماهِرٌ - clever	37.	يَحْمي - to protect
29.	مُتَحَرِّكٌ ، نَقّالٌ - mobile	38.	يَضْغَطُ - to press
30.	مَركَزُ تَسَوُّقٍ ، مَركَزٌ تِجاريٌّ - shopping center	39.	يُعذَرُ - to excuse
			عُذراً ، أعْذُرني .- Excuse me.

B

<table>
<tr><td>

The police patrol (part 2)

Next day Bruce and Omar were accompanying Osama again. They were standing near a big shopping centre when a woman came to them.

"Can you help me please?" she asked.

"Sure, madam. What has happened?" Osama asked.

</td><td>

دَوريَّةُ الشُرطَةِ (الجُزءُ الثاني)

في اليَومِ التالي بروس وَعُمَر كانا مُرافِقَينِ أسامَةَ ثانِيَةً. كانُوا يَقِفُونَ بِالقُربِ مِن مَركَزِ تَسَوُّقٍ كَبيرٍ عِندَما أتَتْ اِمرَأةٌ إلَيهِم .

" أيُمكِنُكُم مِسعَدَتي مِن فَضلِكُم؟" سَألَتْ.

" بِالتَأكيدِ، سَيِّدَتي. ماذا حَدَثَ؟" سَألَ

</td></tr>
</table>

أُسَامَة.

" لَقَدْ فَقَدْتُ هَاتِفِي النَقّالَ. أَعْتَقِدُ أَنَّهُ قَدْ سُرِقَ".

"My mobile phone is gone. I think it has been stolen."

" هَلْ اِسْتُخْدِمَ اليَوْمَ؟" سَأَلَ رَجُلُ الشُرْطَةِ.

"Has it been used today?" the policeman asked.

" لَقَدْ اِسْتَخْدَمْتُهُ قَبْلَ خُرُوجِي مِنْ مَرْكَزِ التَسَوُّقِ،" أجابَتْ.

"It had been used by me before I went out of the shopping centre," she answered.

"فَلْنَذهَبْ إلَى الداخِلِ،" قالَ أُسَامَةُ. دَخَلُوا إِلَى مَرْكَزِ التَسَوُّقِ وَنَظَرُوا حَوْلَهُم. كانَ هُناكَ الكَثِيرُ مِنْ الناسِ.

"Let's get inside," Osama said. They went into the shopping centre and looked around. There were many people there.

" فَلْنُجَرِّبْ حِيلَةً قَدِيمَةً،" قالَ أُسَامَةُ وَهُوَ يُخْرِجُ هاتِفَهُ الخاصَّ، "ما هُوَ رَقْمُ هاتِفِكَ؟" سَأَلَ المَرْأَةَ. أَخْبَرَتْهُ وَاِتَّصَلَ بِرَقْمِ هاتِفِها. رَنَّ هاتِفٌ نَقَّالٌ لَيْسَ بِبَعِيدٍ عَنْهُمْ. ذَهَبُوا إلَى المَكانِ حَيْثُ كانَ الهاتِفُ يَرِنُّ. كانَ هُناكَ طابُوراً. نَظَرَ رَجُلٌ فِي الطابُورِ إلَى رَجُلِ الشُرْطَةِ ثُمَّ أَدارَ بِسُرْعَةٍ رَأْسَهُ بَعِيداً. اِقْتَرَبَ رَجُلُ الشُرْطَةِ مُسْتَمِعاً بِعِنايَةٍ. كانَ الهاتِفُ يَرِنُّ فِي جَيْبِ الرَجُلِ.

"Let's try an old trick," Osama said taking out his own phone, "What is your telephone number?" he asked the woman. She said and he called her telephone number. A mobile telephone rang not far from them. They went to the place where it was ringing. There was a queue there. A man in the queue looked at the policeman and then quickly turned his head away. The policeman came closer listening carefully. The telephone was ringing in the man's pocket.

"Excuse me," Osama said. The man looked at him.	"عُذراً،" قالَ أُسامَة. نَظَرَ الرَجُلُ إِلَيْهِ.
"Excuse me, your telephone is ringing," Osama said.	"عُذراً، هاتِفُكَ يَرِنُّ،" قالَ أُسامَةُ.
"Where?" the man said.	"أَيْنَ؟" قالَ الرَجُلُ.
"Here, in your pocket," Osama said.	"هُنا، فِي جَيْبِكِ،" قالَ أُسامَةُ.
"No, it is not," the man said.	"لا، لَيْسَ كَذَلِكَ،" قالَ الرَجُلُ.
"Yes, it is," Osama said	"نَعَمْ، إِنَّهُ كَذَلِكَ،" قالَ أُسامَة.
"It is not mine," the man said.	"إِنَّهُ لا يَخُصُّنِي،" قالَ الرَجُلُ.
"Then whose telephone is ringing in your pocket?" Osama asked.	"إِذَنْ هاتِف مَنْ الَّذِي يَرِنُّ فِي جَيْبِكِ؟" سَأَلَ أُسامَة.
"I do not know," the man answered.	"لا أَعْرِف،" أَجابَ الرَجُلُ.
"Let me see, please," Osama said and took the telephone out of the man's pocket.	"دَعْنِي أَرَى، مِنْ فَضْلِكِ،" قالَ أُسامَة وَأَخْرَجَ الهاتِفَ مِنْ جَيْبِ الرَجُلِ.
"Oh, it is mine!" the woman cried.	"أوْهِ، إِنَّهُ هاتِفِي!" صاحَتْ المَرْأَةُ.
"Take your telephone, madam," Osama said giving it to her.	"خُذِي هاتِفُكِ، يا سَيِّدَتِي،" قالَ أُسامَةُ وَهُوَ يُعْطِيهِ لَها.
"May I, sir?" Osama asked and put his hand in the man's pocket again. He took out another telephone, and then one more.	"رُبَّما أنا، سَيِّدِي؟" سَأَلَ أُسامَةَ وَوَضَعَ يَدَهُ فِي جَيْبِ الرَجُلِ مَرَّةً أُخْرَى. أَخْرَجَ هاتِفاً آخَرَ، ثُمَّ واحِداً آخَرَ.

"Are they not yours either?" Osama asked the man.

The man shook his head looking away.

"What strange telephones!" Osama cried, "They ran away from their owners and jump into the pockets of this man! And now they are ringing in his pockets, aren't they?"

"Yes, they are," the man said.

"You know, my job is to protect people. And I will protect you from them. Get in my car and I will bring you to the place where no telephone can jump in your pocket. We go to the police station," the policeman said. Then he took the man by the arm and took him to the police car.

"I like silly criminals," Osama Mamdouh smiled after they had taken the thief to the police station.

"Have you met smart ones?" Omar asked.

"وَهٰذانِ لا يَخُصّانِكَ أَيْضاً؟" سَأَلَ أُسامَةُ الرَّجُلَ.

هَزَّ الرَّجُلُ رَأْسَهُ وَنَظَرَ بَعِيداً.

"يا لَها مِنْ هَواتِفَ غَرِيبَةٍ!" صاحَ أُسامَةُ، "تَفِرُّ مِنْ أَصْحابِها وَتَقْفِزُ إِلَى جَيْبِ هٰذا الرَّجُلِ! وَالآنَ تَرِنُّ فِي جُيُوبِهِ، أَلَيْسَ كَذٰلِكَ؟"

"نَعَمْ، هِيَ كَذٰلِكَ،" قالَ الرَّجُلُ.

"أَنْتَ تَعْرِفُ، وَظِيفَتِي أَنْ أَحْمِيَ الناسَ. وَسَأَحْمِيكَ مِنْهُمْ. أُدْخُلْ إِلَى سَيّارَتِي وَسَأُرافِقُكَ إِلَى مَكانٍ حَيْثُ لا يَسْتَطِيعُ هاتِفٌ أَنْ يَقْفِزَ فِي جَيْبِكَ. نَذْهَبُ إِلَى قِسْمِ الشُّرْطَةِ،" قالَ رَجُلُ الشُّرْطَةِ. ثُمَّ أَمْسَكَ الرَّجُلَ مِنْ ذِراعِهِ وَأَخَذَهُ إِلَى سَيّارَةِ الشُّرْطَةِ.

"أُحِبُّ المُجْرِمِينَ الساذِجِينَ،" اِبْتَسَمَ أُسامَةُ مَمْدُوحٌ بَعْدَما أَخَذُوا اللِّصَّ إِلَى قِسْمِ الشُّرْطَةِ.

"هَلْ قابَلْتَ مُجْرِمِينَ أَذْكِياءَ؟" سَأَلَ عُمَرُ.

"Yes, I have. But very seldom," the policeman answered, "Because it is very hard to catch a smart criminal."

Meanwhile two men came into the Express Bank. One of them took a place in a queue. Another one came up to the cash register and gave a paper to the cashier. The cashier took the paper and read:

"Dear Sir,

this is a robbery of the Express Bank. Give me all the cash. If you do not, then I will use my gun. Thank you.

Sincerely yours,

Ramy"

"I think I can help you," the cashier said pressing secretly the alarm button, "But the money had been locked by me in the safe yesterday. The safe has not been opened yet. I will ask somebody to open the safe and bring the money. Okay?"

" نَعَمْ، قَابَلْتُ. لٰكِنْ نَادِراً جِدّاً," أَجَابَ رَجُلُ الشُّرْطَةِ, "لِأَنَّهُ مِنَ الصَّعْبِ جِدّاً أَنْ تُمْسِكَ بِمُجْرِمٍ ذَكِيٍّ".

فِي أَثْنَاءِ ذٰلِكَ دَخَلَ رَجُلانِ إِلَى بَنْكِ اكْسَبْرِيس. أَحَدُهُما أَخَذَ مَكَاناً فِي الطَّابُورِ. وَالآخَرُ أَتَى إِلَى مُسَجِّلَةِ النُّقُودِ وَأَعْطَى وَرَقَةً لِلصَّرَّافِ. أَخَذَ الصَّرَّافُ الوَرَقَةَ وَقَرَأَ:

" سَيِّدِي العَزِيزَ،

هٰذا سَطْوٌ عَلَى لِبَنْكِ اكْسَبْرِيس. أَعْطِنِي كُلَّ النُّقُودِ. إِنْ لَمْ تَفْعَلْ، حِينَئِذٍ سَأَسْتَخْدِمُ مُسَدَّسِي. شُكْراً لَكِ.

المُخْلِصُ،

رامي"

" أَعْتَقِدُ أَنَّهُ يُمْكِنُنِي مُساعَدَتُكَ," قالَ الصَّرَّافُ وَهُوَ يَضْغَطُ خَفِيَّةً عَلَى زِرِّ الإنْذارِ, "لٰكِنَّ النُّقُودَ أُغْلِقَتْ عَلَيْها فِي الخَزِينَةِ أَمْسِ. وَالخَزِينَةُ لَمْ تُفْتَحْ حَتَّى الآنَ. سَأَطْلُبُ مِنْ شَخْصٍ ما أَنْ يَفْتَحَ الخَزِينَةَ وَيُحْضِرَ النُّقُودَ. حَسَناً؟"

"Okay. But do it quickly!" the robber answered.

"Shall I make you a cup of coffee while the money is being put in bags?" the cashier asked.

"No, thank you. Just money," the robber answered.

The radio in the police car P07 began to talk: "Attention all the patrols. We have got a robbery alarm from the Express Bank."

"P07 got it," sergeant Mamdouh answered. He stepped on the gas up to the stop and the car started quickly. When they drove up to the bank, there was no other police car yet.

"We will make an interesting report if we go inside," Omar said.

"You guys do what you need. And I will come inside through the back door," sergeant Mamdouh said. He took out his gun and went quickly to the back door of the bank. Omar and Bruce came into

" حَسَناً. لَكِنْ اِفْعَلْ بِذلِكَ بِسُرْعَةٍ!" أجابَ اللِصُّ.

" هَلْ أُعِدُّ لَكَ فِنْجاناً مِنَ القَهْوَةِ بَيْنَما تُوضَعُ النُّقُودُ فِي الحَقائِبِ؟" سَأَلَ الصَرّافُ.

" لا، شُكراً لَكَ. النُّقُودُ فَقَطْ،" أجابَ اللِصُّ.

بَدَأَ الراديو فِي سَيّارَةِ الشُرْطَةِ P07 يَتَكَلَّمُ: "اِنْتِباهُ كُلِّ الدَوْرِيّاتِ. لَدَينا إنْذارُ سَرِقَةٍ مِنْ بَنْكِ اكسبريس."

" P07 تَسَلَّمَتْهُ،" أجابَ الرَقيبُ مَمْدوح. وَضَغَطَ عَلى البِنْزينِ حَتّى النِهايَةِ وَتَحَرَّكَتْ السَيّارَةُ بِسُرْعَةٍ. عِنْدَما وَصَلوا إلى البَنْكِ، لَمْ يَكُنْ هُناكَ أيُّ سَيّارَةِ شُرْطَةٍ أُخرى حَتّى الآنَ.

" سَنُعِدُّ تَقريراً مُشَوِّقاً لَوْ دَخَلْنا،" قالَ عُمَرُ.

" يا رِفاقُ اِفْعَلا ما تَحْتاجانِ. سَأَدْخُلُ مِنَ البابِ الخَلْفِيِّ،" قالَ الرَقيبُ مَمْدوح. أخْرَجَ مُسَدَّسَهُ وَذَهَبَ بِسُرْعَةٍ إلى البابِ الخَلْفِيِّ لِلبَنْكِ. دَخَلَ عُمَرُ وَبروس إلى البَنْكِ مِنْ

the bank through the central door. They saw a man standing near the cash register. He put one hand in his pocket and looked around. The man who came with him, stepped away from the queue and came up to him.

"Where is the money?" he asked Ramy.

"Ramzy, the cashier has said that it is being put in bags," another robber answered.

"I am tired of waiting!" Ramzy said. He took out a gun and pointed it to the cashier, "Bring all the money now!" the robber cried at the cashier. Then he went to the middle of the room and cried: "Listen all! This is a robbery! Nobody move!" At this moment somebody near the cash register moved. The robber with the gun without looking shot at him. Another robber fell on the floor and cried: "Ramzy! You silly monkey! Damn it! You have shot me!"

"Oh, Ramy! I did not see that it was you!" Ramzy said. At this moment the cashier quickly ran out.

البابِ الرَّئيسِيِّ. شاهَدا رَجُلاً واقِفاً قُرْبَ مُسَجِّلَةِ النُّقودِ. وَضَعَ يَداً بِجَيْبِهِ وناظِراً حَوْلَهُ. الرَّجُلُ الَّذي أتى مَعَهُ، خَرَجَ مِنْ الطّابورِ وأتى إلَيْهِ .

" أيْنَ النُّقودُ؟" هُوَ سَأَلَ رامي.

" رَمْزِيٌّ، قالَ الصَّرّافُ إنَّها تُوضَعُ في حَقائِبَ،" أجالَ اللِّصُّ الآخَرُ.

" لَقَدْ تَعِبْتُ مِنْ الإنْتِظارِ!" قالَ رَمْزي. أخْرَجَ مُسَدَّساً وَصَوَّبَهُ إلى الصَّرّافِ، "أحْضِرْ جَميعَ النُّقودِ الآنَ!" صاحَ اللِّصُّ في الصَّرّافِ. ثُمَّ ذَهَبَ إلى مُنْتَصَفِ الغُرْفَةِ وصاحَ: "أنْصِتوا جَميعاً! هذا سَطْوٌ! لا أحَدَ يَتَحَرَّكْ!" في هذِهِ اللَّحْظَةِ شَخْصٌ ما قَرُبَ مُسَجِّلَةِ النُّقودِ تَحَرَّكَ. اللِّصُّ ذو المُسَدَّسِ بِدونِ أنْ يَنْظُرَ أطْلَقَ النارَ عَلَيْهِ. اللِّصُّ الآخَرُ سَقَطَ عَلى الأرْضِ وصاحَ: "رَمْزي! أنْتَ قِرْدٌ ساذِجٌ! اللَّعْنَةُ عَلَيْكِ! أطْلَقْتُ النارَ عَلَيَّ!"

" أوهْ، رامي! لَمْ ألاحِظْ أنَّهُ أنْتَ!" قالَ رَمْزي. في هذِهِ اللَّحْظَةِ هَرَبَ الصَّرّافُ

"The cashier has run away and the money has not been taken here yet!" Ramzy cried to Ramy, "The police may arrive soon! What shall we do?"

"Take something big, break the glass and take the money. Quickly!" Ramy cried. Ramzy took a metal chair and hit the glass of the cash register. It was of course not usual glass and it did not break. But the chair went back by ricochet and hit the robber on the head! He fell on the floor unconsciously. At this moment sergeant Mamdouh ran inside and quickly put handcuffs on the robbers. He turned to Omar and Bruce.

"I did say! Most criminals are just silly!" he said.

بِسُرْعَةٍ.

"هَرَبَ الصَرّافُ وَالنُّقُودُ لَمْ تُحْضَرْ هُنا حَتَّى الآنَ!" صاحَ رَمْزِي بِرامِي، "رُبَّما تَصِلُ الشُّرْطَةُ حالاً! ماذا يَجِبُ أَنْ نَفْعَلَ؟"

"خُذْ شَيْئاً ما ضَخْمَ وَاكْسِرِ الزُّجاجَ وَخُذِ النُّقودَ. بِسُرْعَةٍ!" صاحَ رامِي. أَخَذَ رَمْزِي كُرْسِيّاً مَعْدِنِيّاً وَضَرَبَ زُجاجَ مُسَجِّلَةِ النُّقودِ. لَقَدْ كانَ بِالطَّبْعِ زُجاجٌ غَيْرُ عادِيٍّ وَلَمْ يَنْكَسِرْ. لكِنَّ الكُرْسِيَّ عادَ بِفِعْلِ الِارْتِدادِ وَضَرَبَ اللِّصَّ عَلَى الرَّأْسِ! وَسَقَطَ عَلَى الأَرْضِ فاقِداً الوَعْيَ. فِي هذِهِ اللَّحْظَةِ دَخَلَ الرَّقيبُ مَمْدوحٌ مُسْرِعاً وَبِسُرْعَةٍ وَضَعَ القُيودَ عَلَى اللُّصوصِ. وَاسْتَدارَ لِعُمَرَ وَبِرُوس.

"لَقَدْ قُلْتُ! مُعْظَمُ المُجْرِمينَ مُجَرَّدُ سَذَجٍ!" قالَ هُوَ.

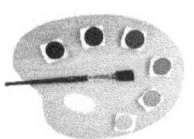

الفَصْلُ التاسِعُ وَالعِشْرُونَ
Chapter 29

البَرْنامَجُ التَبادُليُّ لِقادَةِ المُسْتَقْبَلِ وَجَليسَةُ الأَطْفالِ
Future Leaders Exchange Program (FLEX) and Au pair

A

كلمات

1. اِبْنَةُ - daughter
2. اِتَّصِلْ هاتِفِيّاً - called
3. اِتِّفاقِيَّةُ - agreement
4. اِخْتارَ - chose
5. أَرْسِلْ - sent
6. أَقْرَبُ - nearest
7. أَكْبَرُ - elder
8. البَرْنامَجُ التَبادُليُّ لِقادَةِ المُسْتَقْبَلِ - FLEX

9. الوِلاياتُ المُتَّحِدَةُ الأَمْريكِيَّةُ - United States, USA
10. أَمْريكا الشَماليَّةُ - North America
11. إِمْكانِيَّةٌ - possibility
12. أَمَل - hope; يَأْمُلُ - to hope
13. أَيْضاً - also
14. بَريدٌ إِليكترونيٌّ - e-mail
15. بَلَدُ - country (state); الريفُ - countryside
16. تاريخُ - date
17. تَعَلَّمَ - learning
18. جَليسَةُ أَطْفال - au pair
19. خادِمٌ ، خادِمَةُ - servant
20. خِطابٌ - letter
21. دَفَعَ - paid
22. دَوْرَةٌ ، مَنْهَجٌ - course
23. زارَ - visited
24. شَخْصٌ - person
25. عاشَ - lived

26. غَيْرُ عادِلٍ - unfair
27. قَرْيَةٌ - village
28. قِياسيٌّ - standard
29. كَتَبَ - wrote
30. لَيْلَى - Laila
31. مَرَّ - passed
32. مَرَّةٌ - once
33. مَرَّتانِ - twice
34. مُسابَقَةٌ - competition
35. مُشارِكٌ - participant
36. مُشْكِلَةٌ - problem
37. مُضيفٌ - host
38. مُنْذُ - since (time point), لِأَنَّ - as, since
39. مَوْقِعُ إِنْتَرْنْت - Internet site
40. نوفا - Nova
41. نيويورك - New York
42. يُغَيِّرُ - to change,
43. تَغْييرَ - change

B

FLEX and Au pair

Bruce's sister, brother and parents lived in the United States of America. They lived in New York. The sister's name was Nova. She was twenty years old. She had learned Arabic since she was eleven years old. When Nova was fifteen years old, she wanted to take part in the program FLEX. FLEX gives the possibility for some high school students from North America to spend a year in Egypt, living with a host family and studying in an Egyptian school. The program is free. Airplane tickets, living with a family, food, studying at Egyptian school are paid by FLEX. But by the time when she got the information about the competition date from the Internet site

البَرْنامَجُ التَبادُلِيُّ لِقادَةِ المُسْتَقْبَلِ وَجَلِيسَةِ أَطْفالٍ

أُخْتِ وَأَخُو وَوالِدَيْ بْروس عاشا فِي الوِلاياتِ المُتَّحِدَةِ الأَمْرِيكِيَّةِ. عاشُوا فِي نيويورك. اِسْمُ أُخْتِهِ نوفا. عُمْرُها عِشْرِينَ سَنَةً. تَعَلَّمَت اللُّغَةَ العَرَبِيَّةَ مُنْذُ كانَت فِي الحادِيَةَ عَشْرَةَ مِن عُمْرِها. عِنْدَما كانَت فِي الخامِسَةَ عَشْرَةَ مِن عُمْرِها، أَرادَت أَنْ تَشْتَرِكَ فِي البَرْنامَجِ التَبادُلِيِّ لِقادَةِ المُسْتَقْبَلِ. هٰذا البَرْنامَجُ يُعْطِي الإِمْكانِيَّةَ لِبَعْضِ طُلّابِ المَدارِسِ الثانَوِيَّةِ مِن أَمْرِيكا الشَمالِيَّةِ لِيَقْضُوا عاماً فِي مِصْرَ، يَعِيشُونَ مَعَ عائِلَةٍ مَضِيفَةٍ وَيَدْرُسُونَ فِي مَدْرَسَةٍ مِصْرِيَّةٍ. البَرْنامَجُ مَجّانِيٌّ. فَتَذاكِرُ الطائِرَةِ، وَالعَيْشُ مَعَ عائِلَةٍ، وَالطَعامُ وَالدِراسَةُ بِمَدْرَسَةٍ مِصْرِيَّةٍ مَدْفُوعَةٍ بِواسِطَةِ البَرْنامَجِ التَبادُلِيِّ لِقادَةِ المُسْتَقْبَلِ. لٰكِنْ بِحُلُولِ الوَقْتِ عِنْدَما حَصَلَت عَلَى مَعْلُوماتٍ عَنْ مَوْعِدِ المُسابَقَةِ مِن مَوْقِعِ الإِنْتَرْنَت http://www.americancouncils.org,

كانَ وَقْتُ المُسابَقَةِ قَدْ مَرَّ.

بَعْدَ ذٰلِكَ عَلِمَتْ عَنْ بَرْنامَجِ جَلِيسَةِ الأَطْفالِ. هٰذا البَرْنامَجُ يُعْطِي مُشْتَرِكِيهِ الإِمْكانِيَّةَ لِقَضاءِ سَنَةٍ أَوْ سَنَتَيْنِ فِي بَلَدٍ آخَرَ يَعِيشُونَ مَعَ عائِلَةٍ مَضِيفَةٍ، وَيَعْتَنُونَ بِالأَطْفالِ وَيَدْرُسُونَ فِي دَوْرَةِ لُغَةٍ. وَلِأَنَّ بْرُوس كانَ يَدْرُسُ بِالإِسْكَنْدَرِيَّةِ، كَتَبَتْ لَهُ نُوفا رِسالَةً إِلِكْتْرُونِيَّةً. طَلَبَتْ مِنْهُ أَنْ يَجِدَ لَها عائِلَةً مُضِيفَةً فِي مِصْرَ. بَحَثَ بْرُوس فِي بَعْضِ الصُحُفِ وَمَواقِعِ الإِنْتَرْنَتْ ذاتِ الإِعْلاناتِ. وَجَدَ بَعْضَ العائِلاتِ المُضِيفَةِ مِنْ مِصرَ عَلَى المَوْقِعِ http://www.Aupair-World.net وَعَلَى المَوْقِعِ http://www.PlacementAuPair.com/. بَعْدَ ذٰلِكَ زارَ بْرُوس وَكالَةً لِجُلَساءِ الأَطْفالِ فِي الإِسْكَنْدَرِيَّةِ. كانَ يُنْصَحُ بِواسِطَةِ سَيِّدَةٍ. اِسْمُها لَيْلَى عِزَّتْ.

"أُخْتِي مِنِ الوِلاياتِ المُتَّحِدَةِ الأَمْرِيكِيَّةِ. تَرْغَبُ أَنْ تَكُونَ جَلِيسَةَ أَطْفالٍ مَعَ عائِلَةٍ مِصْرِيَّةٍ. هَلْ يُمْكِنُكَ المُساعَدَةُ فِي هٰذا الشَّأْنِ؟: سَأَلَ بْرُوس لَيْلَى.

http://www.americancouncils.org, the competition day had passed. Then she learned about the program au pair. This program gives its participants the possibility to spend a year or two in another country living with a host family, looking after children and learning at a language course. Since Bruce was studying in Alexandria, Nova wrote him an e-mail. She asked him to find a host family for her in Egypt. Bruce looked through some newspapers and Internet sites with adverts. He found some host families from Egypt on http://www.Aupair-World.net/ and on http://www.PlacementAuPair.com/. Then Bruce visited an au pair agency in Alexandria. He was consulted by a woman. Her name was Laila Ezat.

"My sister is from the United States of America. She would like to be an au pair with an Egyptian family. Can you help on this matter?" Bruce asked Laila.

"I will be glad to help you. We place au pairs with families all over Egypt. An au pair is a person who joins a host family to help around the house and look after children. The host family gives the au pair food, a room and pocket money. Pocket money may be from 400 to 600 dollars. The host family must pay for a language course for the au pair as well," Laila said.

"Are there good and bad families?" Bruce asked.

"There are two problems about choosing a family. First some families think that an au pair is a servant who must do everything in the house including cooking for all family members, cleaning, washing, working in the garden etc. But an au pair is not a servant. An au pair is like an elder daughter or son of the family who helps parents with younger children. To

"سَأَكُونُ سَعِيدَةً لِمُساعَدَتِكَ. نَحْنُ نُوَظِّفُ جَلِيساتِ أَطْفالٍ فِي جَمِيعِ أَنْحاءِ مِصْرَ. جَلِيسَةُ الأَطْفالِ هِيَ الَّتِي تَلْتَحِقُ بِعائِلَةٍ مُضِيفَةٍ لِتُساعِدَ فِي المَنْزِلِ وَتَعْتَنِيَ بِالأَطْفالِ. العائِلَةُ المُضِيفَةُ تُعْطِيها الطَّعامَ، وَغُرْفَةً وَمَصْرُوفَ جيب. مَصْرُوفُ الجَيْبِ يَتَراوَحُ مِنْ 400 إِلَى 600 دُولارٍ. يَجِبُ أَنْ تَدْفَعَ العائِلَةُ المُضِيفَةُ لِدَوْرَةِ لُغَةٍ لِجَلِيسَةِ الأَطْفالِ أَيْضاً،" قالَتْ لَيْلَى.

"هَلْ هُناكَ عائِلاتٌ جَيِّدَةٌ وَأُخْرَى سَيِّئَةٌ؟" سَأَلَ بْرُوس.

"هُناكَ مُشْكِلَتانِ بِخُصُوصِ اخْتِيارِ العائِلَةِ. الأُولَى أَنَّ بَعْضَ العائِلاتِ تَظُنُّ أَنَّ جَلِيسَةَ الأَطْفالِ خادِمَةٌ يَجِبُ عَلَيْها أَنْ تَفْعَلَ كُلَّ شَيْءٍ فِي المَنْزِلِ بِما فِي ذَلِكَ طَهْيِ الطَّعامِ لِكُلِّ أَفْرادِ العائِلَةِ، وَالتَّنْظِيفِ، وَالغَسِيلِ وَالعَمَلِ فِي الحَدِيقَةِ إِلَى آخِرِهِ. لَكِنَّ جَلِيسَةَ الأَطْفالِ لَيْسَتْ خادِمَةً. فَمَنْ يُجالِسُ الأَطْفالَ مِثْلُهُ مِثْلَ ابْنَةٍ أَوْ ابْنٍ أَكْبَرَ لِلعائِلَةِ الَّذِي يُساعِدُ والِدَيْهِ ذُو الأَطْفالِ الأَصْغَرِ.

لِحِمَايَةِ حُقُوقِهِم يَجِبُ عَلَى جُلَسَاءِ الأَطْفالِ أَنْ يَقُومُوا بِعَمَلِ اتِّفاقِيَّةٍ مَعَ العائِلَةِ المُضِيفَةِ. لا تُصَدِّقْ قَوْلَ بَعْضِ وِكالاتِ جُلَسَاءِ الأَطْفالِ أَوْ العائِلاتِ المُضِيفَةِ أَنَّهُم يَسْتَخْدِمُونَ اتِّفاقِيَّةً قِياسِيَّةً. لا تُوجَدُ اتِّفاقِيَّةٌ قِياسِيَّةٌ. تَسْتَطِيعُ جَلِيسَةُ الأَطْفالِ أَنْ تُغَيِّرَ أَيَّ جُزْءٍ مِنَ الاتِّفاقِيَّةِ لَوْ كانَتْ غَيْرَ عادِلَةٍ. كُلُّ شَيْءٍ سَتَقُومُ بِهِ جَلِيسَةُ الأَطْفالِ وَالعائِلَةُ المُضِيفَةُ يَجِبُ أَنْ يُكْتَبَ فِي اتِّفاقِيَّةٍ.

المُشْكِلَةُ الثانِيَةُ هِيَ: بَعْضُ العائِلاتِ تَعِيشُ فِي قُرىً صَغِيرَةٍ حَيْثُ لا تُوجَدُ دَوْراتُ لُغَةٍ وَالقَلِيلُ مِنَ الأَماكِنِ الَّتِي تَسْتَطِيعُ جَلِيسَةُ الأَطْفالِ أَنْ تَذْهَبَ إِلَيْها فِي وَقْتِ الفَراغِ. فِي هٰذِهِ الحالَةِ إِنَّهُ ضَرُورِيٌّ أَنْ تَتَضَمَّنَ الاتِّفاقِيَّةُ أَنَّ العائِلَةَ المُضِيفَةَ يَجِبُ أَنْ تَدْفَعَ تَذْكِرَتَيْ ذَهابٍ وَعَوْدَةٍ إِلَى أَقْرَبِ بَلَدَةٍ كَبِيرَةٍ عِنْدَما تَذْهَبُ جَلِيسَةُ الأَطْفالِ هُناكَ. هٰذا رُبَّما يَكُونُ مَرَّةً أَوْ مَرَّتَيْنِ أُسْبُوعِيّاً."

"أَفْهَمُ ذٰلِكَ. أُخْتِي تَوَدُّ عائِلَةً مِنَ الإِسْكَنْدَرِيَّةِ. هَلْ يُمْكِنُكَ إِيجادُ عائِلَةٍ مُلائِمَةٍ فِي هٰذِهِ المَدِينَةِ؟"

protect their rights au pairs must work out an agreement with the host family. Do not believe it when some au pair agencies or host families say that they use a "standard" agreement. There is no standard agreement. The au pair can change any part of the agreement if it is unfair. Everything that an au pair and host family will do must be written in an agreement.

The second problem is this: Some families live in small villages where there are no language courses and few places where an au pair can go in free time. In this situation it is necessary to include in the agreement that the host family must pay for two way tickets to the nearest big town when the au pair goes there. It may be once or twice a week."

"I see. My sister would like a family from Alexandria. Can you

سَأَلَ برُوس.

"حَسَناً، يُوجَدُ حَوالَي عِشْرِينَ عائِلَةٍ مِن الإِسْكَنْدَرِيَّةِ الآنَ،" أجابَت لَيْلَى. اِتَّصَلَت هاتِفِيّاً بِبَعْضِهِم. العائِلاتُ المُضِيفَةُ كانَت سَعِيدَةً أَن يَكُونَ لَدَيها جَلِيسَةُ أَطْفالٍ مِن الوِلاياتِ المُتَّحِدَةِ الأَمْرِيكِيَّةِ. مُعْظَمُ العائِلاتِ أرادَت أَن تَحْصَلَ عَلَى خِطابٍ وَصُورَةٍ مِن نُوفا. وَبَعْضُهُم أرادَ أَيْضاً أَن يَتَّصِلَ بِها تِلِيفُونِيّاً لِيَتَأَكَّدَ أَنَّها تَسْتَطِيعُ التَحَدُّثَ القَلِيلَ مِن اللُّغَةِ العَرَبِيَّةِ. لِذَلِكَ أعطاهُم بروس رَقْمَ هاتِفِها.

بَعْضُ العائِلاتِ المُضِيفَةِ اِتَّصَلَت بِنُوفا. ثُمَّ أَرْسَلَت لَهُم خِطاباتٍ. وَأَخِيراً اِخْتارَت عائِلَةً مُناسِبَةً وَبِمُساعَدَةِ لَيْلَى قامَت بِعَمَلِ اِتِّفاقِيَّةٍ مَعَهُم. دَفَعَت العائِلَةُ تَكْلِفَةَ التَذْكِرَةِ مِن الوِلاياتِ المُتَّحِدَةِ الأَمْرِيكِيَّةِ إلَى مِصْرَ. أخيراً اِنْطَلَقَت نُوفا إلَى مِصْرَ تَمْلَؤُها الآمالُ وَالأحلامُ.

* * *

find a good family in this city?" Bruce asked.

"Well, there are about twenty families from Alexandria now," Laila answered. She telephoned some of them. The host families were glad to have an au pair from the United States of America. Most of the families wanted to get a letter with a photograph from Nova. Some of them also wanted to telephone her to be sure that she can speak Arabic a little. So Bruce gave them her telephone number.

Some host families called Nova. Then she sent them letters. At last she chose a suitable family and with the help of Laila worked out an agreement with them. The family paid for the ticket from The United States of America to Egypt. At last Nova started for Egypt full of hopes and dreams.

Arabic-English vocabulary

1. أَبٌ - dad
2. أَبٌ - daddy
3. اِبْتِسامَةٌ - smile
4. يَبْتَسِمُ - to smile
5. اِبْتَسَمَ - smiled
6. اِبْتَعِدْ - went away
7. أَبَداً - never
8. اِبْنٌ - son
9. اِبْنَةٌ - daughter
10. أَبْيَضٌ - white
11. أَتَساءَلُ - I wonder
12. اِتَّصِل هاتِفِيّاً - called
13. اِتِّفاقِيَّةٌ - agreement
14. أَتَى ، حَضَرَ - came
15. أَثاثٌ - furniture
16. اِثْنا عَشَرَ - twelve
17. أَثْناءَ ، خِلالَ - during
18. اِثْنانِ - two
19. أَجابَ - answered
20. إِجابَةٌ - answer,
21. يُجيبُ - to answer
22. إِجْرامِي - criminal (adj),
23. مُجْرِمٌ - criminal
24. أَحِبُّ - loved
25. إِحْتِفالُ - ceremony
26. أَحَدُ الوالِدَينِ - parent
27. أَحَدَ عَشَرَ - eleven
28. أَحْزِمَةُ الأَمانِ - seat belts
29. أَحْمَرُ - red
30. أَحْياناً - sometimes
31. أَخٌ ، شَقيقٌ - brother
32. أَخْبِرْ - informed
33. أُخْتٌ ، شَقيقَةٌ - sister
34. اِخْتارَ - chose
35. اِخْتَبَأَ - hid
36. اِخْتِبارٌ ، اِمْتِحانٌ - test
37. يَخْتَبَرُ ، يَمْتَحِنُ - to test
38. أَخَذَ - took
39. آخَرُ - another
40. آخَرُ - else
41. آخَرُ - less
42. آخَرُ - other
43. أَخْضَرُ - green
44. أَخيرٌ - last

45.	يَسْتَمِرُّ - to last	67.	أُسْبُوعٌ - week
46.	أَخيراً ، فِي النِهايَةِ - at last	68.	اِسْتِبْيانٌ ، اِسْتِطْلاعُ رَأْي - questionnaire
47.	Oh! - أداةُ نِداءٍ ، صَوْتٌ لِلدَهْشَةِ	69.	اِسْتِشاراتٌ - consultancy
48.	أدارَ - started (the engine);	70.	اِسْتَطاعَ – could
49.	بَدَأ ، اِنْطَلَقَ - started (to drive)	71.	اِسْتِمارَةٌ، نَمُوذَجٌ - form
50.	أدارَ ، حَوْلَ - turned	72.	أسَدٌ - lion
51.	إدارَةُ المُوَظَّفِينَ - personnel department	73.	أسِرَةٌ - beds
52.	أُذُنَ - ear	74.	أُسْرَةٌ ، عائِلَةٌ - family
53.	أَذهَبُ إلى البَنْكِ - I go to the bank.	75.	أُسْطُوانَةٌ مُدمَجَةٌ - CD
54.	أرادَ - wanted	76.	يُسَمّي ، يُحَدِّدُ ;name - اِسْم name
55.	إرادَةٌ ، وَصِيَّةٌ - will	77.	أسْوَدُ - black
56.	أَرْبَعَةٌ - four	78.	أصْفَرُ - yellow
57.	أَرْبَعَةٌ وَأَرْبَعُونَ - forty-four	79.	أصْلِّي - native
58.	اِرْتِدادٌ - ricochet	80.	أطْفالٌ ، أوْلادٌ - children
59.	أَرْسِلْ - sent	81.	إطْلاقاً - not any
60.	أَرْضٌ - land	82.	أطْلَقَ النارَ - shot
61.	يَهْبِطُ - to land	83.	أظْهَرْ - showed
62.	أرْضِيَّةٌ - floor	84.	إعادَةُ تَأْهِيلٍ - rehabilitation
63.	أزْرَقُ - blue	85.	أعْزَبُ - single
64.	أسْبانِي - Spanish	86.	أعْطى - gave
65.	أسْبانيا - Spain	87.	إعْلانٌ - ad
66.	أسْبِرين - aspirin	88.	إعْلانٌ - advert

89. أَفْضَل - better
90. أَفْضَلُ ، أَحْسَنُ - best
91. أَقْرَبُ - closer
92. أَقْرَبُ - nearest
93. أَقلامُ حِبرٍ - pens
94. أَكْبَرُ - elder
95. أَكْبَرُ - bigger
96. أَكْثَرُ - more
97. أَكِيدٌ - sure
98. الأَرْضُ - earth
99. الإِسْكَنْدَرِيَّةُ - Alexandria
100. الاِسْمُ الأَوْسَطُ - middle name
101. الآنَ - now
102. الآنَ ، بِالفِعلِ - already
103. الآيسُ كْرِيم - ice-cream
104. البَرْنَامَجُ التَبادُلِيُّ لِقادَةِ المُسْتَقْبَلِ FLEX
105. التاسِعُ - ninth
106. الثالِثُ - third
107. الثامِنُ - eighth
108. الجُمْهُورُ - audience
109. الجِنْسُ - sex
110. الخامِسُ - fifth
111. الَّذِي ؛ الَّذِينَ - who
112. الَّذِي ، الَّتِي - which
113. الَّذِي ، الَّتِي (لِغَيرِ العاقِلِ) - which
114. الرابِعُ - fourth
115. الراديو - radio
116. السابِعُ - seventh
117. السادِسُ - sixth
118. السَيِّدُ - mister
119. الشُرْطَةُ - police
120. العاشِرُ - tenth
121. أَلْفُ - thousand
122. الكانجارو - kangaroo
123. اللَيْزَرُ - laser
124. أَلْمانِيٌّ ، اللُغَةُ الأَلْمانِيَّةُ - German
125. الوِلاياتُ المُتَّحِدَةُ الأَمْرِيكِيَّةُ - United States, the USA
126. إلى - نَحْوَ - into
127. إلى آخِرِهِ - etc.
128. إِلى الشارِعِ - into the street,
129. خارِجَ - out of
130. إلى اللِقاءِ - bye
131. إلى اللِقاءِ - goodbye
132. إلى مَسافةٍ أَبْعَدَ - further
133. اليَوْمَ - today
134. أَمْ - mom, mother

135.	أُمّ - mother	159.	آنِسَةُ - miss
136.	أَمامَ - front	160.	أَنْفُ - nose
137.	أَمامَ - in front	161.	أَنْهَى - finished
138.	أَمرّ ، شَأْن - matter, business	162.	أَهْلاً ، هُتاف تَرْحيب - hello
139.	إمْرَأَةُ - woman	163.	أوْ - or
140.	أَمريكا الشَماليَّةُ - North America	164.	أَوَّلُ - first
141.	أَمريكيٌّ - American	165.	أُولئِكَ - those
142.	أَمْسِ - yesterday	166.	أَوَّلاً - at first
143.	إمْكانِيَّةُ - possibility	167.	أوليمبيك - Olympic
144.	أَمَل - hope,	168.	أوول راوند - all-round
145.	يَأْمُلُ - to hope	169.	أَيْ - any
146.	أَنْ - that	170.	أَيْ - أَيّاً مِنْ - any of
147.	أَنا - I	171.	أَيُّ شَيْءٍ - anything
148.	إناءٌ لِلطَهي - cooker	172.	أَيُّ شَيْءٍ - nothing
149.	أَنْتَ، أَنْتُما ، أَنْتُمْ - you	173.	أَيْ مِنْ - either
150.	إنْتِباهُ - attention	174.	أَيْضاً - also
151.	إنْتَظِرْ - waited	175.	أَيْضاً - as well
152.	أُنْثَى - female	176.	أَيْضاً - either, too, also
153.	انجليزي - English	177.	أَيْنَ - where
154.	أنجيلا - Angela	178.	بابٌ - door
155.	إنْدَفَعَ - rushed	179.	بابٌ ، عُنْوانٌ - rubric
156.	إنْذارٌ - alarm	180.	بِإخْلاصٍ - sincerely
157.	إنْسانٌ - human,	181.	بارِدٌ - cold (adj)
158.	آدَمِيٌّ ، إنْسانِيٌّ - human (adj)	182.	بُرُودَةٌ ، بَرْدٌ - coldness

183.	بارِعٌ - sly	207.	بَعدَ - after
184.	بالرَغمِ مِن ، مَعَ أنَّ - although	208.	بَعدَ - past;
185.	بالمُناسَبَةِ - by the way	209.	فِي الثامِنَةِ وَالنِصفِ - at half past eight
186.	بِبُطءٍ - slowly	210.	بَعضُ – some
187.	بترولٌ ، نَفطٌ ، زَيتٌ - oil	211.	بَعضُكُمُ البَعضَ ، كُلُّ الآخَرِ- each other
188.	بِحَذَرٍ , بِعِنايَةٍ - carefully	212.	بَعوضَةٌ ، ناموسَةٌ - mosquito
189.	بَحرٌ - sea	213.	بَعيدٌ - away
190.	بُحَيرَةٌ - lake	214.	بَعيدٌ - far
191.	بَدَأَ - began	215.	بِغَضَبٍ - angrily
192.	بَدَلاً - instead	216.	بِقُوَّةٍ - strongly,
193.	بَدَلاً مِن - instead of	217.	قَوِيٌّ - strong
194.	بَدَلاً مِنكَ - instead of you	218.	بَلَدٌ - country (state);
195.	بِدونِ - without	219.	الريفُ - countryside
196.	بَذرَةٌ - seed	220.	بلور - crystal
197.	بِرِفقٍ - slightly	221.	بليون - billion
198.	بَرنامَجٌ - program	222.	بَنكُ اكسبريس - Express Bank
199.	بروس - Bruce	223.	بِهُدوءٍ - quietly
200.	بَريدٌ إليكترونِيٌّ - e-mail	224.	بِواسِطَةِ - مَعَ - with
201.	بِسَبَبِ؛ لِأَنَّ- as	225.	بولندا - Poland
202.	بِسُرعَةٍ - quickly	226.	بيل - Bill
203.	بَسيطٌ - simple	227.	بَينَ - between
204.	بِصَوتٍ مُرتَفِعٍ - aloud	228.	بَينَما ، أثناءَ- while
205.	بِطاقَةٌ ، تَذكِرَةٌ - ticket		
206.	بِطَلاقَةٍ - fluently		

#	Arabic - English	#	Arabic - English
229.	تاريخٌ - date	252.	ثَلاثَةٌ - three
230.	تَأليفٌ ، إنْشاءُ نَصٍّ - composition	253.	ثَلاثونَ - thirty
231.	تامٌّ ، غامِض - total	254.	ثُمَّ - then
232.	تَحْتَ - under	255.	ثُمَّ - إذَنْ - then
233.	تَحْتَ ، أَسْفَلَ - down	256.	بَعْدَ ذلِكَ - after that
234.	تَحَرَّكَ - moved	257.	ثَمانِيَةٌ - eight
235.	تَحْميلٌ - loading	258.	جائِعٌ - hungry
236.	تَدَفَّقَ - flew away	259.	جارٌ - neighbour
237.	تَذَكَّرَ - remembered	260.	جِدّاً - too;
238.	تَسْجيلُ الأفْكارِ - thought-recording	261.	كَبيرٌ جِدّاً - too big
239.	تِسْعَةٌ - nine	262.	جِدّاً - very
240.	تَصْميمٌ فَنّيٌّ - design	263.	جِدّاً - لِذلِكَ - so
241.	تَعَلُّمٌ - learning	264.	جِدّاً، أيْضاً - too
242.	تَعْليمٌ - education	265.	جِدِّيّاً - seriously
243.	تَفْكيرٌ - thinking	266.	جَديدٌ - new
244.	تليفزيون - television	267.	جَرَّةٌ - jar
245.	تَماماً ، جِدّاً - quite	268.	جَرْوٌ ، كَلْبٌ صَغيرٌ - puppy
246.	تَنْسيقٌ - co-ordination	269.	جُزْءٌ - part
247.	تَنْظيفٌ - cleaning	270.	جِسْرٌ - bridge
248.	تَنْظيفٌ - cleaning	271.	جَلال - Galal
249.	تَوَقَّفَ - stopped	272.	جَليسَةُ أطْفالٍ - au pair
250.	تَيّارٌ - current	273.	جَميلٌ - beautiful
251.	ثانٍ - second	274.	جِنْسِيَّةٌ - nationality
		275.	جِهازُ التليفزيون - TV-set

276.	جِهازٌ لِلرَّدِّ عَلَى المُكالَماتِ - answering machine
277.	جيب - pocket
278.	جَيِّدٌ - good
279.	جَيِّداً ، حَسَناً - OK, well
280.	حاجَةٌ - need
281.	حادِثٌ - accident
282.	حافِلَةٌ - bus
283.	حالاً ، فَوْراً - immediately
284.	حالاً ، قَريباً - soon
285.	حالَةٌ - status,
286.	الحالَةُ العائِلِيَّةُ - family status
287.	حاوَلَ - tried
288.	حُبٌّ - love,
289.	يُحِبِ - to love
290.	حَبَّةُ دَواءٍ - pill
291.	حَتّى - until
292.	حَتّى الآنَ - yet
293.	حَجَرٌ - stone
294.	حَدٌّ - limit
295.	حَديقَةٌ - garden
296.	حَديقَةُ الحَيَوانِ - zoo
297.	حَذَّرَ ؛ مُعتِنٍ - careful
298.	حُرٌّ - مَجّاناً - free
299.	حَرْبٌ - war
300.	حَزينٌ - sad
301.	حَسَناً - okay, well
302.	حَسَناً - جَيِّداً - well
303.	حَقّاً - really
304.	حَقْلٌ - field
305.	حَقيبَةٌ - bag
306.	حَقيرٌ - dirty
307.	حَقيقِيٌّ - real
308.	حُلْمٌ - dream,
309.	يَحْلُمُ - to dream
310.	حِمارٌ وَحْشي - zebra
311.	حَنان - Hanan (name)
312.	حَوالَيْ, بَعْضُ - some
313.	حُوت - whale,
314.	الحُوتُ القاتِلُ - killer whale
315.	حَوْلَ - around
316.	حَوْلَ - round
317.	حَيٌّ - living
318.	حَياةُ - life,
319.	حيلَةٌ ، خُدْعَةٌ – trick
320.	حيلَةُ إنْقاذِ الحَياةِ - life-saving trick
321.	حَيَوانٌ – animal

322.	حَيَوانٌ أَلِيف - pet
323.	خائِفٌ - afraid
324.	خادِمٌ ، خادِمَةٌ - servant
325.	خارِجاً إلَى - outside to
326.	خارِجاً مِن - out of
327.	خاصٌّ بِالأُمّ - mother's
328.	خاصٌّ بِالمَرْأَةِ - woman's
329.	خاصٌّ بِبرُوس - Bruce's
330.	خاصٌّ بِعُمَرٍ - Omar's;
331.	كِتابُ عُمَر - Omar's book
332.	خاصٌّ بِهِيرُوشي - Hiroshi's
333.	خاصَّتَهُ ، مُلِكُهُ - own
334.	خِبْرَةٌ ، تَجرِبَةٌ - experience
335.	خُبْزٌ - bread
336.	خِدْمَةُ الإنْقاذِ - rescue service
337.	خَرِيطَةٌ - map
338.	خَرِيطَةُ الرَجُلِ - man's map
339.	خِزانَةُ كُتُبٍ - bookcase
340.	خَزِينَةٌ - safe
341.	خُصُوصاً - especially
342.	خِطابٌ - letter
343.	خِطابٌ - speech
344.	خُطَّةٌ - plan
345.	يُخَطِّطُ - to plan
346.	خُطْوَةٌ - step,
347.	يَخْطُو ، يَدُوس - to step
348.	خَلْفَ ، وَراءَ - behind
349.	خَمْسَةٌ - five
350.	خَمْسَةَ عَشَرَ - fifteen
351.	خَمْسَةٌ وَعِشرُونَ - twenty-five
352.	دائِماً - always
353.	داخِلَ - inside
354.	دافِئٌ - warm;
355.	يُدَفِّئُ يَسْخُنُ ، - to warm up
356.	دَرَّاجَةٌ - bike
357.	دَرْسٌ - lesson
358.	دَعْنا - let us
359.	دَفَعَ - paid
360.	دَقِيقَةٌ - minute
361.	دلْوٌ - pail
362.	دُمْيَةٌ - doll
363.	دُمْيَةٌ ، لُعْبَةٌ - toy
364.	دَوْرَةٌ ، مَنْهَجٌ - course
365.	دَوْرِيَّةٌ - patrol
366.	دُولار - dollar
367.	دِي فِي دِي - DVD
368.	ذِراعُ - arm,
369.	يُصارِعُ بِالذِراعِ - to arm

370. ذَكَر - male
371. ذَكِيّ - smart
372. ذٰلِكَ - that (conj)
373. ذَيْل - tail
374. رَئيسي - central
375. رائِد ، قائِد - captain
376. رائِع - fine
377. رائِع - wonderful
378. راحَة قَصيرَة - break, pause
379. رادار - radar
380. رَأْس - head;
381. رَئيس - head, chief;
382. يَنْطَلِق - to head, to go
383. رافِقَ ، صاحِب - accompanied
384. رامي - Ramy
385. رَأى - saw
386. رُبَّما - may
387. رُبَّما أذهَبُ إلى البَنْكِ. - I may go to the bank.
388. أيُمْكِنُني مُساعَدَتَكَ؟ - May I help you?
389. رِجال - men
390. رَجُل - guy
391. رَجُل - leg
392. رَجُلُ شُرْطَةٍ – policeman
393. رُخْصَةُ قِيادَةٍ - driving license
394. رِسالَة ، مُلاحَظَة - note
395. رَقيب - sergeant
396. رَمادي - grey
397. رَماديُّ الشَعرِ - gray-headed
398. رَمْزي - Ramzy
399. رَمْل - sand
400. رَنَّ - rang
401. روسي (m), روسِيَّة(f), روسي (adj.) - Russian
402. روسيا - Russia
403. رَوْضَةُ أطفالٍ - kindergarten
404. رياضة - sport;
405. مَتْجَرُ أدَواتٍ رياضِيَّةٍ - sport shop,
406. دَرّاجَةٌ رياضِيَّةٌ - sport bike
407. رِيحّ - wind
408. زائِر - visitor
409. زارَ - visited
410. زَبَد – butter
411. يَدْهَنُ بِالزَبَدِ - to butter
412. زُجاجٌ - glass
413. زِرّ - button
414. زَميلّ - colleague

205

415. زَهْرَةُ - flower
416. ساذَج - silly
417. ساعَةُ - hour
418. بِاسْتِمْرار - hourly
419. ساعَةُ - o'clock
420. إنَّها الساعَةُ الثانِيَةُ. - It is two o'clock.
421. ساعَةُ اليَدِ - watch
422. سَأَلَ - asked
423. سبانيل (نَوْعٌ مِن الكِلابِ) - spaniel
424. سَبَبُ - reason
425. سَبْعَةُ - seven
426. سَبْعَةَ عَشَرَ - seventeen
427. سِتَّةُ - six
428. سِتُّونَ - sixty
429. سِرٌّ - secret
430. سِرّاً ، خُفْيَةً - secretly
431. سُرْعَةُ - speed,
432. المُسْرِعُ - speeder,
433. مُسْرِعَةُ - speeding
434. سِرْوالُ ، بنطلون - trousers
435. سَريرُ - bed
436. سَريعٌ - quick;

437. بِسُرْعَةٍ - quickly
438. سَطْحُ ، سَقْفُ - roof
439. سَعادَةُ - happiness
440. سِعْرُ - price
441. سَعِيدُ ، مُبْتَهِجٌ - happy
442. سَفِينَةُ - ship
443. سَفِينَةُ فَضاءٍ - spaceship
444. سَقَطَ - fell
445. سُقُوطُ - falling
446. سِكَّةٌ حَدِيدِيَّةٌ - railway
447. سكرتيرة ، سكرتير - secretary
448. سَلالِمُ - stairs
449. سِلْكُ ، كابِل – cable
450. سَمّاعَةُ الهاتِفِ - phone handset
451. سَمِعَ - heard
452. سميث - Smith
453. سِنٌّ ، عُمَر - age
454. سَنَةُ - year
455. سُوبَر مارْكت - supermarket
456. سَوْفَ - shall/will
457. سَوْفَ (شَرْطِيَّةٌ) - would (conditional)
458. ... كُنْتُ سَأَقْرَأُ إذاً - I would read if...

459.	سَيِّئٌ - bad	483.	شَوارِعُ - streets
460.	سَيَّارَةُ - car	484.	شَيْءٌ - thing
461.	سَيَّارَةُ أُجْرَة - taxi	485.	شَيْءٌ ما - something
462.	سائِقُ سَيَّارَةِ أُجْرَة - taxi driver	486.	شَيِّقٌ ، مُمْتِعٌ - interesting
463.	سَيِّدَةُ - madam	487.	صاحَ - cried
464.	سِيِّدِي سَيِّد ، - sir	488.	صاحِبُ العَمَلِ - employer
465.	سَيْر - walking	489.	صارِخَ ، زاعِقٌ - howling
466.	سَيْطَرَةُ ، تَحَكُّم - control	490.	صامِت - silent
467.	شاحِبٌ - pale	491.	بِصَمْتٍ - silently
468.	شاحِنَةُ - truck	492.	صَباحُ - morning
469.	شارِعُ - street	493.	صِحَّةُ - health
470.	شاطِئ - shore	494.	صَحَفِيٌّ - journalist
471.	شاطِئُ البَحْرِ - seashore	495.	صَحِيحٌ - correct
472.	شايٌ - tea	496.	بِشَكْلٍ صَحِيحٍ - correctly
473.	شَخْصٌ - person	497.	بِشَكْلٍ غَيْرِ صَحِيحٍ - incorrectly
474.	شَخْصٌ ما - somebody	498.	يُصَحِّحُ - to correct
475.	شَخْصِيٌّ - personal	499.	صَحِيفَةُ - newspaper
476.	شَرِكَةُ - company	500.	صَحِيفَةُ - جَرِيدَة - newspaper
477.	شَرِكَةُ - firm	501.	صَدِيقٌ - boyfriend
478.	شَرِيط فيديو - videocassette	502.	صَدِيقٌ - friend
479.	شَطِيرَةٌ ، شندويتش - sandwich	503.	صَدِيقَةُ - girlfriend
480.	شَعْرُ - hair	504.	صَعْبٌ - difficult
481.	شُعُورٌ - feeling	505.	صَعْبٌ - hard
482.	شَهْرٌ - month	506.	صَغِيرٌ - small

507.	صَغِيرٌ - young		529.	طَافِياً - floating
508.	صَفَارَةٌ ، نَغَمَةٌ عَالِيَةٌ - beep		530.	طَاقَةٌ ، قُوَّةٌ - energy
509.	صَفَارَةُ الإِنْذَارِ - siren		531.	طَالِبٌ - student
510.	صُنْبُورٌ ، حَنَفِيَّةٌ - tap		532.	طَبْعاً - of course
511.	صُنْدُوقٌ ، عُلْبَةٌ - box		533.	طَبَقَ - plate
512.	صَوْتٌ - voice		534.	طِبِّيٌّ - medical
513.	صَوْتُ اِنْفِعَالِي آهٍ ، - ah..		535.	طَبِيبٌ - doctor
514.	صُورَةٌ - picture		536.	طَبِيبٌ بَيْطَرِيٌّ - vet
515.	صَيْدَلِيَّةٌ – pharmacy		537.	طَبِيعَةٌ - nature
516.	صِيغَةُ المَلَكِيَّةِ - your		538.	طَرِيفَةٌ - method
517.	صِيغَةٌ مَلَكِيَّةٌ لِلمُفْرَدِ الغَائِبِ - its (for neuter)		539.	طَرِيقٌ - road
			540.	طَرِيقٌ - way
518.	ضَابِطٌ - officer		541.	طَعَامٌ - food
519.	ضِدَّ - against		542.	طِفْلٌ - child
520.	ضَغَطَ - stepped		543.	طَقْسٌ - weather
521.	ضَمِيرُ الغَائِبِ المُفْرَدِ لِغَيْرِ العَاقِلِ it		544.	طَلَبَةٌ - students
			545.	طَهِي - cooking
522.	ضَمِيرُ المُتَكَلِّمِ مَنْصُوبٌ - me		546.	طَوِيلٌ - long
523.	ضَمِيرُ المُتَكَلِّمِينَ مَنْصُوبٌ – us		547.	طَيَّارٌ - pilot
524.	ضَمِيرُ غَائِبٌ لِلجَمْعِ ، هُمْ - them		548.	ظَهَرَ ، خَلْفَ - back
525.	ضَيْفٌ - guest		549.	عَادَةٌ ، قَاعِدَةٌ - rule
526.	طَائِرٌ - bird		550.	عَادِلٌ - Adel
527.	طَائِرَةٌ - airplane		551.	عَادِي ، مَأْلُوفٌ - usual
528.	طَابُورٌ - صَفٌّ - queue		552.	عَادَةً - usually

553. عاشَ - lived
554. عالٍ - high
555. عالَمٌ - world
556. عامِلٌ - worker
557. عامِلٌ ، عَمَل - working
558. عِبارَةٌ - phrase
559. عَبَرَ ، نَحْوَ - through, across
560. عَثَرَ عَلَى ، وَجَدَ - found
561. عَجَلَةٌ - wheel
562. عَدَدٌ ، رَقْم - number
563. عَرْضٌ جويٌّ - airshow
564. عُرَفَ - knew
565. عَرِيضٌ ، واسِعٌ - wide,
566. عَرِيضاً ، واسِعاً - widely
567. عَزِيزٌ - dear
568. عَشَرَةٌ - ten
569. عِشْرُونَ - twenty
570. عُضْوٌ - member
571. عَظِيمٌ - great
572. عَقْلِي ، ذِهْنِي - mental;
573. ذِهْنِيّاً عَقْلِيّاً - mentally
574. عَلامَةُ النَّجْمَةِ - asterisk
575. عِلْمُ المالِيَّةِ - finance
576. عَلِمَ عَنْ - learned about

577. عَلَى - on
578. عَلَى الأَقَلِّ - at least
579. عَلَى طُولِ - along
580. عِماد - Emad
581. عُمَر - Omar
582. عَمَلٌ - work
583. يَعْمَلُ - to work
584. عَمَلَ - worked
585. عَمَلٌ كِتابِيٌّ - writing work
586. عَمَلٌ يَدَوِيٌّ - manual work
587. عَمِيلٌ - customer
588. عَنْ ، بِشَأْنِ - about
589. عُنْوانٌ - address
590. عَيْنٌ - eye
591. عُيُونٌ - eyes
592. غادَة - Ghada
593. غازٌ - gas
594. غاضِبٌ - angry
595. غَداً - tomorrow
596. غُرَفٌ ، حُجُراتٌ - rooms
597. غُرْفَةٌ ، حُجْرَةٌ - room
598. غُرْفَةُ الحَمّامِ - bathroom;
599. حَمّامٌ يَسْتَحِمُّ - bath
600. غَرِيبٌ - strange

#	Arabic - English	#	Arabic - English
601.	غَرِيبٌ ، أَجْنَبِيٌّ - alien	625.	قَصِيرَ - short
602.	غَسَّالَةٌ - washer	626.	فَضَاء - space
603.	غَسِيلٌ - washing	627.	فَطُورَ - breakfast;
604.	غَلَّايَةٌ - kettle	628.	يَتَنَاوَلُ الفَطُورَ - have breakfast
605.	غَيْرُ عَادِلٍ - unfair	629.	فَعَلَ - did
606.	فَأْر - rat	630.	فَقَطْ - only
607.	فارِغ - blank, empty	631.	فَقَطْ ، بِالضَّبْطِ - just
608.	فارِغٌ ، خالٍ - empty	632.	فَقِيرٌ ، مِسْكِينٌ - poor
609.	فَاقِدٌ لِلوَعْي - unconscious	633.	فِكْرَةُ - idea
610.	فَتَاةٌ - بِنْت - girl	634.	فَنٌّ - art
611.	فَتَحَ - opened	635.	فِنَاء - yard
612.	فَتَحَ ، أدَارَ - switched on	636.	فَنَادِقٌ - hotels
613.	فَجْأَةً - suddenly	637.	فَنَّان - artist
614.	فِراش - mattress	638.	فُنْدُقٌ - hotel
615.	فَرْدِيّاً - individually	639.	فَهِمْ - understood
616.	فُرْصَةُ - chance	640.	فورد - Ford
617.	فَرْمَلَةٌ ، مَكْبَحٌ - brake,	641.	فَوْقَ - over
618.	يُفَرْمِلُ ، يَكْبَحُ - to brake	642.	فِي - in
619.	فَرِيقٌ - team	643.	فِي ، خِلالَ - in,
620.	فُسْتَانٌ ، ثَوْبٌ - dress	644.	خِلالَ سَاعَةٍ - in an hour;
621.	يَرْتَدِي - to put on	645.	فِي السَّاعَةِ الوَاحِدَةِ - at one o'clock
622.	مُرْتَدِي - dressed	646.	فِي ، عِنْدَ - at
623.	فَصْلٌ - class	647.	فِي أَثْنَاءِ ذَلِكَ - meanwhile
624.	فَصْلٌ دِرَاسِيٌّ - classroom		

648.	في الخارِج - outdoors		672.	قِطَّة - cat
649.	فِي الساعَةِ - per hour		673.	قِطَّةٌ صَغِيرَةٌ - kitten
650.	فِي الواقِعِ ، حَقاً - really		674.	قِطَّةٌ صَغِيرَةٌ - pussycat
651.	فيلم - film		675.	قَلَمُ حِبْرٍ - pen
652.	قائِد - leader		676.	قَلِيلٌ - few
653.	قائِمَةٌ - list		677.	قَلِيلٌ - little
654.	قابَلَ - met		678.	قَهْوَةٌ - coffee
655.	قاتِل - killer		679.	قُوَّةٌ - strength
656.	قادَ - drove		680.	قَوِيٌّ - strong;
657.	قالَ - said		681.	بِقُوَّةٍ - strongly
658.	قُبَّعَةٌ - hat		682.	قِياسِيٌّ - standard
659.	قَبْلَ - before		683.	قَيَّمَ - estimated
660.	قُتِلَ - killed		684.	قُيُودٌ - handcuffs
661.	قَدَّمَ - foot		685.	كاتِبٌ - writer
662.	عَلَى الأقدامِ - on foot		686.	كارول - Carol
663.	قَدِيمٌ - old		687.	كاسْبر - Kasper
664.	قِراءَةٌ - reading		688.	كانَ- was
665.	قُرْبٌ - near		689.	كانُوا - were
666.	قَرْجُلٌّ - man		690.	كَبِيرٌ - big
667.	قِرْدٌ - monkey		691.	كِتابٌ - book
668.	قَرِيبٌ - close		692.	كِتابٌ تَعْلِيمِيٌّ - textbook
669.	قَرْيَةٌ - village		693.	كِتابُها - her book
670.	قِصَّةٌ - story		694.	كَتَبَ - wrote
671.	قِطارٌ - train		695.	كَثِيرٌ - lot

696.	كَثيرٌ - many, much	719.	لا - no
697.	كَثيراً ، غالباً - often	720.	لا (تَفْعَلُ) - (do(-es) not
698.	كَذلِكَ ، أَيْضاً - also	721.	لا أَحَدَ - nobody
699.	كُرسِيٌّ - chair	722.	لِأَجْلِ - for
700.	كَريهُ الرائِحَةِ ، نَتِن - stinking	723.	لِأَنَّ - as, since
701.	كُلُّ - every	724.	لِأَنَ ، بِسَبَبِ - because
702.	كُلُّ ، جَميعُ - all	725.	لَحْظَةُ - moment
703.	كُلُّ شَخْصٍ - everybody	726.	لِذلِكَ - so
704.	كُلُّ شَيْءٍ - everything	727.	لِذلِكَ ، جِدّاً - so
705.	كَلْبُ - dog	728.	لَذيذُ المَذاقِ - tasty
706.	كَلِماتْ - words	729.	لِص - robber,
707.	كُلَّما كانَ مُمْكِناً - as often as possible	730.	سَرِقَةُ ، سطو - robbery
708.	كَلِمَةُ - word	731.	لُصوصّ ، لِصّ - thief, thieves
709.	كُلِّيَّةُ - college	732.	لَطيفٌ - nice
710.	كُمْبْيُوتَر - حاسوب - computer	733.	لَعِبَ - playing
711.	كَهْرَبائِيٌّ - electric	734.	لُغَةُ - language
712.	كوبٌ ، كَأْسُ - cup	735.	لُغْزٌ ، سِرُّ - mystery
713.	كَوْكَبُ - planet	736.	لِكُلِّ - فِي - per;
714.	كَيْفَ - how	737.	لَكُما ، لَكُمْ، لَكَ - yours
715.	كيلومتر - kilometer	738.	أَكْسَبُ 10 دُولاراتٍ فِي الساعَةِ. - I earn 10 dollars per hour.
716.	كِيمْياءُ - chemistry	739.	لكِنْ - but
717.	كِيمْيائِيٌّ - chemical(adj)	740.	لِماذا - why
718.	كِيماوِيّاتْ - chemicals	741.	لِمَنْ ، الَّذي ، الَّتي ، الَّذينَ - whose

742.	him - لَهُ ، ضَمِيرٌ لِلمُفْرَدِ الغائِبِ	765.	clever - ماهِر
743.	his; - لَهُ ، مُلِكُهُ	766.	wet - مِبتَلٌّ
	his bed - سَرِيرُهُ	767.	glad - مُبتَهِجّ ، مَسرُورٌ
744.	if - لَوْ ، إذاً	768.	creative - مُبدِعٌ
745.	keyboard - لَوْحَةُ مَفاتِيحٍ	769.	programmer - مُبَرمِجٌ
746.	to me - لِي	770.	shops - مَتاجِرُ
747.	my - لِي ، مَلِكِي	771.	pitching - مُتَأَرْجِحٌ
748.	not - لَيْسَ	772.	shop - مَتجَرٌ
749.	night - لَيْلَةَ لَيلٍ ،	773.	video-shop - مَتجَرُ أفلامِ فيديو
750.	Laila - لَيْلَى	774.	mobile - مُتَحَرِّكٌ ، نَقّالٌ
751.	water - ماءٌ	775.	meter - مِترٌ
752.	hundred - مِائَةٌ	776.	translator - مُتَرجِمٌ
753.	taken - مَأْخُوذٌ	777.	tired - مُتْعَبٌ
754.	what - ماذا	778.	fun - مُتْعَةٌ
755.	What is this? - ما هٰذا؟	779.	park - مُتَنَزَّهٌ ، حَدِيقَةٌ
756.	What table? - أيُّ مِنضَدَةٍ؟	780.	parks - مُتَنَزَّهاتٌ ، حَدائِقُ
757.	past - مارا بِـ	781.	when - مَتِي ، عِنْدَما
758.	Mariam - مارِي	782.	example; - مِثالٌ
759.	still - مازالَ	783.	for example - مَثَلاً
760.	sly; - ماكِرٌ	784.	field - مَجالٌ, حَقلٌ
761.	slyly - بِمَكرٍ	785.	nearby, next - مُجاوِرُ ، تال
762.	machine - ماكِينَةٌ	786.	nearby - مُجاوِرٌ ، قَرِيبٌ
763.	money - مالٌ	787.	magazine - مَجَلَّةٌ
764.	owner - مالِك	788.	editor - مُحَرِّرٌ

789.	مُحَرِّك - engine
790.	مُحْسِن - Mohsen
791.	مَحْشو - stuffed;
792.	مِظَلَّةٌ مَحْشوَّةٍ - stuffed parachutist
793.	مَحَطَّةٌ - station
794.	مُخْتَلِف - different
795.	مُدَرِّس ، مُعَلِّم - teacher
796.	مَدْرَسَةٌ - school
797.	مَدينَةٌ ، بَلْدَةٌ - town
798.	مَدينَةٌ - city
799.	مَرَّ - passed
800.	مَرَّةٌ - once
801.	مَرَّةً أُخْرى ثانِيَةً - again
802.	مَرَّتان - twice
803.	مُرْتَبِك - confused
804.	مِرْحاض - toilet
805.	مَرْحَباً - hi
806.	مَرْكَزُ تَسَوُّقٍ ، مَرْكَزٌ تِجارِيٌّ - shopping center
807.	مُزارِعٌ - farmer
808.	مَزْرَعَةٌ - farm
809.	مَساءٌ - evening
810.	مُسابَقَةٌ - competition
811.	مُساعِدٌ في مَتْجَر - shop assistant
812.	مُساعَدَةٌ - help;
813.	يُساعِد - to help
814.	مَساكِنُ - dorms
815.	مُسْتَديرٌ - turning
816.	مُسْتَشارٌ - consultant
817.	مُسْتَعِدٌّ ، جاهِزٌ - ready
818.	مُسْتَقْبَلٌ - future
819.	مُسْتَمِرٌّ ، ثابِتٌ - constant
820.	مُسَدَّسٌ - gun
821.	مَسْروقٌ - stolen
822.	مُسَلْسَلٌ - serial
823.	مُشارِكٌ - participant
824.	مَشْغَلُ أَسْطُواناتٍ - CD player
825.	مُشْكِلَةٌ - problem
826.	مِصْرُ - Egypt
827.	مَصْرِفٌ - بَنْك - bank
828.	مِصْرِيٌّ - Egyptian
829.	مِصْعَدٌ - lift
830.	مُضْحِكٌ ، مُسِلٌّ - funny
831.	مُضيفٌ - host
832.	مُطارَدَةٌ - pursuit
833.	مَطَّاط - rubber
834.	مَطْبَخٌ - kitchen

835.	مَطَرُ - rain
836.	مِظَلَّةُ هُبُوطٍ - parachute
837.	مُظْلِمٌ - dark
838.	مِظَلِّي - parachutist
839.	مَعاً - together
840.	مُعاوِنٌ - helper
841.	مَعْدِن - metal
842.	مِعْطَف - jacket
843.	مُعَطَّلٌ - out of order
844.	مُعْظَم - most
845.	مَعْلُومات - information
846.	مُغامَرَةٌ - adventure
847.	مُغْلَقٌ ؛ أُغْلِقَ - closed
848.	مُغَنِّي ، مُطْرِبٌ - singer
849.	مُفاجَأَةٌ - surprise
850.	يُفاجِئُ ، يُدْهَشُ - to surprise
851.	مُنْدَهِشٌ - surprised
852.	مِفْتاحٌ - key
853.	مُفَضَّلٌ - favorite
854.	مَفْقُودٌ - gone
855.	مُفَكِّرات - notebooks
856.	مُفَكِّرَةٌ - notebook
857.	مَقْعَدُ - seat,
858.	يَجْلِسُ - to take a seat
859.	مَقْعَدٌ ، مَكْتَبٌ - desk
860.	مَقْهى - café
861.	مَكانٌ - place
862.	يَضَعُ - to place
863.	مُكَبِّرُ الصَوْتِ - microphone
864.	مَكْتَبٌ - office
865.	مَلِيءٌ ، كامِلٌ - full
866.	مَلِكَ - had
867.	مَلِكُنا - our
868.	مَلِكِي - mine
869.	مُمْتازٌ - cool, great
870.	مُمْتَدَّةٌ - running
871.	مُمْكِنٌ - possible
872.	مَمِلٌّ ، رَتِيبٌ - monotonous
873.	مُمِيتٌ - deadly
874.	مِنْ - from
875.	مِنْ - than
876.	عادِلٌ أَكْبَرُ مِنْ حَنانٍ. - Adel is older than Hanan.
877.	مِنْ أَجْلِ ، لِمُدَّةِ - for
878.	مِنْ فَضْلِكَ - please
879.	مُناسِبٌ ، مُلائِمٌ - suitable
880.	مَناضِدُ - tables
881.	مُنْذُ - since (time point),

882.	لِأَنَّ - as, since	906.	نَجْمٌ - star
883.	مُنذُ - ago;	907.	نَحْنُ - we
884.	مُنذُ سَنَةٍ - a year ago	908.	نَسِيَ - forgot
885.	مَنزِلٌ - house	909.	نَشَرَ - publishing
886.	مَنزِلٌ - بَيْتٌ - home, house	910.	نَصٌّ - text
887.	مِنضَدَةٌ - table	911.	نُصْحَ - recommended
888.	مِنضَدَةُ الحَمَّام - bathroom table	912.	نِصْفٌ - half
889.	مَهارَةٌ - skill	913.	نَظَرَ - looked
890.	مِهْنَةٌ - profession	914.	نَظَّفَ - cleaned
891.	مُهَنْدِسٌ - engineer	915.	نَظِيفٌ - clean
892.	مَوْجَةٌ - wave	916.	يُنَظِّفُ - to clean
893.	مَوْسِمٌ ، فَصْلٌ - season	917.	نَعَمْ - yes
894.	مُوسِيقى - music	918.	نَفْسُ الشَيءِ - the same
895.	مَوْقِعُ إِنْتَرنت - Internet site	919.	فِي نَفْسِ الوَقْتِ - at the same time
896.	مَوْقِفٌ ، حالَةٌ - situation	920.	نَقْلٌ - transport
897.	مَوْهِبَةٌ - gift	921.	يَنْقُلُ - to transport
898.	مَيدانٌ - مُرَبَّعٌ - square	922.	نُقُودٌ ، مال - cash,
899.	نادِراً - seldom	923.	مُسَجِّلَةُ النُّقُودِ - cash register,
900.	نادِي - club	924.	صَرّافٌ - cashier, teller
901.	نار - fire	925.	نَمِرٌ - tiger
902.	ناس - شَعْبٌ - people	926.	نِهايَةٌ - finish
903.	نافِذَةٌ - window	927.	يُنْهِي - to finish
904.	ناقِلَةُ بترول - tanker	928.	نَوافِذٌ - windows
905.	نَبَحَ - barked		

929.	نَوْعٌ - kind, type	953.	هِيَ - she
930.	نوفا - Nova	954.	هِيرُوشي - Hiroshi
931.	نَوْمٌ - sleeping	955.	وَ - and
932.	نيويورك - New York	956.	واجِبٌ ، مُهِمَّةٌ - task
933.	هٰؤُلاءِ - these	957.	واجِبٌ مَنْزِلي - homework
934.	هاتِفٌ - telephone;	958.	واحِدٌ - one
935.	يَتَّصِلُ هاتِفِيّاً - to telephone	959.	واحِدٌ آخَرُ - one more
936.	هامٌّ - important	960.	واحِداً بَعْدَ الآخَرِ - one by one
937.	هُتافٌ لِلَفْتِ الإنْتِباهِ - Hey!	961.	واحِدٌ وَعِشرونَ - twenty-one
938.	هٰذا - this;	962.	وَجْبَةٌ - meal
939.	هٰذا الكِتابُ - this book	963.	وَجْبَةٌ خَفيفَةٌ - snack
940.	هٰذا الشَيْءُ - this stuff	964.	وَجْهُ - face
941.	هٰذا هُوَ السَبَبُ - that is why	965.	وَجْهُ - pointed
942.	هَرَبَ - ran away	966.	وَدُودٌ ، بودٌّ - friendly
943.	هَزَّ - shook	967.	وَرَقَةٌ - paper
944.	هُمْ - they	968.	وَرَقَةٌ - sheet (of paper)
945.	هُمْ ، ضَميرُ المَلَكِيَّةِ لِلجَمْعِ - their	969.	وَسَطَ - مَرْكَزٌ - centre
946.	هُنا - here (a place),	970.	وَسَطَ المَدينَةِ - city centre
947.	هُنا - here (a direction),	971.	وَصَلَ - arrived
948.	تَفَضَّلْ - here is	972.	وَظيفَةٌ - job;
949.	هُناكَ (لِلمَكانِ) - there (place)	973.	وَكالَةُ تَوْظيفِ - job agency
950.	هُناكَ (لِلإتجاهِ) - there (direction)	974.	وَظيفَةٌ - position
951.	هُوَ - he	975.	وَقْتٌ - مَرَّةً - time;
952.	هَواءٌ ، جو - air	976.	الوَقْتُ يَمْضي - time goes

217

977.	مَرَّتانِ - two times	1001.	يَتَظاهَرُ بِـ - to pretend
978.	وِكالَةُ - مَكْتَبُ - agency	1002.	يَتَعَلَّمُ - learn
979.	وُلَدَ ، غُلام - boy	1003.	يَتَكَلَّمُ - يَتَحَدَّث - to speak
980.	يُؤَلِّف - to compose	1004.	يَتَوَقَّفُ - to stop
981.	يَأْتي - come	1005.	يُثْبِت - fasten
982.	يَذْهَبُ - go	1006.	يَجِبُ - must
983.	يَأْخُذُ - to take	1007.	يَجِبُ أَنْ أَذْهَبَ. - I must go.
984.	يَأْكُلُ - to eat	1008.	يَجْتازُ - to pass,
985.	يَأْمُرُ - to order	1009.	اِجْتازَ الاِمْتِحانَ - passed exam
986.	يَبْتَعِدُ - to go away	1010.	يَجِدُ - to find
987.	يَبْتَلِعُ - to swallow	1011.	يَجْذِبُ - to pull
988.	يَبْدَأ - to begin	1012.	يَجْري - to run
989.	يُبَدِّدُ ، يُنْفِقُ - to spend	1013.	يُجَفِّفُ - to dry,
990.	يَبْقى - to remain	1014.	جاف - dry (adj)
991.	يَبيعُ - to sell	1015.	يَجْلِبُ ، يُحْضِرُ - to bring
992.	يُبَيِّنُ ، يَظْهَرُ - to show	1016.	جَلْب - bringing
993.	يَتَأَسَّفُ - to be sorry	1017.	يَجْلِسُ - to sit
994.	آسِف. - I am sorry.	1018.	يَجْلِسُ - to sit down
995.	يُتْبَعُ - to be continued	1019.	يُحاوِلُ - to try
996.	يَتَجَمَّدُ ، يُجَمِّدُ - to freeze	1020.	يُحِبُّ - to like, to love
997.	يَتَحَدَّثُ - to talk	1021.	يَحْتَكُّ بِـ - to rub
998.	يَتَدَفَّقُ - to flow	1022.	يَحْدُثُ - to happen,
999.	يَتْرُكُ - to leave	1023.	حَدَثَ - happened
1000.	يَتَّصِلُ هاتِفِياً - to call	1024.	يَحْصُلُ عَلى - to get

1025. يَحْصُلُ عَلَى - to get (something),
1026. يَصِلُ إِلَى - to get (somewhere)
1027. يَحْمِلُ - to carry in hands,
1028. يَنْقُلُ - to carry by transport
1029. يَحْمِلُ - to load,
1030. حَمَّال - loader
1031. يَحْمِي - to protect
1032. يُحَوِّلُ ، يُدِيرُ - to turn;
1033. يَفْتَحُ - to turn on;
1034. يُغْلَقُ - to turn off
1035. يُخْبِرُ - to inform
1036. يُخْبِرُ ، يَقُولُ - to tell, to say
1037. يَخْتَارُ - to choose
1038. يَخْتَبِئُ - to hide
1039. اِخْتِبَاءَ - hiding, hide-n-seek
1040. يَخْجَلُ - to be ashamed;
1041. إِنَّهُ خَجْلَانِ - he is ashamed
1042. يَخْدُمُ - to serve
1043. يَدّ - يُنَاوِلُ - hand
1044. يُدَبِّرُ، يُدِيرُ - manage
1045. يُدَرِّبُ ، يَتَدَرَّبُ - to train
1046. تَدَرَّبَ - trained
1047. يَدْرُسُ - to study
1048. يَدْرُسُ ، يَعْلَمُ - to teach
1049. يَدَعُ ، يَسْمَحُ - to let
1050. يَدْفَعُ - to pay
1051. يَدْفَعُ - to push
1052. يُدَمِّرُ - destroy
1053. يُدِيرُ ، يَبْدَأُ - to start
1054. يُدِيرُ عَجَلَةَ الْقِيَادَةِ - to steer
1055. يَذْهَبُ (عَلَى الأَقْدَامِ) - to go (on foot)
1056. (يَذْهَبُ (بِوَسِيلَةِ إِنْتِقَال - to go (by a transport)
1057. يُرَافِقُ ، يُصَاحِبُ - to accompany
1058. يُرْعِبُ - to panic
1059. يَرْفُضُ - to refuse
1060. يَرْقُصُ - to dance
1061. رَقْص - danced
1062. الرَقْصُ - dancing
1063. يَرْكَبُ - to go by, to ride
1064. يَرْكَبُ الحَافِلَةَ - to go by bus
1065. يَرَى - to see
1066. يُرِيدُ - to want
1067. يُزْعِجُ - to bother
1068. يَسَارُ - left
1069. يُسَافِرُ - to travel
1070. يُسْأَلُ ، يَطْلُبُ - to ask

1071. يَسْبَحُ - to swim
1072. يُسْتَخْدَمُ - to use
1073. يَسْتَشِيرُ - to consult
1074. يَسْتَطِيعُ - can
1075. أَسْتَطِيعُ القِرَاءَةَ - I can read.
1076. يَسْتَلْقِي - to lie
1077. يَسْتَمْتِعُ بِـ - enjoy
1078. يَسْتَمِرُ - to continue;
1079. اِسْتَمَرَّ - continued
1080. يَسْتَمِعُ - يُصْغِي - to listen;
1081. يَسْتَمِعُ إِلَى المُوسِيقَى. - I listen to music.
1082. يَسْتَيْقِظُ - to get up
1083. اِسْتَيْقَظْ! - Get up!
1084. يُسَجِّلُ - to record
1085. يَسْرِقُ - to steal
1086. يَسْقُطُ - to fall
1087. سُقُوطٌ - fall
1088. يَسْكُبُ - to pour
1089. يَشْتَرِكُ - to take part
1090. يَشْتَرِي - to buy
1091. يَشْرَبُ - to drink
1092. يَشْرَحُ - to explain
1093. يُشْعِلُ - to fire

1094. يَشْكُرُ - to thank;
1095. شُكْراً لَكَ - Thank you.
1096. شُكْراً - thanks
1097. يُصْدَمُ، يَضْرِبُ - to hit, to beat
1098. يَصِلُ - to arrive
1099. يُصَوِّرُ - to photograph;
1100. مُصَوِّرٌ - photographer
1101. يَصِيحُ؛ يَصْرُخُ - to cry
1102. صَرَخَاتٌ - cries
1103. يَضْحَكُ - to laugh
1104. يَضَعُ خَطًّ تَحْتَ كَلِمَةٍ - to underline
1105. يَضَعُ رَأْسِيًّا - to put vertically
1106. يَضَعُ أُفُقِيًّا - to put horizontally
1107. يَضْغَطُ - to press
1108. يَضْغَطُ بِقَدَمِهِ - stepping
1109. يُطْعِمُ، يُغَذِّي - to feed
1110. يَطْفُو - to float
1111. يَطْلُبُ عَلَى الهَاتِفِ - to call on the phone;
1112. مَرْكَزُ اِتِّصَالَاتٍ - call centre
1113. مُكَالَمَةٌ هَاتِفِيَّةٌ - call
1114. يُطْلَقُ سَرَاح - to set free
1115. يَطِيرُ - to fly

1116. يَظْهَرُ ، يُطَوِّرُ - to develop
1117. يُعْتَقَدُ - to believe
1118. يَعْتَنِي بِـ ، يَرْعَى - to care
1119. يُعَدُّ - يُصْنَعُ - يَعْمَلُ - to make
1120. ماكِينَةُ الشاي - tea-maker
1121. يُعَدُّ ، يَسْتَعِدُ - to prepare
1122. يُعْذَرُ - to excuse
1123. عُذراً ، أَعْذُرْنِي - Excuse me.
1124. يَعْرِفُ - to know
1125. يَعُضُّ - to bite
1126. يُعْطِي - to give
1127. يَعْنِي ، يَقْصِدُ - to mean
1128. يُعيدُ تَأْهِيلَ - to rehabilitate
1129. يَعِيشُ ، يُقِيمُ - to live
1130. يَغْسِلُ - to wash
1131. يُغْلَقُ - to close
1132. يُغَنِّي - sing
1133. يُغَيِّرُ - to change,
1134. تَغْيِيرَ - change
1135. يُفْتَحُ - to open
1136. يَفْحَصُ ، يَخْتَبِرُ - to check
1137. يُفْرِغُ - to unload
1138. يَفْعَلُ - to do
1139. يَفْقِدُ - to lose
1140. يُفَكِّرُ - to think
1141. يَفْهَمُ - to understand
1142. يُقابِلُ - to meet
1143. يَقْبَلُ - to kiss
1144. يُقَدِّمُ ، يُنْتِجُ - to produce
1145. يُقَدِّمُ تَقْرِيرٍ - to report
1146. صَحَفِيٌّ ، مُراسِلٌ صَحَفِيٌّ - reporter
1147. يُقَدِّمُ طَلَبَ- to apply
1148. يَقْرَأُ - to read
1149. يُقْرَعُ أَوْ يَدُقُّ الجَرَسَ - to ring,
1150. رَنِين - ring
1151. يَقِفُ - to stand
1152. يَقْفِزُ - to jump;
1153. قَفْزَةً - jump
1154. يَقْلَقُ ، يُزْعِجُ - to worry
1155. يَقُودُ - to drive
1156. سائِقٌ - driver
1157. يَقُولُ - to say
1158. يُقِيمُ ، يَثْمِنُ - to estimate
1159. يَكْتُبُ - to write
1160. يَكْرَهُ - to hate
1161. يَكْرَهُ - to mind (to be against something)

1162.	يَكسِبُ - to earn	1181.	يَنْتَظِرُ - to wait
1163.	يُكَلَّفُ - to cost	1182.	يَنْزِلُ ، يَهْبِطُ - to get off
1164.	يَكونُ - to be	1183.	يَنْسَى - to forget
1165.	يَلْعَبُ - to play	1184.	يُنْصَحُ - to recommend;
1166.	يَلْعَنُ - damn	1185.	نَصيحَةٌ - recommendation
1167.	يَلَوِّثُ - to pollute	1186.	يَنْضَمُّ - to join
1168.	بج بلوتكسون - Big Pollutexxon	1187.	يَنْظُرُ - to look
1169.	يَمْتَدُّ ، يَنْتَشِرُ - to spread	1188.	يُنْقِذُ - to rescue
1170.	يُمْسِكُ بِـ - to catch	1189.	يُنْقِذُ - to save
1171.	يَفْهَمُ ، يُدْرِكُ - to catch on	1190.	يَهْتَزُّ - to shake
1172.	يَمْشِي ، يَسيرُ - to walk	1191.	يُوافِقُ - to agree
1173.	يَمْلَأُ - to fill up	1192.	يَوْمَ - day
1174.	يَمْلِكُ - has;	1193.	يَوْمِيّاً - daily
1175.	يَمْلِكُ كِتاباً - He has a book.	1194.	يَوْمَ - day
1176.	يَمْلِكُ - to have	1195.	يَوْمَ الاِثْنَيْنِ - Monday
1177.	يَموتُ - to die,	1196.	يَوْمَ الأَحَدِ - Sunday;
1178.	ماتَ - died	1197.	فَطورُ الأَحَدِ - Sunday breakfast
1179.	يَمينٌ - right	1198.	يَوْمَ السَبْتِ - Saturday
1180.	يَنامُ - to sleep		

English-Arabic vocabulary

about - عَنْ ، بِشَأْنِ

accident - حادِثٌ

accompanied - رافِقٌ ، صاحِبٌ

accompany (v) - يُرافِقُ ، يُصاحِبُ

ad - إِعْلانٌ

address - عُنْوانٌ

Adel - عادِلٌ

adventure - مُغامَرَةٌ

advert - إِعْلانٌ

afraid - خائِفٌ

after - بَعْدَ

again - مَرَّةً أُخْرَى ثانِيَةً

against - ضِدَّ

age - سِنٌّ ، عُمَر

agency - وَكالَةٌ - مَكْتَبٌ

ago - مُنْذُ

agree (v) - يُوافِقُ

agreement - اِتِّفاقِيَّةٌ

ah.. - صَوْتٌ اِنْفِعالِيٌّ آهِ

air - هَواءٌ ، جَوٌّ

airplane - طائِرَةٌ

airshow - عَرْض جَوِّيٌ

alarm - إِنْذارٌ

Alexandria - الإِسْكَنْدَرِيَّةُ

alien - غَرِيبٌ ، أَجْنَبِيٌّ

all - كُلٌّ ، جَمِيعُ

all-round - أوول راوْنْد

along - عَلَى طُولٍ

aloud - بِصَوْتٍ مُرْتَفِعٍ

already - الآنَ ، بِالفِعْلِ

also - كَذلِكَ, أَيْضاً

although - بِالرَغْمِ مِن ، مَعَ أَنَّ

always - دائِماً

American - أَمْرِيكِيٌّ

and - وَ

Angela - أنجيلا

angrily - بِغَضَبٍ

angry - غاضِبٍ

animal - حَيَوانٍ

another - آخَرُ

answer - إِجابَةٌ

answered - أَجابَ

answering machine - جِهازٌ لِلرَدِّ عَلَى المُكالَماتِ

any - أَيْ

any of - أَيْ - أَيّاً مِن

anything - أَيِّ شَيْءٍ
apply (v) - يُقَدِّمُ طَلَبَ
arm - ذِراعٍ
around - حَوْلَ
arrive (v) - يَصِلُ
arrived - وَصَلَ
art - فَنٌّ
artist - فَنَّانٍ
as - بِسَبَبِ ؛ لِأَنَّ
as often as possible - كُلَّما كانَ مُمْكِناً
as well - أَيْضاً
as, since - لِأَنَّ
ask (v) - يَسْأَلُ ، يُطْلُبُ
asked - سَأَلَ
aspirin - أَسْبَرِين
asterisk - عَلامَةَ النَّجْمَةِ
at - فِيَّ ، عِنْدَ
at least - عَلَى الأَقَلِّ
attention - إِنْتِباهَ
Au pair - جَلِيسَةُ أَطْفالٍ
audience - الجُمْهُورُ
away - بَعِيدٌ
back - ظَهْرٌ ، خَلْفَ
bad - سَيِّئٌ

bag - حَقِيبَةٌ
bank - مَصْرِفٌ - بَنْكٌ
barked - نَبْحٌ
bathroom - غُرْفَةُ الحَمَّامِ
bathroom table - مِنْضَدَةَ الحَمَّامِ
be (v) - يَكُونُ
be ashamed - يَخْجَلُ
be continued - إِنَّهُ خَجْلانِ
be sorry - يَتَأَسَّفُ
beautiful - جَمِيلٌ
because - لَأَنِ ، بِسَبَبِ
bed - سَرِيرٍ
beds - أَسِرَّةٍ
beep - صَفَّارَةٌ ، نَغْمَةٌ عالِيَةٌ
before - قَبْلَ
began - بَدَأَ
begin (v) - يَبْدَأُ
behind - خَلْفَ ، وَراءَ
believe (v) - يَعْتَقِدُ
best - أَفْضَلُ ، أَحْسَنُ
better - أَفْضَلُ
between - بَيْنَ
big - كَبِيرٍ
bigger - أَكْبَرُ

bike - دَرَّاجَةٍ	but - لٰكِنْ
Bill - بيل	butter - زَبَدٌ
billion - بِلْيُونٍ	to butter - يُدْهَنُ بِالزَّبَدِ
bird - طائِرٌ	button - زِرٌّ
bite (v) - يَعُضُّ	buy (v) - يَشْتَرِي
black - أَسْوَدَ	by the way - بِالمُناسَبَةِ
blank, empty - فارِغٌ	bye - إلَى اللِقاءِ
blue - أَزْرَقُ	cable - سِلْكٌ ، كابِلٌ
book - كِتابٌ	café - مَقْهىً
bookcase - خِزانَةُ كُتُبٍ	call (v) - يَتَّصِلُ هاتِفِيّاً
bother (v) - يُزْعِجُ	call on the phone - يَطْلُبُ عَلَى الهاتِفِ
box - صُنْدُوقٌ ، عُلْبَةٌ	call - مُكالَمَةٌ هاتِفِيَّةٌ
boy - وَلَدٌ ، غُلامٌ	call centre - مَرْكَزُ إِتِّصالاتٍ
boyfriend - صَدِيقٌ	called - إِتَّصَلَ هاتِفِيّاً
brake - فَرْمَلَةٌ ، مَكْبَحٌ	came - أَتَى ، حَضَرَ
bread - يُفَرْمِلُ ، يَكْبَحُ	can - يَسْتَطِيعُ
break, pause - خُبْزٌ	I can read. - أَسْتَطِيعُ القِراءَةَ
breakfast - فَطُورٌ	captain - رائِدٌ ، قائِدٌ
bridge - جِسْرٌ	car - سَيَّارَةٌ
bring (v) - يَجْلِبُ ، يَحْضُرُ	care (v) - يَعْتَنِي بِ ، يَرْعَى
brother - أَخٌ ، شَقِيقٌ	careful - حَذِرٌ ؛ مُعْتَنٍ
Bruce - بْرُوس	carefully - بِحَذَرٍ , بِعِنايَةٍ
Bruce's - خاصٌّ بِبْرُوس	Carol - كارول
bus - حافِلَةٍ	carry in hands - يَحْمِلُ

carry by transport - يَنْقُلُ	chose - إِخْتارَ
cash - نُقُودٌ ، مالٌ	city - مَدينَةٌ
cash register - مُسَجِّلَةُ النُّقُودِ	class - فَصْلٍ
cashier, teller - صَرّافٌ	classroom - فَصْلٌ دِراسِيٌّ
cat - قِطَّةٌ	clean - نَظيفٌ
catch (v) - يُمْسِكُ بِ	to clean - يُنَظِّفُ
catch on (v) - يَفْهَمُ ، يُدْرِكُ	cleaned - نَظَفَ
CD - أسْطُوانَةٌ مُدمَجَةٌ	cleaning - تَنْظيفٍ
CD player - مَشْغَلُ أسْطُواناتٍ	clever - ماهِرٌ
central - رَئيسِيٌّ	close - قَريبٌ
centre - وَسَطٌ - مَرْكَزٌ	close (v) - يُغْلَقُ
city centre - وَسَطَ المَدينَةِ	closed - مُغْلَقٌ ؛ أُغْلِقَ
ceremony - إحْتِفالٌ	closer - أَقْرَبَ
chair - كُرسِيٌّ	club - نادِي
chance - فُرْصَةٌ	coffee - قَهْوَةٌ
change (v) - يُغَيِّرُ	cold (adj) - بارِدٍ
change - تَغْييرٌ	coldness - بُرُودَةً ، بَرْدٌ
check (v) - يَفْحَصُ ، يَخْتَبِرُ	colleague - زَميلٌ
chemial(adj) - كيمْيائِيٌّ	college - كُلِّيَّةٌ
chemicals - كيماوِيّاتٌ	come - يَأتي
chemistry - كيمْياءٌ	go - يَذْهَبُ
child - طِفْلٌ	company - شَرِكَةٌ
children - أطفالٌ ، أوْلادٌ	competition - مُسابَقَةٌ
choose (v) - يَخْتارُ	compose (v) - يُؤَلِّفُ

composition - تَأليفٌ ، إنْشاءُ نَصٍّ	cup - كوبٌ ، كَأْسٌ
computer - كُمْبيُوتَر - حاسُوبٌ	current - تَيّارٍ
confused - مُرْتَبِك	customer - عَميل
constant - مُسْتَمِرٌّ ، ثابِتٌ	dad - أَبٌ
consult (v) - يَسْتَشيرُ	daddy - أَبٍ
consultancy - اِسْتِشاراتٌ	damn - يَلْعَنُ
consultant - مُسْتَشارٌ	dance (v) - يَرْقُصُ
continue (v) - يَسْتَمِرُّ	dark - مُظْلِمٌ
continued - اِسْتَمَرَّ	date - تاريخٌ
control - سَيْطَرَةٌ ، تَحَكُّمٌ	daughter - اِبْنَةٌ
cooker - إناءٌ لِلطَهْي	day - يَوْمٌ
cooking - طَهْيٌ	deadly - مُميتٌ
cool, great - مُمْتازٌ	dear - عَزيزٌ
co-ordination - تَنْسيقٌ	design - تَصْميمٌ فَنِّيٌّ
correct - صَحيحٌ	desk - مَقْعَدٌ ، مَكْتَبٌ
cost (v) - يُكَلِّفُ	destroy - يُدَمِّرُ
could - اِسْتَطاعَ	develop (v) - يَظْهَرُ ، يُطَوِّرُ
country (state) - بَلَدٌ	did - فِعْلٌ
course - دَوْرَةً ، مَنْهَجٌ	die (v) - يَموتُ
creative - مُبْدِعٌ	different - مُخْتَلِفٌ
cried - صاحَ	difficult - صَعْبٌ
criminal (adj) - إِجْرامِيٌّ	dirty - حَقيرٌ
cry (v) - يَصيحُ ؛ يَصْرُخُ	do (v) - يَفْعَلُ
crystal - بِلَّور	do(-es) not - لا (تَفْعَلُ)

doctor - طَبيبٌ	Egyptian - مِصريٌّ
dog - كَلبٌ	eight - ثَمانِيَةٌ
doll - دُميَةٌ	eighth - الثامِنُ
dollar - دُولارٍ	either - أَيْ مِنْ
door - بابٌ	elder - أَكبَرُ
dorms - مَساكِنُ	electric - كَهرُبائِيٌّ
down - تَحتَ ، أَسفَلَ	eleven - أَحَدُ عَشَّ
dream - حُلمٌ	else - آخَرَ
dress - فُستانٌ ، ثَوبٌ	Emad - عِمادٌ
drink (v) - يَشرَبُ	e-mail - بَريدٌ إليكترونِيٌّ
drive (v) - يَقُودُ	employer - صاحِبُ العَمَلِ
driving license - رُخصَةَ قِيادَةِ	empty - فارِغٌ ، خالٍ
drove - قادَ	energy - طاقَةٌ ، قُوَّةٌ
dry (v) - يُجَفَّفُ	engine - مُحَرِّكٌ
during - أَثناء ، خِلال	engineer - مُهَندِسٌ
DVD - دي في دي	English - انجليزِيٌّ
each other - بَعضُكُم البَعضُ ، كُلُّ الآخَرِ	enjoy - يَستَمتِعُ بِـ
ear - أُذُنٌ	especially - خُصوصاً
earn (v) - يَكسَبُ	estimate (v) - يُقيمُ ، يَثمُنُ
earth - الأَرضَ	estimated - قَيَّمَ
eat (v) - يَأكُلُ	etc. - إلَى آخِرِهِ
editor - مُحَرِّرٌ	evening - مَساءٌ
education - تَعليمٌ	every - كُلُّ
Egypt - مِصرَ	everybody - كُلُّ شَخصٍ

everything - كُلُّ شَيْءٍ	fifth - الخامِسُ
example - مِثالٌ	fill up (v) - يَمْلَأُ
excuse (v) - يُعذَرُ	film - فيلمٌ
experience - خِبرَةٌ ، تَجرِبَةٌ	finance - عِلمُ المالِيَّةِ
explain (v) - يَشرَحُ	find (v) - يَجِدُ
Express Bank - بَنكُ اكسِبرِيس	fine - رائِعٌ
eye - عَيْنٌ	finish - نِهايَةٌ
eyes - عُيونٌ	finished - أَنْهَى
face - وَجْهٌ	fire - نارٌ
fall (v) - يَسقُطُ	fire (v) - يُشعِلُ
falling - سُقوطٍ	firm - شَرِكَةٌ
family - أُسرَةٍ ، عائِلَةٌ	first - أَوَّلٍ
far - بَعيدٌ	five - خَمْسَةٍ
farm - مَزرَعَةٌ	flew away - تَدَفُّقَ
farmer - مُزارِعٌ	FLEX - البَرْنامَجُ التَبادُلِيُّ لِقادَةِ المُسْتَقْبَلِ
fasten - يُثْبِتُ	float (v) - يَطفُو
favorite - مُفَضَّلٌ	floating - طافِياً
feed (v) - يُطعِمُ ، يُغَذِّي	floor - أَرْضِيَّةٌ
feeling - شُعورٌ	flow (v) - يَتَدَفَّقُ
fell - سَقَطَ	flower - زَهْرَةٌ
female - أُنْثَى	fluently - بِطَلاقَةٍ
few - قَليلٌ	fly (v) - يَطيرُ
field - مَجالٌ, حَقلٌ	food - طَعامٌ
fifteen - خَمْسَةَ عَشَرَ	foot - قَدِمَ

229

for - مِنْ أَجْلِ ، لِمُدَّةِ	gave - أَعْطَى
Ford - فورد	German - أَلْمانِي ، اللُّغَةَ الأَلْمانِيَّةَ
forget (v) - يَنْسَى	get (something) - يَحْصُلُ عَلَى
forgot - نَسِيَ	get (v) - يَحْصُلُ عَلَى
form - إِسْتِمارَةً، نَمُوذَجٍ	get off - يَنْزِلُ ، يَهْبِطُ
forty-four - أَرْبَعَةٌ وَأَرْبَعُونَ	get up - ي يَسْتَيْقِظُ
found - عَثَرَ عَلَى ، وُجِدَ	Ghada - غادَةُ
four - أَرْبَعَةً	gift - مَوْهِبَةٌ
fourth - الرابِعُ	girl - فَتاةٌ ، بِنْتٌ
free - حُرٌّ ، مَجاناً	girlfriend - صَديقَةٌ
freeze (v) - يَتَجَمَّدُ ، يُجَمِّدُ	give (v) - يُعْطِي
friend - صَديقٌ	glad - مُبْتَهِجٌ ، مَسْرورٌ
friendly - وَدُودٌ ، بِوُدٍّ	glass - زُجاجٌ
from - مِنْ	go (on foot) - يَذهَبُ (عَلَى الأَقْدامِ)
front, in front - أمامَ	go away - يَبْتَعِدُ
full - مُلِيءٌ ، كامِلٌ	go by bus - يَرْكَبُ الحافِلَةَ
fun - مُتْعَةٌ	go by, to ride - يَرْكَبُ
funny - مُضْحِكٌ ، مُسَلٍّ	gone - مَفْقُودٌ
furniture - أَثاثٌ	good - جَيِّدٌ
further - إِلَى مَسافَةٍ أَبْعَدَ	goodbye - إِلَى اللِقاءِ
future - مُسْتَقْبَلٌ	gray-headed - رَمادِيِّ الشَعرِ
Galal - جَلالٌ	great - عَظيمٌ
garden - حَديقَةٌ	green - أَخْضَرُ
gas - غازٌ	grey - رَمادِي

guest - ضَيْفٌ	her book - كِتابُها
gun - مُسَدَّسٌ	here (a place) - هُنا
guy - رَجُلٌ	Hey! - هُتافٌ لِلَفْتِ الإنْتِباه
had - مَلِكَ الماضي مِنْ فِعْلِ	hi - مَرْحَباً
hair - شَعْرٍ	hid - اِخْتَبَأَ
half - نِصْفُ	hide (v) - يَخْتَبِئُ
Hanan (name) - حَنانٍ	high - عالٍ
hand - يَدٌ - يُناوِلُ	him - لَهُ ، ضَميرٌ لِلمُفْرَدِ الغائِبِ
handcuffs - قُيُودٌ	Hiroshi - هيرُوشِي
happen (v) - يَحْدُثُ	Hiroshi's - خاصٌّ بِهيرُوشِيٍّ
happiness - حَدَثَ	his - لَهُ ، مَلَكُهُ
happy - سَعادَةٌ	hit, beat - يُصَدَمُ، يُضْرَبُ
hard - سَعيدٌ ، مُبْتَهِجٌ	home, house - مَنْزِلٌ - بَيْتٌ
has - يَمْلِكُ	homework - واجِبٌ مَنْزِلِيٌّ
hat - قُبَّعَةٌ	hope - أَمَلٌ
hate (v) - يَكْرَهُ	host - مُضيفٌ
have (v) - يَمْلِكُ	hotel - فُنْدُقٌ
he - هُوَ	hotels - فَنادِقَ
head - رَأْسٌ	hour - ساعَةٌ
health - صِحَّةٌ	house - مَنْزِلٌ
heard - سَمِعَ	how - كَيْفَ
hello - أَهْلاً ، هُتافُ تَرْحيبٍ	howling - صارَخَ ، زاعِقٌ
help - مُساعَدَةٌ	human - إنْسانٌ
helper - مُعاوِنٌ	hundred - مِائَةٌ

hungry - جائِعٌ	jacket - مِعْطَفٌ
I - أَنا	jar - جَرَّةٌ
I go to the bank. - أَذهَبُ إلَى البَنْكِ.	job - وَظِيفةٍ
I wonder - أَتَساءَلُ	join (v) - وَكالَةِ تَوْظِيفِ
ice cream - الآيس كَريم	journalist - يَنْضَمُّ
idea - فِكْرَةٌ	jump (v) - يَقْفِزُ
if - لَوْ ، إذاً	just - فَقَط ، بِالضَّبْطِ
immediately - حالاً ، فَوْراً	kangaroo - الكانجارو
important - هامَ	Kasper - كاسبِر
in - فِيَّ	kettle - غَلّايَةُ
in (time) - فِيَّ ، خِلالَ	key - مِفْتاحٍ
individually - فَرْدِيّاً	keyboard - لَوْحَةُ مَفاتِيحَ
inform (v) - يُخْبِرُ	killed - قُتِلَ
information - مَعْلُوماتٍ	killer - قاتِلٍ
informed - أَخْبِرْ	kilometer - كِيلُومِتر
inside - داخِلَ	kind, type - نَوْعٌ
instead - بَدَلاً	kindergarten - رَوْضَةِ أَطفالٍ
instead of - بَدَلاً مِنْ	kiss (v) - يَقْبَلُ
interesting - شَيِّقٌ ، مُمْتِعٌ	kitchen - مَطْبَخُ
Internet site - مَوْقِعٌ إِنْتَرَنَت	kitten - قِطَّةٌ صَغِيرَةٌ
into - إلَى ، نَحْوَ	knew - عُرِفَ
into the street - إلَى الشارِعِ	know (v) - يُعْرَفُ
it - ضَمِيرِ الغائِبِ المُفْرَدِ لِغَيرِ العاقِلِ	Laila - لَيلَى
its (for neuter) - صِيغَةٌ مَلَكِيَّةٌ لِلمُفْرَدِ الغائِبِ	lake - بُحَيرَةٍ

land - أَرْض	listen (v) - يَسْتَمِعُ - يُصْغِي
language - لُغَة	little - قَلِيلٌ
laser - اللَيْزَرِ	live (v) - يَعِيشُ ، يُقِيمُ
last - أَخِيرٌ	lived - عاشَ
laugh (v) - يَضْحَك	living - حَيٌّ
leader - قائِدٌ	load (v) - يَحْمِلُ
learn - يَتَعَلَّمُ	loading - تَحْمِيلٌ
learned about - عِلْمَ عَنْ	long - طَوِيلٌ
learning - تَعَلُّم	look (v) - يَنْظُرُ
leave (v) - يُتْرَكُ	looked - نَظَرَ
left - يَسارٌ	lose (v) - يَفْقِدُ
leg - رَجُلٌ	lot - كَثِيرٌ
less - آخَرُ	love - حُبٌّ
lesson - دَرَسَ	loved - أَحِبُّ
let (v) - يَدَعُ ، يَسْمَحُ	machine - ماكِينَةً
let us - دَعْنا	madam - سَيِّدَة
letter - خِطابٌ	magazine - مَجَلَّةٌ
lie (v) - يَسْتَلْقِي	make (v) - يُعَدُّ - يَصْنَعُ - يَعْمَلُ
life - حَياةً	male - ذُكِرَ
lift - مِصْعَدٌ	man - قَرْجُلٌ
like, love - يُحِبُّ	man's map - خَرِيطَةُ الرَجُلِ
limit - حَدٌّ	manage - يُدَبِّرُ، يُدِيرُ
lion - أَسَدٌ	manual work - عَمَلٌ يَدَوِيٌّ
list - قائِمَةٌ	many, much - كَثِيرٌ

map - خَرِيطَةُ	mister - السَيِّدُ
Mariam - مارِي	mobile - مُتَحَرِّكُ ، نَقَّالُ
matter, business - أَمرٌ ، شَأنٌ	Mohsen - مُحسِنٌ
mattress - فِراشٌ	moment - لَحْظَةُ
may - رُبَّما	Monday - يَومُ الاِثْنَينِ
me - ضَمِيرُ المُتَكَلِّمِ مَنصُوبٌ	money - مالٌ
meal - وَجْبَةُ	monkey - قِرْدٌ
mean (v) - يَعنِي ، يُقصَدُ	monotonous - مُمِلٌ ، رَتِيبٌ
meanwhile - فِي أَثْناءِ ذَلِكَ	month - شَهرٌ
medical - طِبِّيٌ	more - أَكثَرُ
meet (v) - يُقابِلُ	morning - صَباحٌ
member - عُضْوُ	mosquito - بَعُوضَةٌ ، نامُوسَةٌ
men - رِجالٌ	most - مُعْظَمٌ
mental - عَقْلِيٌ ، ذِهنِي	mother - أُمٌ
met - قابَلَ	mother's - خاصٌ بِالأُمِّ
metal - مَعدِنٌ	moved - تَحَرَّكَ
meter - مِترٍ	music - مُوسِيقَى
method - طَرِيقَةٌ	must - يَجِبُ
microphone - مُكَبِّرُ الصَوتِ	my - لِي ، مَلَكِي
middle name - الاِسمُ الأَوْسَطِ	mystery - لُغْزٌ ، سِرٌ
mind (to be against something) - يَكرَهُ	name - اِسمٌ
mine - مَلَكِي	nationality - جِنسِيَّةٌ
minute - دَقِيقَةٌ	native - أَصلِيٌ
miss - آنِسَةٌ	nature - طَبِيعَةٌ

234

near - قُرْبَ	Nova - نُوفا
nearby - مُجاوِرٌ ، قَرِيبٌ	now - الآنَ
nearby, next - مُجاوِرٌ ، تالٍ	number - عَدَدٌ ، رَقْمُ
nearest - أَقْرَبَ	o'clock - ساعَةٌ
need - حاجَةَ	of course - طَبْعاً
neighbour - جارٍ	office - مَكْتَبٌ
never - أَبَداً	officer - ضابِطٌ
new - جَدِيدٌ	often - كَثِيراً ، غالِباً
New York - نيويورك	oil - بِثْرُولٍ ، نَفْطٌ ، زَيْتٌ
newspaper - صَحِيفَةٌ ، جَرِيدَةٌ	OK, well - جَيِّداً ، حَسَناً
nice - لَطِيفٍ	old - قَدِيمٌ
night - لَيْلَةُ لَيْلٍ ،	Olympic - أوليمْبيك
nine - تِسْعَةٌ	Omar - عُمَر
ninth - التاسِعِ	Omar's - خاصٌ بِعُمَرٍ
no - لا	on - عَلَى
nobody - لا أَحَدَ	once - مَرَّةٍ
North America - أمْريكا الشَمالِيَّةُ	one - واحِدٌ
nose - أَنفٌ	one by one - واحِداً بَعْدَ الآخَرِ
not - لَيْسَ	one more - واحِدٌ آخَرُ
not any - إِطلاقاً	only - فَقَطْ
note - رِسالَةٌ ، مُلاحَظَةٌ	open (v) - يَفْتَحُ
notebook - مُفَكِّرَةٌ	opened - فَتْحَ
notebooks - مُفَكِّراتٌ	or - أوْ
nothing - أَيُّ شَيْءٍ	order (v) - يَأْمُرُ

other - آخَرُ	past - بَعْدُ
our - مِلْكُنا	patrol - دَوْرِيَّةٌ
out of - خارِجاً مِن	pay (v) - يَدْفَعُ
out of order - مُعَطَّلٍ	pen - قَلَمُ حِبْرٍ
outdoors - فِي الخارِجِ	pens - أَقْلامُ حِبْرٍ
outside to - خارِجاً إلى	people - ناس، شَعْبٌ
over - فَوْقَ	per - لِكُلِّ، فِي
own - خاصَّتِهِ، مِلْكُهُ	per hour - فِي الساعَةِ
owner - مالِكٌ	person - شَخْصٌ
paid - دَفَعَ	personal - شَخْصِيٌّ
pail - دَلْوٌ	personnel department - إدارَةُ المُوَظَّفِينَ
pale - شاحِبٌ	pet - حَيَوانٌ أَلِيفٌ
panic (v) - يُرْعِبُ	pharmacy - صَيْدَلِيَّةٌ
paper - وَرَقَةٌ	phone handset - سَمّاعَةُ الهاتِفِ
parachute - مِظَلَّةُ هُبوطٍ	photograph (v) - يُصَوِّرُ
parachutist - مِظَلِّيٌّ	phrase - عِبارَةٌ
parent - أَحَدُ الوالِدَيْنِ	picture - صورَةٌ
park - مُتَنَزَّهٌ، حَدِيقَةٌ	pill - حَبَّةُ دَواءٍ
parks - مُتَنَزَّهاتٌ، حَدائِقُ	pilot - طَيّارٌ
part - جُزْءٌ	pitching - مُتَأَرْجِحٌ
participant - مُشارِكٌ	place - مَكانٌ
pass (v) - يَجْتازُ	plan - خُطَّةٌ
passed - مَرَّ	planet - كَوْكَبٌ
past - مارّاً بِـ	plate - طَبَقٌ

play (v) - يَلْعَبُ	publishing - نَشْرٌ
playing - لَعِبٌ	pull (v) - يَجْذِبُ
please - مِن فَضْلِكَ	puppy - جَرْوٌ ، كَلْبٌ صَغِيرٌ
pocket - جَيْبٌ	pursuit - مُطارَدَةٌ
pointed - وَجْهُ	push (v) - يَدْفَعُ
Poland - بولندا	pussycat - قِطَّةٌ صَغِيرَةٌ
police - الشُرْطَةُ	put vertically - يَضَعُ رَأسِيّاً
policeman - رجل شرطة	questionnaire - اِسْتِبْيانٌ ، اِسْتِطْلاعُ رَأي
pollute (v) - يُلَوِّثُ	queue - طابُورٌ - صَفٌّ
poor - فَقِيرٌ ، مِسْكِينٌ	quick - سَرِيعٌ
position - وَظِيفَةٌ	quietly - بِسُرْعَةٍ
possibility - إِمْكانِيَّةٌ	quite - بِهُدُوءٍ
possible - مُمْكِنٌ	radar - تَماماً ، جِدّاً
pour (v) - يُسْكَبُ	radio - رادار
prepare (v) - يُعِدُّ ، يَسْتَعِدُّ	railway - الراديو
press (v) - يَضْغَطُ	rain - سِكَّةٌ حَدِيدِيَّةٌ
pretend (v) - يَتَظاهَرُ بِ	Ramy - مَطَرٌ
price - سِعْرٌ	Ramzy - رامي
problem - مُشْكِلَةٌ	ran away - رَمْزي
produce (v) - يُقَدِّمُ ، يُنْتِجُ	rang - هَرَبَ
profession - مِهْنَةٌ	rat - رَنَّ
program - بَرْنامَجٌ	read (v) - فَأْرٌ
programmer - مُبَرْمَجٌ	reading - يَقْرَأُ
protect (v) - يَحْمِي	ready - قِراءَةٌ

real - مُسْتَعِدٌّ ، جاهِزٌ
really - حَقيقِيٌّ
reason - فِي الواقِعِ ، حَقّاً
recommend (v) - سَبَبٌ
recommended - يُنصَحُ
record (v) - نَصيحَةً
red - نُصْحٌ
refuse (v) - يُسَجِّلُ
rehabilitate (v) - أَحْمَرَ
rehabilitation - يَرْفُضُ
remain (v) - يُعيدُ تَأْهيلَ
remembered - إعادَةَ تَأْهيلٍ
report (v) - يُقَدِّمُ تَقْريرٌ
rescue (v) - يُنْقِذُ
rescue service - خِدْمَةَ الإِنْقاذِ
ricochet - اِرْتِدادٌ
right - يَمينٍ
ring (v) - يَقْرَعُ أَو يَدُقُّ الجَرَسَ
road - طَريقٌ
robber - لِصٌّ
roof - سَطْحٍ ، سَقْفٌ
room - غُرْفَةٌ ، حُجْرَةٌ
rooms - غُرَفٍ ، حُجُراتٌ
round - حَوْلَ

rub (v) - يَحْتَكُّ بِـ
rubber - مَطَّاطٍ
rubric - بابٌ ، عُنْوانٌ
rule - عادَةً ، قاعِدَةً
run (v) - يَجْري
running - مُمْتَدَّةً
rushed - إِنْدَفَعَ
Russia - روسيا
Russian - روسي ، رُوسِيَّة ، رُوسِي
sad - حَزينٌ
safe - خَزينَةَ
said - قالَ
sand - رَمْلٌ
sandwich - شَطيرَةً ، شندويتش
Saturday - يَوْمَ السَبْتِ
save (v) - يُنْقِذُ
saw - رَأى
say (v) - يَقُولُ
school - مَدْرَسَةٌ
sea - بَحْرٍ
seashore - شاطِئُ البَحْرِ
season - مَوْسِمٌ ، فَصْلٌ
seat - مَقْعَدٌ
seat belts - أَحْزِمَةُ الأَمانِ

second - ثانٍ	shook - هَزَّ
secret - سِرٌّ	shop - مَتْجَرٌ
secretary - سكرتيرَةُ ، سكرتيرٌ	shop assistant - مُساعِدٌ فِي مَتْجَرٍ
secretly - سِرّاً ، خَفْيَةً	shopping center - مَرْكَزُ تَسَوُّقٍ ، مَرْكَزٌ تِجارِيٌّ
see (v) - يَرَى	shops - مَتاجِرَ
seed - بَذَرَةً	shore - شاطِئٌ
seldom - نادِراً	short - قَصِيرٌ
sell (v) - يَبِيعُ	shot - أَطْلَقَ النارَ
sent - أَرْسَلَ	show (v) - يُبَيِّنُ ، يَظْهَرُ
sergeant - رَقِيبٌ	showed - أَظْهَرَ
serial - مُسَلْسَلٌ	silent - صامِتٌ
seriously - جَدِّيّاً	silly - ساذِجٌ
servant - خادِمٌ ، خادِمَةٌ	simple - بَسِيطٌ
serve (v) - يَخْدُمُ	since (time point) - مُنْذُ
set free - يُطْلَقُ سَراحٌ	sincerely - بِإخْلاصٍ
seven - سَبْعَةٌ	sing - يُغَنِّي
seventeen - سَبْعَةَ عَشَرَ	singer - مُغَنِّي ، مُطْرِبٌ
seventh - السابِعُ	single - أَعْزَبُ
sex - الجِنْسُ	sir - سَيِّدِي سَيِّدٌ ،
shake (v) - يَهْتَزُّ	siren - صَفّارَةُ الإنذارِ
shall/will - سَوْفَ	sister - أُخْتٌ ، شَقِيقَةٌ
she - هِيَ	sit (v) - يَجْلِسُ
sheet (of paper) - وَرَقَةٌ	sit down - يَجْلِسُ
ship - سَفِينَةٌ	situation - مَوْقِفٌ ، حالَةٌ

six - سِتَّةٌ	space - فَضاءٌ
sixth - السادِسُ	spaceship - سَفينَةُ فَضاءٍ
sixty - سِتُّونَ	Spain - أَسبانيا
skill - مَهارَةٌ	spaniel - سبانيل (نَوعٌ مِن الكِلابِ)
sleep (v) - يَنامُ	Spanish - أَسباني
sleeping - نَومٌ	speak (v) - يَتَكَلَّمُ - يَتَحَدَّثُ
slightly - بِرِفقٍ	speech - خِطابٌ
slowly - بِبُطءٍ	speed -
sly -	speeder -
slyly - ما بِمَكرٍ	speeding - سُرعَةٌ
	المُسرِعُ
	مُسرِعَةٌ
small - صَغيرٌ	spend (v) - يُبَدِّدُ ، يُنفِقُ
smart - ذَكِيٌّ	sport - رِياضَةٌ
smile - إبتِسامَةٌ	spread (v) - يَمتَدُّ ، يَنتَشِرُ
smiled - إبتَسَمَ	square - مَيدانٌ - مُرَبَّعٌ
Smith - سَميث	stairs - سَلالِمٌ
snack - وَجبَةٌ خَفيفَةٌ	stand (v) - يَقِفُ
so - لِذلِكَ ، جِدّاً	standard - قِياسِيٌّ
some - حَوالَي, بَعضُ	star - نَجمٌ
somebody - شَخصٍ ما	start (v) - يُديرُ ، يَبدَأُ
something - شَيءٌ ما	started (the engine) - أَدارَ
sometimes - أَحياناً	station - مَحَطَّةٌ
son - إبنٌ	status - حالَةٌ
soon - حالاً ، قَريباً	

steal (v) - يَسرِقُ	supermarket - سُوبَر مارْكِت
steer (v) - يُديرُ عَجَلَةَ القِيادَةِ	sure - أَكيدٌ
step - خُطْوَةٌ	surprise - مُفاجَأَةٌ
stepped - ضَغَطَ	swallow (v) - يَبْتَلِعُ
stepping - يَضْغَطُ بِقَدَمِهِ	swim (v) - يَسْبَحُ
still - مازالَ	switched on - فَتَحَ ، أَدارَ
stinking - كَرِيهُ الرائِحَةِ ، نَتِنٌ	table - مِنْضَدَةٌ
stolen - مَسْروقٌ	tables - مَناضِدَ
stone - حَجَرٌ	tail - ذَيلٍ
stop (v) - يَتَوَقَّفُ	take (v) - يَأْخُذُ
stopped - تَوَقَّفَ	take part - يَشْتَرِكُ
story - قِصَّةٌ	taken - مَأْخوذٌ
strange - غَريبٌ	talk (v) - يَتَحَدَّثُ
street - شارِعٌ	tanker - ناقِلَةُ بِتْرُولٍ
streets - شَوارِعَ	tap - صُنْبورٍ ، حَنَفِيَّةٌ
strength - قُوَّةٍ	task - واجِبٌ ، مُهِمَّةٌ
strong - قَوِيٌّ	tasty - لَذيذُ المَذاقِ
student - طالِبٌ	taxi - سَيّارَةُ أُجْرَةٍ
students - طَلَبَةٌ	tea - سائِقُ سَيّارَةِ أُجْرَةٍ
study (v) - يَدْرُسُ	teach (v) - شايٍ
stuffed - مَحْشوٌّ	teacher - يَدْرُسُ ، يَعْلَمُ
suddenly - فَجْأَةً	team - مُدَرِّسٌ ، مُعَلِّمٌ
suitable - مُناسِبٌ ، مُلائِمٌ	telephone - هاتِفٌ
Sunday - يَوْمَ الأَحَدِ	television - تليفزيونٌ

tell, say - يُخْبِرُ ، يَقُولُ	those - أُولَئِكَ
ten - عَشَرَةٌ	thought-recording - تَسْجِيلُ الأَفْكارِ
tenth - العاشِرِ	thousand - أَلْفٌ
test - اِخْتِبارٌ ، اِمْتِحانٌ	three - ثَلاثَةٌ
text - نَصٌّ	through, across - عَبَرَ ، نَحْوَ
textbook - كِتابٌ تَعْلِيمِيٌّ	ticket - بِطاقَةٍ ، تَذْكِرَةٌ
than - مِنْ	tiger - نَمِرٌ
thank (v) - يَشْكُرُ	time - وَقْتٌ - مَرَّةً
that - أَنْ	tired - مُتْعَبٌ
that is why - هَذا هُوَ السَبَبُ	to me - لِي
the same - نَفْسُ الشَيْءِ	today - اليَوْمَ
then - ثُمَّ	together - مَعاً
then - ثُمَّ - إِذَنْ	toilet - مِرْحاضٌ
there (place) - هُناكَ (لِلمَكانِ)	tomorrow - غَداً
these - هَؤُلاءِ	too (as well) - أَيْضاً
they - هُمْ	too - جِدّاً
thief - لِصٌّ	too, either, also - أَيْضاً
thing - شَيْءٌ	took - أَخَذَ
think (v) - يُفَكِّرُ	total - تامٌّ ، غامِضٌ
thinking - تَفْكِيرٌ	town - مَدِينَةٌ ، بَلْدَةٌ
third - الثالِثِ	toy - دُمْيَةٍ ، لُعْبَةٌ
thirty - ثَلاثُونَ	train - قِطارٍ
this - هَذا	train (v) - يُدَرِّبُ ، يَتَدَرَّبُ
this stuff - هَذا الشَيْءُ	translator - مُتَرْجِمٌ

transport - نَقْل
travel (v) - يُسافِرُ
trick - حِيلَةً ، خُدَعَةً
tried - حاوَلَ
trousers - سِرْوالَ ، بنطلون
truck - شاحِنَةٌ
try (v) - يُحاوِلُ
turn (v) - يُحَوِّلُ ، يُدِيرُ
turned - أدارَ ، حَوَّلَ
turning - مُسْتَدِيرِ
TV-set - جِهازِ التليفزيونِ
twelve - إثنا عَشَرَ
twenty - عِشْرُونَ
twenty-five - خَمْسَةٌ وَعِشْرُونَ
twenty-one - واحِدٌ وَعِشْرُونَ
twice - مَرَّتانِ
two - إثْنانِ
unconscious - فاقِدٌ لِلوَعْي
under - تَحْتَ
underline (v) - يَضَعُ خَطٌّ تَحْتَ كَلِمَةٍ
understand (v) - يَفْهَمُ
understood - فَهِمَ
unfair - غَيْرُ عادِلٍ
United States, the USA - الوِلاياتُ المُتَّحِدَةُ الأَمْرِيكِيَّةُ
unload (v) - يَفْرُغُ
until - حَتَّى
us - ضَمِيرُ المُتَكَلِّمِينَ مَنْصُوبٌ
use (v) - يُسْتَخْدَمُ
usual - عادِيٌّ ، مَأْلُوفٌ
very - جِدّاً
vet - طَبِيبٌ بَيْطَرِيٌّ
videocassette - شَرِيطُ فيديو
video-shop - مَتْجَرُ أفلامِ فيديو
village - قَرْيَةٌ
visited - زارَ
visitor - زائِرٌ
voice - صَوْتٌ
wait (v) - يَنْتَظِرُ
waited - إنْتَظَرَ
walk (v) - يَمْشِي ، يَسِيرُ
walking - سَيْرٌ
want (v) - يُرِيدُ
wanted - أرادَ
war - حَرْبٌ
warm - دافِئٌ
was - كانَ

wash (v) - يَغْسِلُ	why - لِماذا
washer - غَسّالَةً	wide - عَرِيض ، واسِعٌ
washing - غَسِيلُ	will - إرادَةً ، وَصِيَّةً
watch - ساعَةِ اليَدِ	wind - رِيحٌ
water - ماءٌ	window - نافِذَةٌ
wave - مَوْجَةٍ	windows - نَوافِذُ
way - طَرِيقٌ	with - بِواسِطَةٍ ، مَعَ
we - نَحْنُ	without - بِدُونِ
weather - طَقْسٌ	woman - إمْرأةٍ
week - أسْبُوعٌ	woman's - خاصٌّ بِالمَرْأةِ
well - حَسَناً ، جَيِّداً	wonderful - رائِعٌ
went away - إبْتَعِدَ	word - كَلِمَةٌ
were - كانُوا	words - كَلِماتٌ
wet - مُبْتَلٌّ	work - عَمَلٍ
whale - حُوتٌ	worked - عَمَلَ
what - ماذا	worker - عامِلٌ
wheel - عَجَلَةٌ	working - عامِلٌ ، عَمَلَ
when - مَتي ، عِنْدَما	world - عالِمٌ
where - أيْنَ	worry (v) - يَقْلَقُ ، يُزْعِجُ
which - الَّذِي ، الَّتِي (لِغَيرِ العاقِلِ)	would (condition.) - سَوْفَ (شَرْطِيَّةٌ)
while - بَيْنَما ، أثْناءَ	write (v) - يَكْتُبُ
white - أبْيَضُ	writer - كاتِبٌ
who - الَّذِي ؛ الَّذِينَ	writing work - عَمَلٌ كِتابِيٌّ
whose - لِمَنْ ، الَّذِي ، الَّتِي ، الَّذِينَ	wrote - كَتَبَ

yard - فِناءٌ
year - سَنَةٌ
yellow - أَصْفَرُ
yes - نَعَمْ
yesterday - أَمْسِ
yet - حَتَّى الآنَ

you - أَنْتَ، أَنْتُما، أَنْتُمْ
young - صَغِيرٌ
your - صِيغَةُ المَلَكِيَّةِ
yours - لَكُما، لَكُمْ، لَكَ
zebra - حِمارٌ وَحْشِيٌّ
zoo - حَديقَةُ الحَيَوانِ

www.ingramcontent.com/pod-product-compliance
Lightning Source LLC
Chambersburg PA
CBHW080334170426
43194CB00014B/2561